MACHADO DE ASSIS AND NARRATIVE THEORY

BUCKNELL STUDIES IN LATIN AMERICAN LITERATURE AND THEORY

Series editor: Aníbal González, Yale University

Dealing with far-reaching questions of history and modernity, language and selfhood, and power and ethics, Latin American literature sheds light on the many-faceted nature of Latin American life, as well as on the human condition as a whole. This highly successful series has published some of the best recent criticism on Latin American literature. Acknowledging the historical links and cultural affinities between Latin American and Iberian literatures, the series productively combines scholarship with theory and welcomes consideration of Spanish and Portuguese texts and topics, while also providing a space of convergence for scholars working in Romance studies, comparative literature, cultural studies, and literary theory.

Selected Titles in the Series

Rebecca E. Biron, *Elena Garro and Mexico's Modern Dreams*
Persephone Brahman, *From Amazons to Zombies: Monsters in Latin America*
Jason Cortés, *Macho Ethics: Masculinity and Self-Representation in Latino-Caribbean Narrative*
Tara Daly, *Beyond Human: Vital Materialisms in the Andean Avant-Gardes*
Earl E. Fitz, *Machado de Assis and Female Characterization: The Novels*
Earl E. Fitz, *Machado de Assis and Narrative Theory: Language, Imitation, Art, and Verisimilitude in the Last Six Novels*
Thomas S. Harrington, *Public Intellectuals and Nation Building in the Iberian Peninsula, 1900–1925: The Alchemy of Identity*
David Kelman, *Counterfeit Politics: Secret Plots and Conspiracy Narratives in the Americas*
Brendan Lanctot, *Beyond Civilization and Barbarism: Culture and Politics in Postrevolutionary Argentina*
Adriana Méndez Rodenas, *Transatlantic Travels in Nineteenth-Century Latin America: European Women Pilgrims*
Andrew R. Reynolds, *The Spanish American Crónica Modernista, Temporality, and Material Culture*
Elisa Sampson Vera Tudela, *Ricardo Palma's Tradiciones: Illuminating Gender and Nation*
Mary Beth Tierney-Tello, *Mining Memory: Reimagining Self and Nation through Narratives of Childhood in Peru*

MACHADO DE ASSIS AND NARRATIVE THEORY

Language, Imitation, Art, and Verisimilitude in the Last Six Novels

EARL E. FITZ

Bucknell University | University Press
Lewisburg, Pennsylvania

Library of Congress Cataloging-in-Publication Data

Names: Fitz, Earl E., author.
Title: Machado de Assis and narrative theory : language, imitation, art, and verisimilitude in the last six novels / Earl E. Fitz.
Description: Lewisburg, PA : Bucknell University Press, 2019. | Series: Bucknell studies in Latin American literature and theory | Includes bibliographical references and index.
Identifiers: LCCN 2018057884 | ISBN 9781684481125(pbk. : alk. paper) | ISBN 9781684481132 (cloth)
Subjects: LCSH: Machado de Assis, 1839–1908—Technique. | Narration (Rhetoric)
Classification: LCC PQ9697.M18 Z634 2019 | DDC 869.3/3—dc23
LC record available at https://lccn.loc.gov/2018057884

A British Cataloging-in-Publication record for this book is available from the British Library.

∞ The paper used in this publication meets the requirements of the American National Standard for Information Sciences—Permanence of Paper for Printed Library Materials, ANSI Z39.48-1992.

www.bucknell.edu/UniversityPress

Distributed worldwide by Rutgers University Press

Manufactured in the United States of America

To Julita, Lilliana, and Sam B.

CONTENTS

ABBREVIATIONS

The works of Machado de Assis:

BC *The Posthumous Memoirs of Brás Cubas,* trans. Gregory Rabassa (Oxford: Oxford University Press, 1997).

CA *Counselor Ayres' Memorial,* trans. Helen Caldwell (Berkeley: University of California Press, 1972).

DC *Dom Casmurro,* trans. Helen Caldwell, foreword Elizabeth Hardwick (New York: Farrar, Straus and Giroux, 1991).

EJ *Esau and Jacob,* trans. Helen Caldwell (Berkeley: University of California Press, 1966).

OC *Obra Completa,* 3 vols., ed. Afrânio Coutinho (Rio de Janeiro: Editôra José Aguilar, 1962).

Psy *The Psychiatrist and Other Stories,* trans. William L. Grossman and Helen Caldwell (Berkeley: University of California Press, 1963).

QB *Quincas Borba,* trans. Gregory Rabassa (Oxford: Oxford University Press, 1998).

A NOTE ON TRANSLATIONS

Unless otherwise noted, translations are mine.

MACHADO DE ASSIS AND NARRATIVE THEORY

INTRODUCTION

In this book I argue that the last six novels of Machado de Assis's career,[1] the "texts" that compose his "great," or mature, period,[2] stem from a single but powerfully unifying theoretical stalk: his exploration of the nature of language and its unique relationship to human reality, narrative art, and mimesis. While Machado has long been celebrated as a great writer, indeed, "the best Latin American fiction writer of the century" and "one of the best of all time anywhere," he has not, oddly enough, been seriously regarded as a theoretician of the novel form.[3] I assert that he was and that he needs to be appreciated as such, in Brazil, in Spanish America, in North America, and in the Western tradition. Moreover, I also view Machado de Assis as epitomizing the kind of writer such scholars of world literature as Sarah Lawall, David Damrosch, Pascale Casanova, Franco Moretti, and Héctor Hoyos today urge their readers to know better. In my estimation, Machado not only "invents" "modern Latin American narrative," as Alfred Mac Adam has argued, but also creates, for the Western tradition and globally, the modern language novel, the text that is deliberately constructed around the essential ambiguity of language itself.[4]

Read from this perspective, the need for which was suggested by K. David Jackson in his recent *Machado de Assis: A Literary Life*,[5] we can see that Machado takes up the issues so famously engaged by Plato, in *Cratylus* (often regarded as Plato's first discussion of language) and *Phaedrus*,[6] and Aristotle in *The Poetics* and that he adapts them to issues of modern literary theory and practice. In doing so, the Brazilian writer engages what is one of Western art's most core issues: the imitation of nature by language. My belief is that, within the increasingly complex and innovative verbal webs that Machado puts into play in his later novels, there is embedded a steady and constant interrogation of narrative as an imitative art form, one that, moreover, becomes more and more sophisticated as his theoretical acumen and technical expertise increase. And the consequences reveal themselves to be not merely aesthetic in nature but philosophical and political as well. My method is deductive; that is, I base my argument on what the texts of the novels themselves reveal when a close reading is applied to them. As much as possible, I let the texts speak for themselves, paying close attention, however, to how they speak to the reader, to themselves and their constituent parts (their self-referentiality), and to each other. Taken together, they form, I contend, an identifiable unit, one unique in Western literature and one characterized by a new kind of thinking about language as an imitative medium, a new vision of literary Realism, and, finally, a more accurate and honest way of thinking about ourselves and the worlds in which we live.

In contrast to Plato, who tended to concern himself with the Ideal and with the concept of eternal, unchanging forms, Aristotle, his great student, was (like Machado de Assis) very much of this world. In Aristotle's view, the world, including human reality, could be understood only by means of an ongoing interplay between our vision of the Ideal (Plato's concern with imperishable forms or ideas) and our engagement with the material (the matter that constitutes what we call existence). Importantly, however (and especially so for the argument about language, art, and narrative that I will be making in this study), this latter category, the "material," or *Stoff*, of everyday existence, gains what we think of as artistic reality only when it is acted upon by form, that is, when the artist selects and organizes certain aspects of reality and imposes a new and cohesive structure on them. This is what Machado does in his later narratives with men and women in action and, to echo the famous words of Aristotle in *The Poetics*, who are both higher (as in tragedy) and lower (as in comedy) than we are.[7] Thus do we have in Machado's work the full spectrum of human existence, the tragic figure of "Dom Casmurro" as well as the comic figure of Marcella, in *The Posthumous Memoirs of Brás Cubas*, and everything in between.

Although Machado is undeniably a philosophic and political aware writer, I regard him here only as a fiction writer, an artist who imitates human reality by means of language, albeit one who is keenly aware of doing so. My focus is thus limited to how Machado de Assis, the literary artist who seeks to imitate the world of women and men in action and of different classes and social settings, employs language as the most complete way of apprehending and reproducing as art what men and women do, say, and think, about themselves and their world. In his final six novels, I believe, Machado concentrates less on the "what" his narratives imitate, or re-present (the human condition as played out by his very Brazilian characters), than on the question of "how they do so," which turns on the question of how language produces meaning. The peculiar and highly distinctive self-referentiality that marks Machado's final six novels is not, in my reading of it, an idle stylistic fillip;[8] it derives, rather, from what I believe Machado has come to see as two defining and inescapable qualities of language—that it generates meaning (and counter meanings) by referring constantly to itself and that said meaning must therefore be forever in flux, an unstable function, in the literary realm, of the similarly unstable relationship between author, text, and reader.

His new theorizing about language and the nature of its functioning directly determine, I contend, how he will create his post-1878 linguistic art. For this late

Machado, language, in a sense, becomes his main character, his main protagonist. And because, as a consequence of this new realization about how language works—how it affects the clearly and closely related processes of writing, reading, and thinking—words are incessantly sending signals to, and receiving signals from, other words, the reader, who comes in for particular attention in Machado's later novels and who, Machado insists, must become less of a passive receiver of meaning and more of an active producer of it, finds herself in a bit of a quandary as to what to make of Machado's self-conscious, multilayered, and ironically charged texts. Machado, I posit, discovers, between *Iaiá Garcia* (1878) and *The Posthumous Memoirs of Brás Cubas* (1880–81), what Ferdinand de Saussure will demonstrate some thirty-plus years later and what Fredric Jameson will elucidate in *The Prison-House of Language* (1972)—that ambiguity in language derives from its semantic mutability, an essential, non-eradicable, and unavoidable characteristic that stems from the "structure of language itself."[9]

While men and women may use language poorly or carelessly, and while they may misinterpret things and while (as in so many of the mature Machado's novels) they may even choose to prevaricate and distort what they think is true (or verisimilar), there is always another level of ambiguity at work in his texts, and it arises from the nature of language and its function as a signifying system. This discovery, on Machado's part, will change everything, from what and how he writes to how the reader responds to it. After 1878, Machado realizes this; indeed, it is what separates the earlier Machado from the later one. Beginning with *The Posthumous Memoirs of Brás Cubas,* and his rejection of conventional Realism, Machado begins to explore what this new thinking about language would mean, for men and women living out their lives and for the new language-based novel that he was now determined to write. Machado's newly acquired sense of language as a powerful ontological and epistemological force, as opposed to a neutral and undistorting lens through which everything can be seen, understood, and imitated allows him to re-create the external lives of his characters at the same time that it allows him to illuminate and give a uniquely language-driven form to their darker, more inchoate, and more tangled inner worlds, the murky, constantly changing realm of motivation, desire, and interpretation. I will also argue that Machado viewed language, in all its semantic instability and productivity, as the most valid way of understanding the often contradictory nature of the human being, the medium of imitation that most fully reproduces the human condition, which depends so profoundly on language use for its sense of being and its struggle to know. It is, I maintain, this new focus on language's semantic instability that pervades Machado's late narratives. For Aristotle, then, as for Machado de Assis, form must be imposed on reality in order for it to be comprehended and transformed into art.

But what is most distinctive about Machado's novels after 1880 is that, for him, the form in question is language, and this had serious artistic and intellectual implications. It meant, for example, that the world was suddenly a much more unstable and ultimately unknowable place than had previously been thought. When Carlos Faraco writes, of Machado's post-1878 fictional world, that "tudo é relativo" (everything is relative) and that "nada é absoluto" (nothing is absolute), he is correct, and particularly so when Machado's late narratives are judged from a thematic perspective.[10] Writing, again correctly, that, for the mature Machado, "the puzzle" is prized over "certainty," Chris Power, citing two of Machado's translators, Jack Schmitt and Lorie Ishimatsu, argues that Machado's famous ambiguity stems, "in part," from "his subjective, relativistic world view, in which truth and reality, which are never absolutes, can only be approximated."[11] What this means is that, in Machado's late narratives, where, I believe, the unstable nature of language itself now takes center stage, "no character relationships are stable, no issues are clear-cut, and the nature of everything is tenuous."[12]

What has remained a mystery for scholars of Machado de Assis, however, is exactly how this distinctive and quintessentially modern worldview came to be. What could explain the dramatic leap forward that marks extraordinary *The Posthumous Memoirs of Brás Cubas* and the very good novel, *Iaiá Garcia*, that preceded it? A long-standing and quite plausible explanation has been that Machado simply matured, as a writer and a social commentator, and that the later novels and stories are the logical result of this process of intellectual and artistic growth. There is undoubtedly much truth to this position, and it does help explain how and why Machado began, with *The Posthumous Memoirs of Brás Cubas,* to leave his old style behind and write as he now did. And, speaking both technically and thematically, the earlier novels do share some traits with the later ones; they are not entirely unrelated. So the Machado de Assis as maturing writer theory does have its legitimacy.

But as I argue in the pages that follow, there is another factor that needs to be considered—what I believe is Machado's new thinking about language and its relationship to the human condition and to both art and imitation. As Machado appears to have clearly recognized in 1878, at this decisive juncture in his career as a man of letters and as a citizen of the new Brazil that was fast emerging, the human creature who wanted a truly realistic view of things would have to come to grips with all the many repercussions, from thoughts about the meaning of words and actions to thinking about personal identity, relationships, politics, and social structures that would issue from these prescient and deeply destabilizing ideas about the self-referentiality and semantically relative nature of language. Machado probes these and other theoretical and critical questions in essays he writes between the last novel of his early period (*Iaiá Garcia*) and the first of his final, brilliantly innovative period (*The Posthumous Memoirs of Brás Cubas*).[13]

For my purposes here, however, his most important theoretical statements are the two pieces he wrote about the work of his contemporary, the Portuguese novelist Eça de Queirós. It is here that Machado makes clear the revolutionary nature of his new thinking about language, its potential as an imitative art form, and Realism. Although his incisive commentaries on Eça are valuable in and of themselves, as scholars of Luso-Brazilian literature have long known, what is more important, I contend, is that in critiquing the theoretical assumptions of the Portuguese master, Machado begins to shape his own, radically new theory of language and narrative art. Thanks to his close and rigorous examination of Eça's very estimable writing, Machado begins to see that the prevailing ideas, in Western literature, about Realism and Naturalism were based on a series of misapprehensions about language and its relationship to reality, human existence, and art. Crucially, Machado's iconoclastic thinking about these issues meant (as I believe Machado had come to realize) that his preferred mode of imitation, language, was inescapably self-referential, semantically ambiguous, and constantly in flux. In this, language differed radically from imitations done by sound (music), pigments (painting), and stone (sculpture).

And when an artist imitates human reality by means of language, the outcome, wherein the question of artistic verisimilitude reigns supreme, must be different. There is, I believe Machado begins to see, a degree of fixity in these other modes of imitation that does not exist in language, which, semantically speaking, generates its own deconstruction at the very moment of its construction. Language exists, in other words, in a constant state of flux, and it is this quality that imparts the distinctive sense of uncertainty, or ambiguity, that permeates the Brazilian's late narratives. Writing in an imitative mode, Machado now understands, language is fundamentally different, and this difference affects all aspects of the human experience, from art and philosophy to politics and issues of human interaction and thought. The theories, practices, and assumptions of the old Realism would have to be jettisoned. A new theory of narrative art would have to be promulgated and explored.

Further, I contend, Machado's post-1878 realizations about language and his work as a writer were also going to be true for his reader as well, which meant that a new kind of reader was going to have to be created, one who could accept the protean quality of meaning and who could apply this to the process of living. While in *The Life and Opinions of Tristram Shandy, Gentleman* (1760–67), Laurence Sterne had also played with the idea of a different kind of reader, Machado, perhaps inspired by Sterne's narrative, takes a different tact; whereas the Irish writer was influenced by the ideas of philosopher John Locke, who believed that the mind is formed by an often illogical, even random association of ideas, the Brazilian writer was interested in a more basic question, the association of words and how one word gives rise to another in a seemingly endless process of signification. For Machado's reader and for his fast emerging new theory of narrative, this would have profound consequences.

As a form of imitation, Machado demonstrates, language was not like the other imitative modes Plato and later Aristotle discuss; it was radically different. As

Machado had come, by 1878, to realize, language was not merely something to be listened to, gazed upon, or viewed as a way to tell a story. It imbues everything we do, perceive, and imagine with life, energy, and meaning. It affects not merely our sense of who we are and what we do but how we think about it all, how we seek to make sense of it. Like the other kinds of imitation, narrative could become an art form itself (as poetry had been for Plato) but, unique among them all, it was, at the very moment of its creation, also the medium by which we discuss its nature and its significance, both personal and political. As humans, we use language to discuss language, whether this be in literature, politics, law, religion, history, or relationships. While painting, music, and sculpture (images of which figure prominently in Machado's work) all rely on language to bring them to life and make them, via thought and analysis, meaningful to human experience, only language *is* the very thing it simultaneously creates and interrogates. Meaning, Machado realizes, exists by, through, and in language. And it is from this that his narrative revolution ensues.

In Machado's later novels, as in Aristotelian criticism, the main elements of literary art (principally, for a narrativist, plot, characterization, point of view, theme, and language) come felicitously together to arouse certain emotions, thoughts, and reactions. A key difference, however, is that these same elements, for Machado, do not produce the cathartic effect that Aristotle had advocated as being essential to effective tragedy. While in Machado's towering human tragedy *Dom Casmurro* the reader certainly feels horror at what has happened and is repulsed by it, she is not purged of her emotions, as Aristotle dictated. Instead, Machado, the harbinger of the modernist malaise, plunges his reader into the seemingly inescapable ambiguity that envelops our lives and that renders us anxious and alienated, unable to know and to be with the level of certainty that, as sentient human beings, we yearn to have. It is this very ambiguity that Machado, understanding it, I contend, as a function of language itself, will now explore, chart, and plumb in his final novels. In doing so, in electing to examine the effects and consequences of eradicable ambiguity as opposed to showing how the great mysteries of life can (as in the mechanics of plot) be unraveled and resolved to the reader's satisfaction, he realizes that he can no longer provide his reader with the kinds of even artfully done denouements that had structured his earlier novels.[14] After 1878 and his growing frustrations with orthodox Realism, Machado appears to decide that the doubts, fears, confusions, and uncertainties of life must not be elided from the dramatically different texts he now determines to write. Indeed, they must be given prominence; ambiguity thus inflects everything, including the reader's best efforts to understand and decipher with what I suspect Machado would have said was an unjustified confidence, at least insofar as finding a single, perfect, and unchanging interpretation was concerned. When (in the Epps translation) Aristotle writes that "tragedy . . . is an imitation . . . of a serious, complete, and ample action by means of language rendered pleasant at different places in the constituent parts by each of the aids [used to make language more delightful], in which imitation there is also effected through pity and fear its catharsis of these and similar emotions," he is showing Machado how and why the artistic elements involved in the production of great and lasting literature must be selected, organized, and structured, but he is also giving the Brazilian writer his point of departure, the point at which he will break with tradition and create a new narrative for a new age.[15] It is here that, as early as 1880, Machado de Assis begins to present himself as the quintessentially modernist writer.

For Machado already in 1880, as for Marshall McLuhan some eighty years later, the medium is the message. In Machado's case, of course, the medium in question is language, understood not as a mechanism that delivers a neutral and untainted message but as a self-referential and semantically protean semiotic system. But, Machado would emphasize, the message (the nature of life in the language-inscribed world in which we humans exist and that gives rise to literature) is also the medium, and for a writer this would change everything, and drastically. Understanding this, Machado had come to realize, would have incalculable consequences, not merely for reading and writing narrative but for all aspects of life, how we live, how we set standards and make decisions, and how, most critical of all, we determine meaning. It would even affect how we think about the process of thinking itself. In Machado's late narratives, language does not merely imitate the human condition but defines it, and in all its myriad forms, manifestations, and mysteries. We cannot escape it. In the process, his post-1878 writing gains a significance about being and knowing that painting, music, and sculpture do not possess.

This same realization about the nature of language, its peculiar ability to create or imitate and its ability to simultaneously explicate (or obfuscate) what it has already created or imitated, would, I argue in the pages to come, lead Machado to produce two landmark contributions to American, European, and world literature: a new theory about the nature of narrative and an actual, and corresponding, "new narrative," one that, after 1878, is designed to imitate human reality by emphasizing the inherently fluid and productive (and therefore sometimes frustrating) nature of signification.

Although I do not wish to push this comparison of Aristotle and Machado too far, I will say that I believe it was on Machado's mind, part of his theoretical strategizing. As I will show, in several of his later works, perhaps most notably *The Posthumous Memoirs of Brás Cubas*, *The Psychiatrist*, *Dom Casmurro*, and *Counselor Ayres' Memorial*, Machado does seem to call his reader's attention to the Greek sage, and to do so rather openly, as if inviting her to make the connection. If this is true, but even if it is not, it is still quite possible to read the later, mature Machado de Assis as a narrative theoretician of major importance and as a practitioner of a radically inventive "new narrative," one that explores the relationship between language used in this fashion and reality, and, with respect to this latter term, in much the same sense as Aristotle spoke of it in *The Poetics*. It is not outlandish, I maintain, to read Machado de Assis as one of Western literature's most egregiously overlooked narrative theoreticians, one directly related to the still pertinent issues of art, imitation, and verisimilitude first brought up by Aristotle but also as a writer who, steeped in the art and thought of the Western tradition, showed us how a new, language-based novel might be written.

In doing this, I propose that Machado de Assis casts new light on the transition of narrative art from that of Flaubert to that of such modern masters as Proust, Woolf, Mann, and Joyce. Between 1880 and 1908, and in a systematic and coordinated fashion, the novels of Machado de Assis transform the dominant narrative mode of the nineteenth century, Realism, into the new modes of the early twentieth century and the modernist novel.[16] While the Western tradition has been slow to recognize Machado's genius, few writers have ever been more cognizant of it, its aesthetic and intellectual characteristics, and its greatest authors, artists, and thinkers than Machado was. And, for all his post-1878 originality and iconoclasm, he was a product of the Western tradition as well as an astute and discerning commentator on it. He comes shawling out of it. As he does from out of global literature, of which he was also deeply informed.[17] And yet Machado and his art remain all but unknown to those who do not toil in the fields of Luso-Brazilian, or even Latin American, literature. As if to demonstrate the full extent of this obliviousness and its consequences, the editors of the Macmillan *Literature of the Western World*, Brian Wilkie and James Hurt, could, as late as 1984, still write that "a group of remarkable writers, including Gabriel Garcia [*sic*] Márquez, Jorge Amado, Julio Cortázar, and Mario Vargas Llosa, have transformed Latin American literature, in the last quarter of a century" (basically, the Boom years) "from a placid backwater of world literature into an important current in the main stream."[18] The mere fact that scholars of the novel genre have for so long largely ignored the power and singularity of Machado's work, a point that Jackson makes quite forcefully and that Wilkie and Hurt (by mentioning Brazil's Amado but not Machado) imply, does not justify his continued exclusion from the ranks of the Western novel form's most sophisticated theoreticians and practitioners. Machado was deeply rooted in the art and thought of Western culture even if Western culture has been woefully slow to recognize his genius. It is high time this error was corrected. As Power writes, of Machado, his work, and the parallels that exist between him and his European, American, and Spanish American counterparts, the "chilling shadow" of Poe "falls across 'The Hidden Cause' and 'The Fortune Teller'" while "The Alienist," also known as *The Psychiatrist*, "glitters with Swiftian satire. Machado's shrewd, even devious work with the point of view of his narrators positions him alongside Henry James. Numerous stories anticipate the moral ambiguity of Chekhov' mature work, in particular 'A Singular Occurrence.' Machado's literary mapping of Rio [de Janeiro] reaches back to the St. Petersburg of Gogol and Dostoevsky, and anticipates the Dublin of

Joyce. Finally, some of his more obviously strange works (nearly all of it is strange to some degree, which is part of its brilliance) evoke Borges and Kafka. Given all this, it's little wonder that writer and critic Keven Jackson would feel confident to claim that Machado 'invented literary modernity, sui generis.'"[19]

The road to understanding the modern novel, I contend, must now be seen as leading through Brazil and Machado de Assis. In considering the above quote, it is clear that Jackson is wrong only in asserting that Machado's genius was "sui generis" (uniquely his own). In truth, he was born and bred in the Western intellectual and artistic tradition, and it is this same tradition that, as far as the art of fiction is concerned, he stands on its head beginning in 1880. The problem in reading a writer like Machado de Assis as a radically renovating contributor to the Western literary tradition is the same problem that confronts all writers who, no matter their level of skill or their originality, come not from the heart of this tradition but from its margins: Can they ever gain the respect they deserve? Or are they forever condemned to be regarded as mere imitators of breakthroughs already achieved by the European masters, as inconsequential inheritors of their world? I believe the answer to this latter question must be a firm and resolute no, that writers from the far-flung (and less commonly studied) outposts of the Western artistic citadel can equal their European compatriots and, as in the case I present here, sometimes exceed them by breaking new ground themselves. Machado is a writer who does precisely this, and we must recognize him for doing so.

Brazilian critic and theorist Roberto Schwarz has underscored the importance of our recognizing this very point. In a 2010 essay, Schwarz demonstrates how one of Machado's 1894 *crônicas* drolly rewrites the canonical European tale of Lucrecia's rape and subsequent suicide and, in the process, inverts (and subverts) the conventionally understood relationship between the venerated "European core" and the supposedly imitative "colonial periphery."[20] In revealing how the story works, that is, how and why Machado puts it together as he does, and by demonstrating exactly how Machado makes use of Livy's original account of the episode in question, Schwarz shows how a superbly talented writer like Machado de Assis exists simultaneously on the periphery, or margin, and in the core—the heart—of the European tradition. And this dual condition, with all its many tensions, makes a tremendous difference in terms of artistic and intellectual preparation and perspective. To speak any longer of Machado as a marginalized writer only is, Schwarz rightly suggests, a serious, misleading, and ultimately demeaning mistake; in truth, Machado is not only writing from within the European tradition, he is enhancing it. He is adding luster to it. But, crucially, he is doing so even as he is keenly aware of being automatically prejudged, as a Brazilian writer, to be, at best, a mere imitator of it. This blindly prejudicial attitude must change.

Merging arguments made by both Casanova and Moretti about the viability of world literature and how one might study it (particularly if one hails from a fertile and diverse, if too long ignored, culture like Brazil), Schwarz proves conclusively that the European "core" and the "colonial periphery" are not separate entities, with one commonly thought to be superior to the other, but mutually enriching occupants of the same, global literary system.[21] It can no longer be countenanced to speak of Latin American literature as being "a placid backwater of world literature";[22] in point of fact, this was never the case. As all scholars of Latin American literature know full well, and as writers as diverse as Sor Juana Inés de la Cruz, Gregório de Matos, José Basílio da Gama, Aluísio Azevedo, and Rubén Darío demonstrate, from the beginning the literatures of Spanish America and Brazil were fully and creatively engaged with Western and, especially in the case of Brazil, world letters. "In suggesting that the" productive "interaction between core and periphery" can be beautifully demonstrated by a supposedly "marginal" writer like Machado de Assis, Schwarz proves "the point captured in Moretti's term, 'distant reading'—namely, that core and periphery are not different spaces" in conflict with each other but the same space, one in which each party benefits.[23]

Interestingly, this same point, long understood by Brazilian writers, artists, intellectuals, and critics, and codified by the Brazilian Anthropophagy Movement of 1928, still seems to come as a surprise to readers and critics not in the Luso-Brazilian ken or aware of it.[24] That such a condition even exists today is a clear sign of the continuing problem faced by writers who work on what some still regard as the margins of the old, fast-fading Western literary empire. They are routinely passed over or, if noted at all, given short shrift. The case of Machado de Assis epitomizes this no longer tenable situation: "Everyone who reads him," writes Michael Wood, professor of English and comparative literature at Princeton University, "thinks he is a master, but who reads him, and who has heard of him? When I talk to people about Borges, I often have to say the name carefully, but I don't always have to say who he is."[25]

But the times are changing. Paris, as lovely and influential as it is, is no longer the center of the literary world.[26] Nor is New York, London, Rome, or Berlin. Today, places like Rio de Janeiro, with their long histories of global circulation and cultural interaction, are leading the way.[27] And as they do, too-long-ignored writers like Machado de Assis are finally getting their due. "In superbly funny books," writes Jackson, Machado "depicted the abnormalities of alienation, perversion, domination, cruelty and madness. He deconstructed empire with a thoroughness and an esthetic equilibrium that place him in a class by himself."[28] This is a point that, in various ways, Brazilian critics have long made. And yet Machado has still not received the respect he deserves not merely as an outstanding writer but also as a theoretician of the novel form. It is high time for him to be so recognized. As Machado shows in his comic but sharp-edged chronicle, and as Schwarz makes clear in his commentary, parody, as powerful a weapon as it is in gaining legitimacy for the so-called marginal voices from the edges of the empire, is not the only possible response to the disruptive interplay between the margins and the venerable cultural centers of the past, between the core and the periphery.[29] Sometimes, literary works from the colonies are simply better; sometimes they surpass those of the metropole and stand on their own as superior works of art and theory.[30] And Machado de Assis offers us a particularly compelling case in point.

The author of *The Posthumous Memoirs of Brás Cubas*, praised in 1990 by Susan Sontag for its extraordinary modernity,[31] was thoroughly versed in the authors, texts, traditions, and values of the Western tradition even as he was deeply invested in those of world literature and culture.[32] But in spite of this, his marginalizing identity as a Brazilian who wrote in Portuguese, and not in English, French, or German (all languages that he knew), has long prevented him from being welcomed as the innovator he was into the ranks of the Western literary elite. Yet this awkward fact can no longer lead us to diminish his achievement, to undervalue his work, or to blithely assume that it does not measure up to what his European compatriots were achieving. "Still neglected" by readers who work only in, or primarily in, the still too-often-privileged languages of the modern European tradition, for example, "the Brazilian writer is one of the very greatest of the early modern era."[33] One's nationality and native tongue cannot be allowed to determine one's artistic and intellectual evaluation. To do so is not just, and, in an age when we are thinking globally about literary production and circulation, it must not be tolerated, much less practiced, any longer.[34] As literary scholars and honest brokers of literary excellence, we must recognize greatness wherever and whenever we find it and not allow ourselves to be blinded by prejudice, by ignorance, or by long-standing hierarchies of culture and language.

The current study therefore addresses itself not to specialists in Machado de Assis, who are already well aware of his excellence, but to those students and scholars of literature who do not know who he is, who may not read Portuguese, and who therefore cannot benefit from the extensive body of criticism that exists in that language. Machado has been a staple of Brazilian critical thought ever since he first began to publish, in the mid-nineteenth century, and major studies have come from such critical luminaries as Alfredo Bosi, Luis Augusto Fisher, Sérgio Paulo Rouanet, João Cézar de Castro Rocha, João Alexandre Barbosa, Abel Barros Baptista, Marta de Sena, Ronaldes de Melo Sousa, and Gustavo Bernardo Krause, plus others like Schwarz and Antônio Cândido. Schwarz's *A Master on the Periphery of Capitalism: Machado de Assis* stands as an example of the excellent scholarship achieved by these, and other, Brazilian scholars.[35]

Spanish American writers and critics, too, have written important pieces about Machado, with Carlos Fuentes's *Machado de la Mancha* being a case in point.[36] While a few of these insightful books and articles exist in English translation (the John Gledson translation of Schwarz's work is a notable example), most do not, and so they are beyond the reach of those who do not read Portuguese, a language, though global in nature and rich in its literary heritage, is not as widely studied as are French, English, Italian, Russian, and German, the languages normally associated with the Western canon. This lack of Portuguese, or, more precisely, this lack of respect for Portuguese-language literature, it could be said, is another of the obstacles that must be overcome if Machado de Assis is to gain the recognition he deserves as one of Western literature's great figures. My goal with this book, therefore, is to bring Machado to the attention of scholars who work not inside but outside of the world of Luso-Brazilian literature, and to do that, I rely more heavily on criticism written in, or translated into, English.

In terms of my concentration on the novels written between 1880 and 1908, my argument here also builds upon that of Jorge de Sena and his well-known consideration of Machado's final five novels as the Brazilian writer's "Carioca quintet" (writer's dissection of Rio de Janeiro society at the time).[37] In contrast to Sena, however, I believe, as I have said, that the connecting thread is a new awareness, on Machado's part, of the nature of language and its ability to imitate nature, the real world around it. In my judgment, the salient issue is less thematic than theoretical. Machado does not cultivate ambiguity, for example, as a theme per se; he engages it, I believe, because it is the defining property of language itself. It is an inescapable by-product of imitation by language, which, unlike imitation by paint, stone, and sound, is fundamental to all aspects of the human experience. By 1878, I contend, Machado had come to realize that "language is figurative through and through," and that this fact would necessarily affect both how he wrote his novels and how they would have to be read.[38] And while they do have some traits in common, there is a huge difference between the pre-1880 novels and those of the post-1880 period. Something fundamental changes with respect to Machado's understanding of narrative and what he wants to do. But the real, and still unanswered, question remains: What happened? Or, as Wood puts it, referring to what happens in Machado's thinking between 1878 and 1880, "What do we make of the sudden change in method, the move from graceful, third-person storytelling to extravagant modernist antics, including tangled time lines, reflexive commentary, digressions, deeply unreliable first-person narrators, proliferating allusions, canceled or incomplete stories, pages filled with dots, idiosyncratic chapter titles, constant references to the bookishness of the books, and teasing addresses to a variety of imaginary readers?"[39] The current study seeks to offer an explanation of why this spectacular but still mysterious metamorphosis took place.

In the Western tradition, Machado de Assis is, I contend, the first novelist to build an entire corpus of texts around this new theory of language, narrative, and imitation.[40] While it is true that other, earlier writers were concerned with a host of language-related issues, I contend that it is only with Machado that the nature of language itself becomes the subject not merely of a novel or two but of an entire corpus of work. It is with the Brazilian writer and theoretician Machado de Assis that the production of meaning receives its first full exploration. This innovative understanding of language, and its relation to narrative art, helps explain, I believe, why his final six novels are as distinctive as they are. And it is why his post-1878 novels feature so many allusions to painting and music and how they compare to narrative as a mode of imitation. He is concerned, as a theoretician of the novel form, with how the reproduction of life by narrative language measures up to the same process as it is achieved through other means. But it also explains why Machado is so valuable to both literary scholars, on the one hand, and historians and social scientists, on the other. His radically new understanding of language, as both an imitative medium and an unstable but endlessly productive semiotic system, is crucial to the work of both camps.[41] His novels succeed, and brilliantly, at the level of recognizable human interaction and, more specifically, at offering acute insights into the Brazil of the nineteenth century. But, at the level of narrative theory and innovation, they also demonstrate a new, indeed radically new, theory of language and its semantically fertile mechanisms. It is this latter quality, I propose, that separates his early novels from his late novels. Machado's post-1878 novels stand out, in other words, as both insightful social documents and a radically new form of linguistically driven art. "Machado's breakthrough," as Wood correctly concludes, "is simultaneously aesthetic and political."[42]

Like Aristotle, Machado is concerned with questions of genre, though for the Brazilian the focus is primarily on narrative and how it compares, in its artistic verisimilitude, to painting and music (both of which appear frequently in these last six novels) and sculpture. As Machado's six post-1878 novels show, the imitation of human life by language can achieve levels of truthful representation that cannot be attained in any of these other imitative modes. Though visual art, or representation by painting, can create powerful and convincing levels of verisimilitude, and while music can achieve levels of harmony that cannot be attained in any other imitative form, the imitation of human life by language, and most especially by narrative, has a unique ability to capture the full range of the human experience, the seen and the unseen, the known and the unknown, and the balanced as well as the imbalanced. Although it is language that allows an artist like Machado de Assis to achieve these levels of insight and representation, it is also language that struggles with the ever elusive and protean problem of meaning. To accept imitation by language, Machado will show us, is to accept the reality of human life as semantic instability and uncertainty. And, again like Aristotle, Machado seems to have believed that change is a fundamental aspect of nature. For Machado, however, an artist who is acutely conscious of imitating what occurs in nature (specifically, the human condition) by means of language, change (understood by Machado primarily as semantic flux) is also an inherent part of meaning, as this is ceaselessly produced by language itself.[43] This is the critical issue.

Whereas Plato had objected that even narrative poetry could do little more than represent how life seems, or appears, to be, it failed to reflect, touch on, or even require any real knowledge of the thing imitated. Such imitation was, according to Plato, fated to be inescapably superficial. Going beyond even Aristotle's famous defense of poetry, Machado de Assis demonstrates that imitation by language requires not only a thorough understanding of human actions and motivations but a similarly thorough understanding of language as a determiner of how we understand who we are and how we claim to know things. Imitation by language, Machado will show us in the final six novels, resolves Plato's complaint, though, as he will also demonstrate, it cannot do this perfectly. Owing to the fact that they are functions of language, perfect knowledge and perfect communication cannot be attained through language use and cannot be represented through linguistic imitation of human action.

The true nature of language, Machado will show, does not permit this level of perfection, either in reality or in its imitation (by language). While the imitation of human life by narrative, Machado's artistic craft, can, his texts will contend, more truthfully represent the entire spectrum of the human experience, the physical details of the outer world as well as the mysteries and contradictions of the murky inner world of desire and motivation, it cannot, as a function of language and its semantic slippage, reproduce life except as a process of constant change, instability, and undecidability. But, as I seek to demonstrate in this study, this is precisely the nature—the true nature—of the reality in which the human creature lives, and so it is this new, ambiguity-laced Realism that Machado seeks to explore in his later novels. Adding to the complexities of language as a driver of change are the issues of time, memory, circumstance, self-consciousness, meaning, and desire, all of which are treated in depth by Machado in his late novels.[44] Like Aristotle, then, but much more emphatically, Machado de Assis, by 1880, regards language as a creative and, I believe he would insist, a necessarily disruptive, or unsettling, force, one that constantly undercuts our best efforts to seek and establish the certainty of meaning and understanding that, as human beings, we seek and need, in our personal lives, in our sense of history, and in our social, political, economic, legal, and religious structures.[45] That we fail to achieve this accounts, I believe, for the acute and, I would argue, unsettling sense of modernity that permeates his late novels.

And here we touch on the primary difference between Aristotle and Machado as concerns this key point; the latter intensifies his examination of language (and its relationship with both form and meaning, both of which he comes to understand as inherently fluid) much more than the former, who does little more than note it and catalog its basic parts.[46] Whereas for Aristotle language is a medium writers use to imitate nature and men and women in action, for Machado it is all of that plus an inescapable tendency to self-interrogation that constantly destabilizes its own efforts to establish a single, stable meaning. We can, in fact, observe Machado cultivating precisely this aspect of language, its semantic instability, in his last six novels. On page after page, and in character after character, he shows us that while language leads us to articulate what we want (what, it turns out, we can never have—certainty of knowing and being and a clear, unchanging sense of identity), it also prevents us (by means of its inescapably fluid production of meaning) from ever achieving these same ends. As his narrators, especially, demonstrate, even that mysterious entity we term the "self" is flexible and evolving, not static. And the same is true of meaning. Eventually, and painfully, we humans come to realize this. And we have to learn to live with all that comes from this jarring realization.

What Hazard Adams says of Aristotle's defense of poetry can, I contend, be equally applied to Machado's new thinking about language, narrative, and the novel form: "The poet," whom we can here think of as Machado, "makes the meaning of events by making their structure, and he does this in a medium, which is words."[47] The medium (language) Machado utilizes to achieve his new narrative art makes him, as Aristotle had theorized, both an imitator of reality and a creator of new, elusive, and language-based realities. The deep verisimilitude of Machado's late novels is thus the verisimilitude of language itself. This explains, I argue in the pages that follow, how it is that Machado seems simultaneously a writer whose texts have a strong sense of the verisimilar (the appearance of truth) to them even as they remain forever ambiguous as to exactly what they mean. As functions of language, they have to—unless (as they clearly do not) they wish to continue with what Machado would say is the false and meretricious Realism of the past. This dual quality—the deliberate merging in his narratives of the verisimilar and the semantically ambiguous (which defines the "extraordinary process" that he and his narrator discuss in the novel that bears his name; *BC*, 5)—I argue, is the heart and soul of Machado's new, post-1880 narrative.

My goal here also tracks, though on a smaller, more limited scale, that of Erich Auerbach in *Mimesis*; that is, I consider how Machado's final novels examine the means by which he seeks an "interpretation of reality through literary representation or 'imitation.'"[48] In doing so, however, I defend the kind of "modern narrative" that (as I believe is embodied in Machado's late work) Auerbach derides.[49] Auerbach is especially harsh in his judgments of modern novels in the *Ulysses* mode, maintaining that there is, in them, "something that is hostile to the reality which they represent" and concluding that, because of their "haziness" and their "vague indefinability of meaning," they "leave the reader with an impression of hopelessness."[50] These latter two criticisms are, I believe, particularly important to my discussion here of Machado's late novels because they (Auerbach's comments) speak to what many of Machado's readers and critics have taken to be his alleged pessimism, nihilism, and ambiguity. My argument thus extends one already made by Jackson, who also speaks of Machado's "central role in transforming literary realism into modernist prose."[51] It is this question about the "vague indefinability of meaning," however, that is the critical touchstone, the one issue broached by Auerbach that ties all these threads together and that forms the core of the argument I proffer in this book. It is my contention that this very vagueness of meaning derives from conclusions he had reached about the nature of language and its relationship to the human condition. Although Auerbach did not approve of the novels of Virginia Woolf either, he was able to say, of them, that they were written with "insight and mastery."[52] I believe he would come to the same conclusion about the novels of Machado de Assis, and this is why his comments about narrative art, representation, and mimesis are pertinent to the current project. But while the subject of Auerbach's famous study (based on his reading of Plato's discussion of mimesis in book 10 of *The Republic*) was "the representation of reality through literary representation or 'imitation,'" the focus of this study is the nature of Machado's language use in his last six novels.[53]

My basic argument is that, in the conception and writing of his post-1880 novels and short stories, Machado effectively achieved the status of what we would today term a narrative theorist. I further believe that he has not yet been accorded the credit he deserves as such. The current study seeks to begin to correct that critical lacuna. While I think there are close technical ties that link Machado's novels to his stories, which are also superb and deserving of their own study along the lines I propose here, I also contend that it is a question of genre, or form—the difference between the art of the novel and the art of the short story—that the Brazilian master is most concerned with. The demands of the story form are different from those of the novel form. In the interests of space, however, I here limit my study to a consideration of his final five novels, plus the novella *The Psychiatrist*. Specifically, I show how each of these texts explores, in distinct ways, the relationship between language and both the writing and the reading of the art form we refer to as "the novel." In short, I argue that Machado de Assis had a particular concern with the novel as a unique kind of artistic expression and that his novelistic production amounts to a lifetime of experimentation with it. He is, I maintain, a more important contributor to our better understanding of the modern novel genre than he has been given credit for.

As a key part of this thesis, I also show how it is the Brazilian author's groundbreaking approach to the concept of verisimilitude that binds these narratives together. Appearing as a constant motif in his novels (even, on and off, in his early ones), but manifesting itself in more and more decisive ways in his last six novels, the question of how a writer achieves a truthful appearance of life emerges as the pivotal theoretical problem Machado sought to plumb. And, as I argue, the true nature of literary verisimilitude can be perceived only through an understanding of the true nature of language and its imitative capacities. Language, the post-1880 Machado appears to have realized, enjoys a special relationship with artistic imitation, a relationship that he not infrequently compares in his novels to painting, music, and (less commonly) sculpture. One learns a language, for example, largely by the process of imitation itself. And part of this process involves the realization that, far from being a passive medium of imitation, language produces more language. In terms of its ability to generate meaning, it is endlessly productive, a fact that, for Machado, had tremendous consequences, both aesthetic and political, or civic. Concerned, I believe, not merely with the story that gets told, nor even with how it gets told and received (though these are clearly fundamental aspects of his work), Machado comes, after 1880 and *The Posthumous Memoirs of Brás Cubas*, to understand verisimilitude in literature as a function of language. Crucially, however, Machado comes to understand language not in the traditional way, as a more or less neutral instrument of imitation that expresses a writer's vision and that clearly represents the world around us (which would be the old Realism), but as a semantically fluid and inherently self-referential semiotic system. This is where Machado parts company with earlier theoreticians of novelistic technique, such as Mark Schorer, for whom "technique is the means by which the writer's experience is the only means he has of discovering, exploring, developing his subject, of conveying its meaning, and, finally, of evaluating it."[54] For the Brazilian master, it is the nature of this new thinking about language as a closed, semantically organic system that comes to dictate how narrative fiction must work. What is true of language, Machado concludes, must also be true not only of both narrative and the novel form but of verisimilitude itself.

It is from this realization, I argue, that Machado's "new narrative" is born. His great self-conscious and utterly unreliable narrator/protagonist Brás Cubas announces as much in the 1880 novel (or anti-novel) that bears his name. The four novels that then follow are, I believe, additional explorations into both the theoretical and formal consequences of this radically new assessment of the nature of language and narrative verisimilitude. "By 1880," however, Machado had indeed "completed the transition from realism to modernist author par excellence."[55] Of this there can be no doubt. What we need to understand more clearly is the exact nature of this crucial transition. This study offers one possible answer to that question. I believe that between 1878 and 1880, Machado begins to theorize a radically new theory of narrative, one deriving from a similarly new theory about language and one that will demonstrate itself in the first novel of Machado's mature period. While the seeds of this "new narrative" are there to be seen even in the earlier novels, it is only with *The Posthumous Memoirs of Brás Cubas* that we see, and feel, the full impact of his new thinking about language, narrative, and imitation. While the creative gap that separates the 1880 text from the previous one, *Iaiá Garcia* (1878), usually thought to be the best of the four early novels, is great, the signs of what was to come were already there.

As readers of this book will soon discover, there is one point on which I depart from established thinking as regards Machado and his narrators: Pursuant to my main argument, I believe that, beginning with *The Posthumous Memoirs of Brás Cubas* and running through to *Counselor Ayres' Memorial*, Machado articulates his new theories about narrative art, and the particular nature of imitation by means of narrative, largely through his narrators. Unreliable as they are in so many other ways, these same narrators do, I believe, convey Machado's seismic decision to write novels in accordance with his new thinking about the fundamental semantic fluidity of language. Part of their unreliability is precisely that of their advocacy of Machado's "new narrative" and the new, ambiguous kind of narrative Realism that must stem from it. And, if it is to be "true" or "realistic," in terms of Machado's new thinking about language and meaning, the fiction that is built from this realization about meaning's inherently protean nature must itself reflect these basic characteristics of language. This, I contend, is the genesis of Machado's new theory of what a true literary Realism must look like. Except for what his otherwise unreliable narrators tell us, comically and ironically, about the stories they are telling, about how they and their tales differ from what has come before, about how they should be read, and, more and more, about how well these narratives can imitate nature, or reality, Machado's post-1880 novels make the reader engage with the experiments in narrative art and imitation that he is undertaking.

My contention in the current critical study, then, is that between 1880 and 1908 (the year of his death) Machado de Assis undertakes a series of closely related and closely orchestrated experiments concerning the nature of imitation in the narrative mode and how this relates directly to both the nature of language and, concomitantly, the nature of the novel form. As a kind of corollary to this main argument, I show that, in the process of carrying out these formal divagations concerning novelistic technique, the nature of language, narrative, and linguistically based verisimilitude, Machado invents not merely Latin America's first "new novel" but the first "new novel" of the Americas, where Machado unquestionably ranks as "one of the greatest writers ever produced" by our hemisphere.[56] Breaking away, and dramatically so, from the tradition of the conventional realistic novel, which, I believe, Machado had come to understand as an essentially "closed" text that had only one, real meaning and that rendered the reader a passive "*consumer* of a fixed meaning," Machado created magnificently "open" texts that turned his reader into a "*producer*" of multiple and indeterminate meanings.[57] Finally, I contend that because of his creation of a radically new kind of narrative fiction, Machado de Assis deserves to be read not merely as one of the greatest fiction writers of the late nineteenth and early twentieth centuries but as one of the period's greatest theoreticians as well.

MACHADO DE ASSIS AND THE NEW NARRATIVE: FROM THEORY TO PRACTICE

One of the primary markers of Brazilian and Spanish American literature of the twentieth century is its concern with the nature of language and its function as an imitative mode. As Uruguayan critic and former Yale professor Emir Rodríguez Monegal put it, the "new novel" of Spanish America and Brazil (both of which he knew intimately) "is not only the most complete poetic object for the exploration of reality, but also the richest instrument to transmit that other parallel reality: the reality of language."[58] For the Latin American "new novelists" of the 1960s, the great step forward, both conceptually and technically speaking, was their realization that "language is the ultimate 'reality' of the novel."[59] While in this essay Rodríguez Monegal does not mention Machado de Assis, in a very important book appearing three years later, *El Boom de la novela latinoamericana*, he discusses Machado extensively as one of the main forerunners of the Boom era's famed "new novel."[60] But Rodríguez Monegal is right in calling attention not merely to the excellence of Latin American literature but, as he does in his 1969 essay, to the particular excellence—and originality—of the modern Latin American novel. It was, at this time, unmatched anywhere in the extent of its thematic, technical, and theoretical innovativeness. Writing in the late 1960s, but thinking backward in time to Latin America's rich narrative traditions, Rodríguez Monegal avers, with confidence and justifiable pride, that modern "Latin America can offer the work of at least three or four generations of novelists which continue an incessant renewal of the" novel form.[61] "Can this," he asks, "be said of many other literatures?"[62]

Rodríguez Monegal's comment is important to my discussion of Machado de Assis here because much of what, from his post at Yale, the Uruguayan critic will say about the very unique ways the new Latin American novelists of the 1960s treat language reflects directly on experiments undertaken by Machado, in Brazil, between 1880 and 1908. While the "new novel" of Machado de Assis and his later Latin American progeny emphasizes "the 'fictional' quality of all narrative," it also "sets up right in its core the negation of its 'truth'; it creates and destroys," and "ends up by demolishing the carefully built edifice of its own fiction," its self-conscious status as an art form that imitated life and that could, and did, contain certain immutable truths put there by the author and available to the reader who trusted in her author and text and who wanted to find them.[63] This is what the old realistic novel did, and it is what its readers expected. But today we realize that "the reading process . . . is an extremely complicated activity in which the mind . . . is at once and the same time relaxed and alert, expanding meanings as it selects and modifies them, confronting the blanks and filling them with constantly modifiable projections produced by inter-textual and intra-textual connections. Because of the nature of the reading process," a point Machado drove home in his later narratives, "each reading remains as 'indeterminate' as the text that it is a response to."[64] As Machado and his different post-1878 narrators insist, "the identification of one idea among many others is," as in the case of *Dom Casmurro* and the question of Capitú's guilt or innocence, "only one step toward a more complete and dynamic reading," which is what Machado wanted.[65]

By approaching Machado's late novels from this perspective, one in which his "new narrative" is matched with a "new reader" of his creation, it becomes "plausible to suggest that by enabling" readers "to tolerate and confront ambiguities and uncertainties in the reading process" itself, Machado helps them "learn to deal with the uncertainties and ambiguities that they themselves generate in the process of writing their own texts" and their own lives, both private and civic.[66]

Whether in choosing whom to vote for or in responding to a work of literary creation, the processes of writing, reading, and thinking are a shared and closely interrelated endeavor. Writing that "a novel," like life, "is but a collection of words and devices until it is read," or subjected to interpretation by a reader (who uses her own system of words to contemplate another system of words), the celebrated scholar and translator Gregory Rabassa has averred that the "new Latin American writers," that is, those from both Spanish America and Brazil, "are the ones who have come closest in this essential understanding of the importance of collective creation in literature the same as in the other arts."[67] This quality, the necessarily collaborative relationship between author, text, and reader, characterizes modern Latin American literature, a term that, both technically and thematically, must include Machado de Assis. The ability to identify "one idea among many" is a skill as necessary to the task of the good citizen as it is to that of the reader of literature, a point that underscores Wood's argument that the revolution wrought by Machado de Assis was both aesthetic and political. Machado, I believe it is fair to say, is the first of the Latin American new novelists. And he is still one of the greatest, perhaps, when one factors in what I believe was his radical new theory about language, narrative, imitation, human reality, and verisimilitude, the greatest of all time. It is entirely possible to think so, as, indeed, Roberto González Echevarría does.[68]

But within the framework Rodríguez Monegal lays out, the case of Machado de Assis emerges as a very special one. It is with the Brazilian writer, I maintain, that Rodríguez Monegal's very accurate and influential argument first comes to light. And it is with Machado that Rodríguez Monegal's thesis sees its full flowering. Spanish American fiction would have nothing similar until the 1930s and the era of Jorge Luis Borges and the *ficciones,* which, while not novels, were certainly comparable examples of a new narrative. When, in 1985, J. Hillis Miller wrote that "the great writers are all 'deconstructionists,'" he could easily have been describing the Machado de Assis of his late, 1880 to 1908 period.[69] Building on the arguments of both Monegal and Miller, I propose that we go further and consider Machado as the first novelist of the Western tradition to explore, in a series of interconnecting narratives, what a novel built around the principles of language, signification, and reader response that define "deconstruction" as a strategy for reading and writing would actually be like. In doing this, we can see Machado theorizing the nature of our first "new narrative" and inventing our first "new novel." For this achievement, he deserves much more recognition than he has so far received.

Although I concur with Rodríguez Monegal in the main, and certainly with his argument about the central importance of language to the Latin American new novel, I part company with him as regards the role of Machado de Assis in this grand tradition. In my estimation, Machado is not merely a Brazilian forerunner of the later, and predominantly Spanish American, new novel; he is the creator, already in 1880 and the appearance of *The Posthumous Memoirs of Brás Cubas*, of not only a new narrative and a new novel but a new reader as well. On this point, he is, to invoke the term once again, "sui generis," and while he knew the European and world masters, their approval and validation are not required for us to see his genius and originality. When Machado declares, in the late 1870s, that while reality is infinitely interesting to him he finds Realism to be boring, ill conceived, and superficial in both its practice and its theoretical base, he is, in effect, declaring his independence from it. Further, I think that in the two intervening years, between 1878 and 1880, Machado, having made the above-mentioned declaration, is now hard at work envisioning and then writing the new kind of novel that is born of his similarly new thinking about narrative, language, imitation, and the novel form. It is here, between 1878 and 1880, that Machado's egregiously overlooked contribution to narrative theory comes most clearly and vividly to the fore. It is here that his new thinking about the nature of narrative, long smoldering in his work, burst into full flame and begins to take shape in the novels of his later period. As many have surmised, if Machado had written in English, French, or German, he would long ago have been recognized for being the great iconoclast, innovator, and renovating force that those of us who work in the ken of Luso-Brazilian literature know him to be.[70] Yet beyond our discipline, Machado is shamefully little known, much less celebrated. It is high time that, as scholars interested in a more complete understanding of the Western narrative tradition, we correct this critical and theoretical lacuna.

Although we do not know what his exact thinking was, we do know that, in terms of Machado's growth as a novelist, in terms of what I believe was his chaffing at the restrictions and artificialities of traditional Realism, and in terms of what I argue was his concentrated thinking about the new kind of novel he wanted to write (a kind of novel that itself would be the direct result of his also radical thinking about the nature of language and how it seeks to achieve literary verisimilitude), by the latter date Machado had written a wildly new and inventive novel, one that brazenly and often comically calls attention to its own distinctiveness even as it tells us that it is also continuing in Western literature's grand novelistic tradition. And, as if anticipating the trouble he knows his readers are going to have with his hitherto unseen "new narrative" and his own, quite distinctive "new novel," he takes pains, throughout his narrative, to create a new reader as well, one who will not be as passive as the old reader and who will engage with the text (that is, with language) as Machado deems it necessary to do.[71]

If, as I suggest we do, we imagine Latin America has having not one but two great literary traditions, the Spanish American and the Brazilian, then having Machado de Assis in such an integrated vision changes forever how we understand our common narrative history. The beginning, in 1880, of his so-called "mature period" marks, for me, the beginning of not only Latin America's first "new narrative" but the first "new narrative" of the Americas generally. And, I further contend, if we consider that *Epitaph of a Small Winner* first appeared only twenty-three years after *Madame Bovary*, then we can easily consider it as marking the end of Realism as a reigning force in Western narrative theory and production. It is with *Epitaph of a Small Winner* that the modernist novel begins.

As we begin to think of Machado as a novelistic innovator who was keenly interested, as was his contemporary and North American counterpart Henry James, in the art of the novel, we can see that his approach to issues related to technique—how a novel gets conceived, written, and read—recalls Schorer's famous essay, "Technique as Discovery." The main difference between James and Machado as theoreticians is that James wrote a number of his positions on novel writing in the form of lengthy and fairly detailed "Prefaces" to his different works, whereas Machado did not; while he did make use of prefaces, they tended, as did his fiction, to be short, elusive, and enigmatic. As I show, even the famous "To The Reader" section that Machado uses to introduce the wildly different *The Posthumous Memoirs of Brás Cubas* (authored, ostensibly, by Brás Cubas himself) to his public and the critical establishment is carefully shrouded in comic distancing and semantic ambiguity. What she is here about to experience is, for the reader, only hinted at; it is not explained. In contrast to James, who takes pains to elaborate his thinking about the novel form in narratives that are clearly distinct from what he considers his fiction, the post-1878 Machado builds his theoretical innovations into the very texts he now determines to write. They are woven into it, becoming, finally, its defining characteristics. As a result, Machado never left us with a separate explanatory text like James's *The Art of the Novel* (1884); instead, we get a series of fictional and sometimes interrelated texts replete with theoretical discussions of language and meaning larded, often comically, into them.

Still, we would be wrong to think that Machado was not interested in criticism and theory or that he did not practice them, for he did, and with considerable relish and acumen.[72] Where we find the most concentrated and telling statements about Machado's thinking about narrative theory are in his post-1880 novels and stories. Embedded in these are his theoretical divagations made concrete; typical of his later style, Machado *shows* us what he is thinking, he does not *tell* us. In this, and in the other aspects of his work, Machado, Merquior declares, is "utterly modern—indeed, far more modern than . . . James."[73] Virtually everything about these later narratives—their plot structures, their characterizations, what their characters say, their points of view, their ambiguities, their differing levels of reliability, their effects on the reader, and their often ironic tonal shifts, among other things—shows the mark of a powerfully innovative narrative theoretician.

When one rereads Schorer's study, however, and applies it to Machado's pre- and post-1880 narratives, it becomes immediately clear how the Brazilian's later efforts are guided by a vastly different sense of (or sureness about) how the semantically and symbolically unstable nature of language affects issues of narrative technique and imitation. For Schorer, "the uses to which language, as language, is put to express the quality of the experience in question" is, along with point of view, one of the two main concerns of any novelist.[74] This is a position with which Machado would surely have agreed. Further, I also believe the Brazilian would have also agreed with Schorer that, broadly defined, technique would also serve as the "means" by which "our apprehension of the world of action is enriched or renewed."[75] But for Machado, the matter of technique is nevertheless less (much less) a matter of language being a stable and semantically neutral mechanism by which we objectively re-represent the human experience than it is a self-referential system of tropes that constantly offset, undermine, and otherwise call into question whatever interpretive stance we apply to what we are reading. Not to put too fine a point on it, one might well conclude that, for the late Machado, technique is not so much something that the author does to language as it is how the author responds to what he now realizes language is doing to him and his ability to write, to compose narrative. And to the reader's response to it. In telling us, via his introductory comments, about the "new narrative" he is about to write, the acutely self-conscious narrator/protagonist Brás Cubas takes pains to explain what he provocatively declares is his unusual technique not as the advocacy of a new style but, I argue, as a direct exploration of the nature of language itself.

Already in 1880, I further contend, Machado de Assis is, in anticipation of Ferdinand de Saussure's linguistics, showing us that his texts are, as functions of language, necessarily fluid semantic systems in which each word, each "signifier," leads not to some "signified" that lies outside of the system but only to other signifiers. This helps explain not just that Machado's late texts speak to themselves, and to each other, but, more importantly, why they do. In, especially, literary art, such as Machado wants to write, the words (or signs) that form the artistic whole, its structure, speak to each other. They have to because this is how language itself works, how it produces both meaning and change. Needing to be understood before one considers the notion of literature, language, Machado demonstrates, is alive, and nowhere more so than in its semantic mutability. Before what I do not hesitate to term the Machadoan revolution, in Brazil and in the Western tradition, the "conventional view of language" was that words were "similar to a window through which" the reader could "glimpse an extralinguistic concept or referential object known as the signified. . . . According to this perspective," language was nothing more than "a convenient means for designating," describing, and explaining "objects existing in an independently existing phenomenal world."[76] Style, largely a matter of diction, syntax, and point of view, of how the author handled language, was thought to be how one achieved this end. In this view, language was, like paints and brushes, stone and the sculptor's tools, or the sounds a musician could make, the instrument by which reality could be imitated. This was the understanding of language that the old Realism, the Realism that the late Machado so clearly rejects, was based upon. Machado's "new narrative," driven by its radically new and ontologically and epistemologically linguistic essence, subverts the theoretical basis of the old Realism and replaces it with a radically new theory of language, imitation, the production of meaning, and the reader's role in it.

If we accept the venerable argument of Robert Scholes and Robert L. Kellogg that prose fiction divides itself into two basic categories, the "representational" and the "illustrative," we can see that, in novels from *The Posthumous Memoirs of Brás Cubas* (1880) to *Counselor Ayres' Memorial* (1908), Machado's new narrative and new novel both cultivate the "illustrative," showing it to function as a symbolic system of signification while also showing the "representational" mode as being more mimetic, understood in the conventional sense of the word.[77] For Machado, who, I believe intentionally, makes considerable use of painting and other forms of artistic reproduction and expression (music, for example) in his later novels (and in some of his earlier ones as well), the literary artist, the one who works with words, has both restrictions that artists who work in other mediums do not have and hitherto unseen opportunities. If Machado's novels had been considered by Erich Auerbach in *Mimesis*, which seeks to evaluate the tradition of Western narrative in terms of his rather restricted view of mimetic Realism, he would have found it problematic, just as he found problematic all so-called "modern" narrative and for the same reasons. Like Joyce (whose *Ulysses* Auerbach judged, famously, or perhaps infamously, to be a hopelessly obscure "hodgepodge," full of "blatant and painful cynicism" and "uninterpretable symbolism"),[78] Machado grew, as a narrative artist, frustrated with the limitations imposed on him by the conventions and techniques of Realism and so began, even in the novels of his early phase (which move, technically speaking, steadily in this same direction), to lard them with more and more of the techniques (like a newly deployed symbolism) associated with "illustrative" narrative art. Both *Helena* (1876) and, more pointedly, *Iaiá Garcia* (1878) move in this direction.[79] But while Scholes and Kellogg maintain that "illustration differs from representation . . . in that it does not seek to reproduce actuality but to present selected aspects of the actual, essences referable for their meaning not to historical, psychological, or sociological truth but to ethical and metaphysical truth," Machado goes further.[80] Considerably further, I maintain.

The active and productive interaction of these two narrative modes, the "representative" and the "illustrative," in Machado's fiction, and most especially in his late fiction, is what allows more historically and sociologically inclined critics even now to read his novels, stories, and crônicas as penetrating insights into the institutions and tension of nineteenth-century Brazil at the same time that it allows literary scholars to see him break new ground in terms of narrative experimentation and the reader's role in it. If we view his use of the "representational" as a kind of seemingly realistic hook that draws readers in to a representation of a society they think they recognize and relate to, then his subtle but immensely dislocating use of the "illustrative," or symbolic, forces that same reader (or, at least, the one who will accede to Machado's numerous urgings, all of which come, charmingly, from the mouths of his unreliable narrator/protagonists) to confront and consider the fundamental instability of life and our attempts to impose meaning on it. Interpretation, Machado's late texts tell us, is everything, in literature and in life and with both being categorized, analyzed, and understood via language.

This, perhaps, touches on the genius of Machado de Assis—that he was able, in his new narrative art, to meld this radically different sense of what language is (a system of interlocking symbols) and how it actually works with a solid sense of how human society works. Far from being in conflict with each other, or with leading the reader too far in either direction, Machado was able to create texts, aesthetic and intellectual systems, that undercut the seemingly (or superficially) secure representations of certainty, conventional thinking, and bourgeois smugness that they appear, on one level, to be offering. Human institutions, to say nothing of human ideas, beliefs, and motivations (long recognized as turf Machado cultivates), are all the products of language use, and so, he deftly insists, they must be understood, in all their mutable, uncertain glory. Many of the best extraliterary studies on Machado that we have deal, in fact, with his brilliant dissection of a welter of historical, philosophical, sociological, political, and economic issues important to Brazil—and Western culture—in the second half of the nineteenth century.[81] Much of John Gledson's work, especially *Ficção e História* (1986), as well as Raymundo Faoro's *A Pirâmide e o Trapézio* (1974), Roberto Schwarz's *Ao Vencedor as Batatas* (1979) and *Um Mestre na Periferia do Capitalismo: Machado de Assis* (1990), and the work of Antônio Cândido, falls into this same socially conscious category. So while it is undoubtedly true that Machado "was more concerned with the perfection of his art than with taking a militant role in social causes," it is also true that Machado was keenly interested in Brazil's future as a modern nation-state and in the social, political, and economic forces that were shaping its development.[82] That he could do both, in fact, and with consummate skill, could be taken, as it is with Joyce or Faulkner, as a sign of his genius.

For my purposes here, however, it is, in the world of Machado's late novels, the play of language that comes to the fore, undercutting itself at both the micro level of diction and syntax and at the macro level of his novels' overall structuring and storytelling. Impressed as I am by Machado's extraliterary acumen, what interests me in the current study is how his last six novels order their clever, often acerbic, and always skeptical asides, their fascinating characters, their individual scenes, and their not infrequently funny chapters, and how, reflective of how language itself operates, they show us how and why they develop their circular, self-reflective, and metafictive structures. It is, I believe, this consistent offsetting, or semantic undercutting, that gives rise to Machado's famous ambiguity. For Machado, I contend, this ambiguity is less a function of a complex worldview (which he surely had) or a theme that is built into his narratives than a function of language itself.

It is precisely here, in this deliberate utilization of the modes of both the representational and the illustrative, that, again as in the case of Joyce (and the differences between his early works and his later ones), we can see more clearly how Machado manages to make his greatest novels appeal to both historians and literary critics and narrative theoreticians. It is clear, even in the first of these, *The Posthumous Memoirs of Brás Cubas* in 1880, that while he absolutely intends, consciously and deliberately, to create a new and different narrative, he does not intend to even pretend to break from the larger novelist tradition. Indeed, he has his self-conscious and (though we do not at first know it) ferociously unreliable narrator/protagonist tell us exactly this, albeit in a comically symbolic manner that gains our trust. One result of this is that only the truly engaged and thinking reader, the very new reader Machado will take pains to create through the run of this novel, will see what is happening here and how it needs to be read and appreciated. We can no longer be naïve or innocent about language use, not in the world of novels and not in the real world either. All is a matter of thoughtful, engaged interpretation.

In my view, then, modern Latin American literary history has two "new narratives," one beginning in Brazil with Machado de Assis in the period between 1878 and 1880 and the other beginning, in terms of narrative theory, with Borges and his "ficciones" in the 1930s. In the Spanish American narrative tradition, there would, and more specifically related to the novel genre, be other "new" narratives appearing in inchoate form around 1946, as in the latter half of Asturias's *El Señor Presidente*. What we think of as the Spanish American "new novel," however, really bursts into full bloom in the 1950s and 1960s, with texts like Juan Rulfo's *Pedro Páramo*, Julio Cortázar's *Hopscotch*, and Gabriel García Márquez's *One Hundred Years of Solitude*, among many others. Less widely known to those outside the ken of Brazilian literature is the extraordinary line of experimental narrative that is being produced in Brazil from the time of Machado de Assis to the 1950s and 1960s. Writers like Euclides da Cunha, Mário de Andrade, Oswald de Andrade, Patrícia Galvão, Graciliano Ramos, Raquel de Queirós, Hélio de Seixas Guimarães Rosa, and Clarice Lispector broke new ground in terms of how language, structure, and genre could be imagined and practiced. The great revolution in narrative theory, form, and technique that had begun in Brazil during the latter decades of the nineteenth century (a revolution that parallels that of Spanish American poetry during the same period) continues on unabated into the twentieth century. For Afrânio Coutinho, in fact, the 1920s and 1930s amount to a "golden age" for innovative and experimental Brazilian narrative.[83] Seen from the perspective of the comparative Latin Americanist, what we can conclude from an examination of Spanish American and Brazilian narrative between, roughly, 1880 and the 1960s is that it is an exceptionally rich and fecund period, one in which some of Western culture's most inventive and original stories and novels are being produced and in which exciting new theories about language and literary art are being promulgated. And central to all of this is the work of Brazil's Machado de Assis.

Understood as a problem of ontology and epistemology, and not as a function of stylistic adornment or the *mot juste* (precise word) of Flaubert, language, for the Latin Americans, had to do with how human beings perceived the world, how they imitated it in literary art, and how readers responded to it. Language itself became a touchstone for the Spanish American and Brazilian "new novelists," a subject that, for them, during the 1960s especially, directly affected how we view the world, how we seek to understand it, and how we struggle to define and cope with our multiple identities. This is the gist of Monegal's argument. While we see this concern most clearly in prose fiction, it is also present in much Latin American poetry as well. Vicente Huidobro, working in the same vein as Pierre Reverdy and Guilhaume Apollinaire, originates a new poetic aesthetic that he terms "Creacionismo," in which the poetically charged word possesses a creative force akin to that of God, while Borges, more known for his later "ficciones," is an early enthusiast of "Ultraísmo," an avant-garde movement with roots in the work of European expressionism and Dadaism. His 1960 poem "El otro tigre" expresses in poetic form what he had achieved earlier in his "ficciones," the creation of verbal structures so vivid and so verisimilar that they seemed both tangible and magical. In Brazil, too, as we see in the work of Manuel Bandeira, Cecília Meireles, and Carlos Drummond de Andrade, the new poetry of this fecund period is emphasizing the peculiar power of language not merely to imitate, or reproduce, but to create its own, self-sustaining structures. One of the greatest poets of the twentieth century, Mexico's Octavio Paz, believed that, for human beings, the word is Logos, and that the "worded" man or woman, that is, the woman or man who seeks identity and meaning through language use, knows that "to destroy words," or to use them deceitfully or carelessly, "is to destroy oneself."[84] For Paz, as he explains in works like *El arco y la lira* (1956), *Corriente alterna* (1967), and *Los hijos del limo* (1974), language must be understood never as mere decoration but as a living, breathing force essential to human comprehension and expression and, in the final analysis, to human existence itself. But while a great many Brazilian and Spanish American poets have dealt with language in this way, it is in the narrative tradition of Brazil that we see it explored most profoundly. In the literary history of Latin America, moreover, and in the literary history of the Americas generally, it is Brazil's Machado de Assis who, beginning in 1880, first plumbs the depths of this issue, the nature of language and its relationship to art, to understanding, and to the human experience.

THE REJECTION OF TRADITIONAL REALISM AND THE CREATION OF A NEW, LANGUAGE-BASED REALISM

We know that, already in 1878, Machado was cogitating, critically and iconoclastically, about Realism, about its basic assumptions and limitations, its relationship to reality, and about how language, as opposed to another art form, painting (as I will show, a common motif in his later works), imitates it. But, I posit, at the core of this new thinking about linguistic imitation (and artistic verisimilitude) was a view of language as a semantically arbitrary and fluid signifying system. In his still controversial 1878 essays on the Portuguese writer Eça de Queirós and his novels, *O Crime do Padre Amaro* and *O Primo Basílio*, Machado recommends that we "Voltemos os olhos para a realidade, mas excluamos o Realismo, assim não sacrificaremos a verdade estética" (Let's return our eyes to reality, but let's exclude Realism, so as not to sacrifice the aesthetic truth; *OC*, 3:913). Then again, and this time more sharply, as if he were making up his mind about an important point (which is precisely what I believe he is doing), in 1879 Machado avers that "A realidade é boa, o Realismo é que não presta para nada" (Reality is good; it's Realism that isn't worth anything; "A Nova Geração," in *OC*, 3:830). At this point in his analysis, Machado is less concerned with Eça, whom he praises for being the superb writer that he is, and more concerned with his new and rapidly emerging theory of language and literary art. Condemning Realism "in the name of reality," Machado begins to define himself as a writer who will change the ways narrative is conceived and practiced.[85] What we have here, then, in the years 1878 and 1879, is a definitive break with conventional Realism, its precepts, and its modes of expression, and the beginning of Machado's theorizing of a new narrative and, by 1880 and *The Posthumous Memoirs of Brás Cubas*, a new novel as well, one unique in the Americas and in the Western tradition generally.

Until the time of Machado, Realism in literature, as we have seen, had claimed to "to be all-inclusive in subject matter" and "objective in method."[86] For M. H. Abrams, Realism involves a kind of writing in which "the subject is represented, or 'rendered,' in such a way as to give the reader the illusion of actual experience. It is well, however," Abrams cautions, "to reserve the term 'realist' for writers who render a subject seriously, and as though it were a direct reflection of the causal order of experience, without too patently shaping it . . . into a tightly wrought comic or ironic pattern. . . . The technical term, 'realistic novel,' however, is most usefully applied to works which are realistic both in subject and manner, and throughout the whole rather than in parts."[87] Since the time of Aristotle and his *Poetics*, Realism has been a consistently sought-after objective, or parameter, of art. "Realism in the wide sense of fidelity to nature," notes Wellek, "is indubitably a main stream of the critical and creative tradition of both the plastic arts and literature."[88] "Still," as the same critic points out, "the pitfall of realism lies not so much in the rigidity of its conventions and exclusions as in the likelihood that it might, supported as it is by its theory, lose all distinction between art and the conveyance of information or practical exhortation."[89] Although "in its lowest reaches realism constantly" declines "into journalism, treatise writing," and "scientific description, in short, into non-art," at its "highest" reaches, which, I will argue, is represented by the late novels of Machado de Assis, a reconsidered Realism could create not only new "worlds of imagination" but also, as we see in the case of Machado de Assis, new, more language-sensitive ways of thinking about them.[90]

An important step in this same direction has been taken by José Luiz Passos, who, in his discerning 2000 essay on the nature of "moral reasoning" within the Realism of Eça de Queirós and Machado's lacerating criticism of it, addresses himself to the question of "narrative verisimilitude" and to the peculiar nature of the "syntax of life" in Machado's mature work.[91] Also noting the apparent connection between Machado's incisive critique of Eça's adherence to the French school and what I term his invention of Latin America's (and the New World's) first "new narrative," Passos feels that, in his two reviews, "Machado seems to put forward a view that stresses not necessarily a verisimilar representation of objects and events, but rather a plausible depiction of motivation and inner life," one, I would add, that stems from Machado's plumbing of how language works, how it creates, or generates, meaning even as it is working to undercut certainty and lead one to consider, virtually ad infinitum, other semantic alternatives.[92] By the late 1870s, Machado had come to realize that within any verbal structure, from shopping lists to sonnets, words—what Saussure would later define as linguistic signs—generate meaning more in relation to each other than in relation to the reality that they point to. Once he arrived at this conclusion, he also understood, I contend, why conventional Realism posed "a serious challenge to our understanding of the relations between artistic representation and reality."[93]

While it is true, as Passos points out, the old Realism (the one to which Machado objects; see above) leads us to pretend that what we are reading is, or is close to being, reality, the Brazilian master's unsettling realization about what this meant, for readers of literature and for citizens tasked with making political decisions (themselves a function of language use), takes us to an even more radical understanding.[94] Machado had come to see that, in all its semantic mutability, language touched on the great ontological and epistemological questions of life: Who are we and how do we claim to know things? Do we possess a single, unchanging identity, or do we become different people according to circumstance and motivation? How can we tell what is true and what is false? Are these concepts stable and eternal, or do they change too? How can we know the difference, if there is one? And how, since we use language to discuss it, can we ever hope to get beyond language? It is this radically new realization about language, being, and reality, I believe, that brings about the extraordinary "new narratives," and their struggle to create "new readers" (which, as I will show, we can also think of as new, more aware citizens, charged with interpreting the words/symbols that form societies, value systems, and political states) that define Machado's mature period.

I propose that we go further, however; that when we begin to consider Machado's new thinking about words as linguistic signs, or symbols that signify only in terms of other symbols within the same structure, we take the next logical step and begin to consider the possibility that the famous ambiguity that permeates Machado's world comes not so much from his consideration of a common theme but from the destabilizing nature of semantic production in language itself. Read as works of art, his late novels offer a series of attempts to explore what this realization would mean for the writing and reading of what we still rather cavalierly term "fiction," this being a term that cannot mean what we like to think it does since, as Machado had come to realize, all language use is a "fiction," a symbol of something else. And, as Machado would also have understood, since human beings are known as the "language animal," the one for whom language is key to its very existence, what is true of language must also be true of human existence itself, whether this be manifested in literature or in the entire span of social, political, philosophical, and ethical structures and systems. A novel written from this perspective would have characteristics very different from one written from the perspective of the old Realism, the one in which writers and readers both have an unjustified confidence in the close and essentially stable connection between a text written in the traditional realistic mode and the new kind that Machado, beginning in 1880, begins to explore.

Perhaps most salient, however, for the argument I wish to make here, is that between 1878 and 1880, when he published his withering critiques of Portuguese Realist Eça de Queirós, I believe Machado comes to the same conclusion about literary Realism that René Wellek reaches in 1963, namely, that "the theory of realism is ultimately bad aesthetics because all art is 'making' and is a world in itself of illusion and symbolic forms."[95] For Machado, the problem was that, in his view, Eça was slavishly devoted to the precepts, aesthetics, and "doctrines" of this old Realism, and to its cousin, Naturalism, and that this had led the Portuguese writer to create literary texts that, while well written, were overly preoccupied with the "external" and, most damning, that were "superficial" in their depictions, or representations, of human life and society.[96] Brazilian critic Celso Favaretto comes to a similar conclusion, noting that after 1880, Machado's "method of composition" amounts to "a displacement that implies a critique of literature, of mimetic Naturalism," and, I would add, of Realism as well, and "of the novels then in fashion."[97]

Implying that the old Realism, as practiced by Eça and others, failed to get beneath of surface of things, where, for Machado, the real drama of the human condition lay, his critique of Portuguese writer's novels allows him, I believe, an opportunity to clarify his new theory about the nature of narrative and artistic representation. Machado's final six novels are, I believe, a demonstration of this position as regards the new, and, with respect to the old Realism, "anti-realistic" kind of literary art that he is imagining and now creating. I conclude, therefore, that Machado's devastating critique of Eça and his novels should be read as less of an attack of Eça and his work, which he praises as being exemplary of a certain kind of narrative fiction (albeit one he now eviscerates), than as the moment when, theoretically speaking, Machado rejects the rote Realism of the past and begins to write novels in accordance with his new vision of what happens (of what *has to happen*) when an artist uses the medium of language to imitate nature and create verisimilitude.

By 1880, the year widely taken to be the point of departure for the astonishing novels of his mature period, Machado, who knew French well and who was deeply informed about French literature and critical thought, also had the example of Stéphane Mallarmé behind him. This, I believe, is important to Machado's thinking about language and literature. And to the "new narrative" he is about to begin creating. Like Mallarmé, Machado understands language to be a system of symbols. And, also like the French poet, he understands the unique power of syntax to alter the meaning of individual words, or signs, in a literary line as well as the often very different ways an engaged reader might respond to them, creating innumerable possibilities of meaning in the process. Semantically speaking, Mallarmé and Machado have come to realize words, and especially words organized in unusual ways in a sentence (or organized into a striking image or metaphor) by syntactic innovation, open themselves up, in the mind of a good reader, to a perhaps infinite number of interpretations, with each interpretation giving rise to yet another in a never ending process.

Machado, I believe, would agree that, because it cultivates precisely these qualities, poetry constitutes a very special kind of language use, one that emphasizes, and cultivates, the semantic productivity of words. "A poem concentrates," George Steiner insists, "it deploys with the least regard to routine or conventional transparency, those energies of covertness and of invention which are the crux of human speech. A poem is maximal speech."[98] And while Machado would continue to do his best, most experimental work in what, even now, we tend to think of as "prose fiction," his final six novels consistently demonstrate how, when blended with those of prose, the techniques of poetry can produce a radically new form of narrative, one that, in its linguistically rooted ambiguity, imitates the human experience more authentically than the old Realism could ever do. Sensing this already in 1866, Machado now begins quite intentionally and strategically to create a hybrid text, one that consciously makes use of the best qualities of both prose and poetry (OC, 3:847).[99] In doing so, he writes what is arguably Western literature's first "lyrical novel."[100] Inherently, Machado now realizes, words (and especially words used in this fashion) open things up; they do not close things down, and creative writing that tries to do this (to fix meaning), or that tries, by way of its traditional forms and definitions, to do so, is going against the grain, the very nature, of language. From *The Posthumous Memoirs of Brás Cubas* to *Counselor Ayres' Memorial*, Machado's post-1978 novels offer Western literature a slate of sometimes literally interconnecting narratives that explore the kind of writing—and reading—that would come from the new theory of language, art, and imitation that he was now pursuing. Limited by its conventional thinking about the superficial differences between poetry and prose, the old Realism is, at its core, deeply unrealistic, and it is against this misconception that Machado and his "new narrative" rebel.

Pushing the Machado/Mallarmé comparison further, one could argue that the 1880–81 novel *The Posthumous Memoirs of Brás Cubas* breaks with narrative tradition as much as the 1897 poem, "Un coup de dés jamais n'abolira le hazard" (A play/roll/throw of the dice will never abolish/eliminate/do away with chance), does with the Western poetic tradition. Even allowing for the demands of different genres, the two texts strike the reader in remarkably similar ways. While the French poet is better known in this respect, both he and Machado are, I contend, similarly experimental and iconoclastic. Even physically, as they exist, in unconventional fashion, on the page, the two texts share a number of traits. While both *seem*, initially, to be accessible to the reader, they very quickly show themselves not to be so, with discombobulating syntax and (especially notable in the case of Machado) unusual structurings at the level of the chapter that lead endlessly to different possible meanings and to meanings that seem to offset, or even cancel, one another. Both, moreover, achieve their extraordinary breakthroughs on the strength of what appear to be breathtakingly new understandings of language, how it works, and how it produces meaning. In both the poetry of Mallarmé and the narrative of Machado, language is shown to be always moving itself "away from certainty and stasis."[101] Finally, and again in both cases, constant semantic mutability, which produces a kind of constant undecidability (more discussed as ambiguity in Machado's case), comes to reign supreme. It is an embracing of this essential undecidability, or indeterminacy, that I believe both Machado and Mallarmé find to be inherent in language itself, that defines their respective revolutions.

Machado came to realize, I maintain, that while the meanings produced by individual words are unstable and relative more to other words (and other linguistic signs) than to any reality outside the particular structure (a chapter, a scene, or an image) to which they collectively give form, they are exponentially more so when their fundamental semantic fluidity is expanded to their functions in a line, a chapter, or an entire novel. Beginning in 1880, I believe that the heart of Machado's "new narrative" is what I have termed his use of the "metaphoric method," a kind of very deliberate writing that emphasizes, and builds upon, language's status as a symbolic system, a series of interlocking and self-referential metaphors. It is at this point, I suggest, that Machado parts company with the traditional modes of Realism and invents a new kind of fiction, one that now enriches itself via the techniques of poetry, that exemplifies his signature style, and that stands as the first "new narrative" not merely of Latin America and the Americas but of the Western tradition as well. After 1880, a word, Machado now seems to understand, is not the thing it stands for or describes but a representation of it, a representation, moreover, that is innately unstable in terms of its meaning. There is a separation between the word and its object, and, when understood by both writer and reader, this changes everything, at least as far as fiction writing is concerned. Working from this realization, Machado sees clearly that a work of literature has to be not a "realistic" depiction, or imitation, of reality in the old sense of the term but a structure made of symbols in which every word/symbol means something only in relation to other words/symbols in the same structure. Words, I believe Machado had, by 1878, come to realize, were figurative and iconic; they were not and could not *be* the things they pointed to and sought to imitate, and to think that they could, or even that they could objectively represent these things, was to be mistaken. And it was essential that both writer and reader understood this. Parting company with the old Realism, the narratives of the late Machado de Assis consciously celebrate "the troubled relation of the word to what it represents."[102] In literature (a very specific kind of language use), words, functioning as symbols, speak more to each other than to anything outside their common structure. To the extent that they do, this will be accomplished by the reader, who will extrapolate meaning from the text and apply it to life outside the piece of literature being read. It is for this latter reason that, in all of Machado's mature novels, the role of the new, aware, and engaged reader is so constantly stressed. A "new narrative," Machado now realizes, requires a "new reader."

And while Machado makes light of the reader's role in his late novels, the point he makes about how his "new reader" is a very serious one, one that speaks directly to how she is to respond to his "new narrative." Machado's "new reader" cannot any longer be a passive, unthinking consumer of a literary work, as she had been able to do with the novels and stories of the old Realism. Now, and beginning, comically but importantly, with *The Posthumous Memoirs of Brás Cubas*, much more would be demanded of Machado's reader. On this point, the connections between deconstruction, understood here as a reading strategy, and Machado's late novels become evident, for, as Miller has argued, "all good readers are and always have been deconstructionists."[103] This is so, Miller contends, because "reading is itself a kind of writing, or writing is a trope for the act of reading. Every act of writing is an act of reading, an interpretation of some part of the totality of what is."[104] Because, in each of his late novels, he gives primacy to both writing and reading, this is a point, I believe, with which the post-1878 Machado would surely agree.

As Gledson suggested in one of Machado's most seminal critical studies, *The Deceptive Realism of Machado de Assis* (1984), the Brazilian writer's Realism is more subtle than many, perhaps most, of traditional Realism's usual paragons. But the issue is complicated, and not without its ideological dimensions. "For Gledson," Alfred J. Mac Adam asserts, "'realism' is not a literary style or movement as practiced by Flaubert or Galdós but a value. A literary work of art is good if it can be demonstrated to be 'realistic,'—which means to be a kind of history writing with imaginative touches."[105] Arguing nevertheless that Machado creates "a profoundly original realism," Gledson identifies Machado as "the first truly great novelist to have written in Latin America."[106] I believe he is all that and more. Much more. Following esteemed Brazilian critic Schwarz, who, in a similar vein, finds Machado to have been "a great and consequent realist," one whose novels, "in their larger structures and their small details, are conformed by the realities of a slave-owning, favour-ridden, dependent, provincial society," Gledson and others have offered us insightful readings of Machado that convince us of his social awareness and his abilities to re-create the forces that drove the Brazil (and especially the urban Brazil) of his time.[107] In support of this position, Schwarz and Gledson cite three characteristics that have nevertheless confused generations of critics who have sought to fully explicate the true nature of Machado's unusual Realism: (1) "an extraordinarily pervasive and ingenious irony"; (2) his creation of "first-person narrators who seem much more reliable than they are"; and (3) his "experimentalism."[108]

But in contrast to Gledson, who ultimately finds Machado to be essentially a realist (albeit a quite singular one), I find him to be a modernist, a "deceptive" one, to invoke Gledson's thinking, in that, for me, the Brazilian is a modernist who offers us a radically new and language-based version of Realism. So while I agree that Machado's post-1878 novels most certainly do fly "in the face of Realism," they do so "deceptively" and in a way that does not ban from the text the "real" world that Gledson not unreasonably requires in his sense of Realism.[109] It is still there for Machado, but it is no longer the narrative's main objective; indeed, it is there largely to show why, as a mode of artistic imitation, it needs to be jettisoned. To imitate the true nature of human reality requires, Machado suggests, a new kind of Realism, one that achieves a new and (Machado will theorize) more "real," more authentic verisimilitude. More specifically, and in an attempt to explain the true (and distinctively unique) nature of the Brazilian writer's late narratives, I regard the mature Machado to be a modernist in a most profound and revolutionary fashion—one that in its essence prefigures the new linguistics of Saussure. And Saussure, I believe, merits recognition not merely as a revolutionary linguist (one who changed forever how we think about language) but as the last of the revolutionary thinkers of the nineteenth and early twentieth centuries, a list that includes such luminaries as Darwin, Marx, Freud, and Einstein. With Saussure, working in the early years of the twentieth century, the essential ambiguity inherent in the linguistic sign becomes clear, but with Machado, beginning already in 1880, it becomes the heart of his fictive universe.

My reasons for invoking Saussure in the context of explaining what I argue is Machado's new theory of narrative stem from the main points advanced by the Swiss linguist in his famous *Course in General Linguistics* (1916): that a linguistic sign is composed of two parts, the signifier (the *significant*) and the signified (the *signifié*); that a language had to be studied as a closed structure or self-referential system of differences *without positive terms*;[110] that "in the system of signs which constitutes language, the relationship between a given sound and the mental image it evokes is completely arbitrary, based on convention only"; that "languages seem to constitute world of convention independent of each other and of the physical world"; and that "'Reality' comes to mean the self-referential sign/language system which has adopted us."[111]

An additional point, and also one important to the case I am making here, is that Saussure "warns that language's radical arbitrariness makes it a unique medium," this being a proposition of immense importance for understanding how imitation via narrative art might be achieved.[112] This last point is germane to Aristotle's *The Poetics* in that it is precisely this point—how language imitates nature—that the Greek polymath does not delve into in depth. Nor does he get to a discussion of comedy, which, particularly as irony is concerned, is so important to our reading and understanding of Machado's late novels. All four of Saussure's arguments about the nature of language apply directly, I maintain, to the nature and form of Machado's last five novels. Since these radically innovative positions about language did not become public until the years between 1907 and 1911, when Saussure began to offer them to his students at the University of Geneva, it would be virtually impossible for Machado, who died in 1908, to have known about them and so be influenced by them. There are very few scenarios by which this could have happened, though it is possible that news about Saussure's lectures could have gotten to Rio de Janeiro and gain Machado's attention. So we are essentially free to conclude both that Machado's new thinking about language, narrative art, structure, and meaning almost certainly comes about independently of Saussure's groundbreaking work and that, in point of fact, it exemplifies it, much in the ways the Borges *Ficciones* epitomized (mostly via French translations) how the theories of French structuralism would look when given form in creative fiction.

But, and again deceptively, Machado achieves his iconoclastic understanding of how words relate to reality and to each other in a deliberately crafted structure (the literary work of art) by a writer aware of the semiotic fluidity of his materials (language and the structures into which he chooses to construct them) by choosing, very strategically, to work within the norms of the conventional novel form. Machado, we might say, is a revolutionary who elects to work within the system. Beginning with *The Posthumous Memoirs of Brás Cubas*, his conception of the new "anti-novel" he wanted to write has no meaning outside the context of the traditional novel itself. Without the model of the "novel," the idea of an "anti-novel" means little or nothing, and Machado understood this. He undertakes his subversive (of the traditional novel form) work while remaining solidly within the traditions of the novel form. In doing this, in revolutionizing the novel genre by staying more or less within its traditionally defining definitions and boundaries, Machado effectively does for extended narrative fiction what Mallarmé had earlier done for modern poetry—using a traditional form to feature a nontraditional technique to highlight a new approach to, or implementation of, the old form. But while the French poet dramatized the semantic play and ambiguity of language within the sonnet form, Machado does so within the notably expansive confines of the novel form.

On the surface, Machado's novels deal with the people, issues, social structures, and institutions that reconstruct middle- and upper-class urban Brazil in the second half of the nineteenth century. This is where Machado's traditional Realism shows through most clearly. It is why we can read him, as we regularly and rightly do, as a writer of great historical, social, and political insight. And he is all of this. But inside, at the level of language, syntax, structure, and semantics, his texts (the products of his new views about how language works) destabilize everything, turning what, seen from the outside, seems orderly, stable, and "realistic," into ambiguity and the constant play of *différance* that Derrida, following Saussure, argues is characteristic of all language and of all language use. And, as I have argued elsewhere, part of this new sense of how language constantly undercuts itself, Machado is also led, in his later novels, to connect the liberation of the black slaves to the need to liberate Brazil's women as well, a move that, in modern critical parlance, involves the undercutting of not merely logocentrism but phallogocentrism as well.[113] Because, in fact, of his assiduous cultivation of what many critics think of as language's inherent "indeterminacy" (which stems, in Machado's case, first, from his unorthodox syntactical linkages, and, second, from the unexpected sequencing of seemingly [but not truly] discontinuous images and scenes, this being also an issue of syntax, though on the macro level), Machado can be thought of as much of a proto-poststructuralist as Mallarmé had been for a number of French theorists, from Lacan and Barthes to Derrida himself. In Machado's post-1880 novels, with their emphasis on how words generate sometimes contradictory or inconsistent meanings in consort with other words, it is not difficult to see, as critic Raman Selden argues is characteristic of all poststructural prose, that "the signifier floats away from the signified, *jouissance* [enjoyment] dissolves meaning, the semiotic disrupts the symbolic, *différance* inserts a gap between signifier and signified, and power disorganises established knowledge."[114]

To pursue this comparison a bit more, we could, after reading Machado, easily conclude that he "disappears" from his late novels in ways that parallel the "disappearance" of Mallarmé into his poetry. It is true that the "disappearance" of Mallarmé in a poem like "L'Après-midi d'un faune" (first written in 1865 but published in 1876) differs from the "disappearance" of Machado in his five late novels, but the difference has more to do with the demands of genre (lyric poetry versus narrative fiction) than anything else. Machado, for example, makes extensive use, as I will show, of a variety of unreliable narrator/protagonists to tell his tale. He engineers his own effacement at the hands of these acutely self-conscious storytellers. In both cases, however, it is the endlessly productive play of language that takes over and dominates not only the text itself but the reader's uncertain and evolving response to it. For Mallarmé, poetry, which is to constantly test the potentialities of language, resides in "the *contemplation* of things, in the image emanating from the reveries which things arouse in us."[115] For the French master, poetry "does not *name*, it *suggests*," a concept Machado would now extend to his own thinking about narrative and, indeed, to all language use.[116] In the view of Mallarmé and Machado, literature, a function of language, cannot be mere imitation; it is that, but it is also something more, a kind of reality itself. For Mallarmé and Machado, this new reality, the one they are now most concerned with, is that of language-driven artistic reality; for them, "Reality is the poem," or the narrative, "itself," a self-contained and self-referential system of symbols, or figures, that, while it may exude points of contact with external reality that the astute reader may choose to make, answers, ultimately, to its own artistic devices.[117] Because what Mallarmé and Machado are now seeking to do is a function of language, and not paint, stone, or sound, and because the reader's response to it will also take place in language, their art is radically different from these other modes of imitation. In their verbal constructs, language will be speaking to itself, both in the text and in the mind of the reader. While Mallarmé's poetry goes further in this direction, becoming, at times, quite hermetic, Machado's late novels, I contend, are built on the same principle: while they do, indisputably, have clear social relevance, they are, at the same time, and again indisputably, self-contained and self-referential linguistic structures. This, I believe, is the basis of their antirealistic and iconoclastic art and of their status as language conscious "new narratives." It is what makes them so different. At bottom, then, neither the poet nor the narrativist is primarily concerned with "teaching the reader, or copying nature, but rather searching out and capturing an elusive reality in words, perhaps even *making* reality in words."[118]

In this same context, however, it is important to bear in mind that each reader's response is itself conducted by means of language as well (and it need not be the language in which the text is written). Because of this, what Machado causes to be happening in his texts is what is happening to the reader as she seeks to decipher what Machado's texts, scenes, and metaphors mean, or might mean. For both Machado and Mallarmé, then (this being the point the latter writer makes in 1895, with *The Book: A Spiritual Instrument*), it is as if the particular linguistic forms their texts take (or are finally given by their language-conscious authors) function like a powerful steel spring, which, when released (by the act of reading) into the mind of the reader (whose process of reading and thinking is also a function of language), sets off an effectively endless chain reaction of possible readings, lines of interpretation, and potential meanings, at least some of which may well undermine each other. This, I believe, is the source of Machado's famous ambiguity, which he demonstrates, after 1880, to be less external (that is, imposed from the outside, as in the case of an author wishing to complicate plots, relationships, characterizations, and utterances) than internal, an unavoidable function of language itself, of symbols ceaselessly sending and receiving messages, or inchoate signals (suggestions or intimations, moments of insight or new thoughts about the same text or image), and with each word (or sign) generating not closure (a feeling of certitude about what is meant) but more words and more possible meanings. In 1896, and the essay "Mystery in Literature," Mallarmé will lay out a very similar argument about the unavoidably opaque nature of literary language use.

In approaching Machado's late novels from this perspective, however, it is also important to bear in mind that while, in my estimation, at least, he does reject the basic tenets of conventional Realism, he also invents, and offers to the reader, a new kind of Realism, one that is much more derived from the nature of language and its unstable processes of signification than the earlier, more stylistically oriented Realism was. Favaretto, moving in this same direction, concludes that "Machado articulates a very personal realism," one that "resists easy interpretations based on psychological projection and identification with characters or on the establishment of pathologies and predetermined traits—elements typical of the novelists of his time."[119] The new Realism of Machado's "new narrative" is thus more able than the old Realism ever was to capture the mystery, uncertainty, and ambiguity of life and the human experience. The narrative Realism of Machado's last five novels is, in short, more realistic, surprising as this may seem, than conventional Realism could ever be. The "realism" of Machado's anti-Realism gets at the true nature of the human condition, the degree to which the experience of being human is a function of language. And language, Machado demonstrates (and as Saussure will later prove), is inherently arbitrary and relative in terms of its ability to produce meaning. In moving away from traditional thinking about Realism, Machado should be read in the context of such other Western giants as Proust, Woolf, Joyce, Mann, Kafka, and Faulkner who, like Machado, sought to "break away from the aims, attitudes, and techniques of realism."[120] And, as in the cases of these other luminaries, Machado's readers and critics were utterly "unprepared" for what he was seeking to do.[121]

Like the Proust of *À la recherche du temps perdu* (1913–27), but earlier and coming at it from the perspective of what we now think of as semiotics, Machado's later novels excel at showing the endlessly destabilizing role of language in recapturing thoughts, sensations, and people from past time, and at developing characters (Marcel, for example, and Brás Cubas) who serve as both narrator and character. "Time and its destructive passing" are the warp and woof of Machado's post-1880 narratives, and, "as Proust would define in *Swann's Way*" more than three decades later, and our painfully human desire to recapture the past cannot be achieved and, indeed, can be approximated only by "the action of involuntary memory."[122]

And, in advance of Woolf, Machado understands, already in 1880, that "life is not a series of gig lamps symmetrically arranged," which, for him, would describe what Realism had sought to do, "but a luminous halo, a semi-transparent envelope surrounding us from the beginning of consciousness to the end."[123] For Machado, this "luminous halo," this "semi-transparent envelope," was not merely an as yet poorly understood entity called "consciousness"; it was a function of language, without which this mysterious, evanescent, ever metamorphosing thing we term "consciousness" could not be named or discussed. Language, which we need not only to give "consciousness" its name but to plumb, and establish, its potential meanings, was the key.

In comparison to Joyce, who began to publish after Machado had died, we can see how, like the Irish writer, Machado was committed to the rejection of Realism and to the writing of experimental narratives that emphasized the essential uncertainty of life and our attempts to imbue it with meaning. Importantly, Joyce was, like Machado, a great comic writer, though they both envisioned life as fragmented and lacking the unity, depth, and meaning that only great narrative art can provide. In *Dubliners*, a collection of fifteen stories begun in 1905 but not published until 1914, Joyce makes use of a technique, the story line that coalesces around not external event or action but interconnecting structures and patterns of images, symbols, and motifs, that Machado had been experimenting with since 1880. It is no accident, I believe, that the last story of *Dubliners*, "The Dead," which many regard as the collection's greatest achievement, is eerily reminiscent of many of Machado's post-1878 stories and of sections of his later novels as well, *Quincas Borba* and "Midnight Mass" perhaps most particularly.[124] A powerful sense of missed opportunity permeates both texts. For Machado, as for these other, later modernists, the devices and techniques of poetry are brought to bear on the creation of a new, imagistic kind of narrative fiction.

In the case of Mann (whose first novel, *Buddenbrooks*, published in 1900, he might have known or read about), Machado would have seen how effectively symbolism could be made use of in narrative and, even more important for Machado's fame as an acute social commentator in Brazil, he would likely have responded to the theme of the conflict between artist and citizen that so permeates Mann's work, as it does that of Joyce. In my opinion, however, a major part of Machado's greatness lies in his realization that this conflict need not be fatal or tragic; indeed, if one understands the semantic mutability of language, then both artist and citizen can better deal with the vicissitudes, confusions, self-delusions, and, on occasion, the outright deceptions that define human reality.

And like Kafka, Machado had begun to see the human being as trapped in a tangle of systems that she or he could neither control nor understand. And yet it is within this tangle of systems, with all the confusion and uncertainty that ensues from it, that the human creature must exist. There is no other alternative. To a large extent, language determines our existence; murky and unstable, this is the nature of our existence, and it must be dealt with as it is. The act of doing so, of dealing with it, becomes the record of human experience, and it is the imitation of this, through language, that Machado seeks. But from his post-1878 novels, we can also see that while Machado is grappling with the problem of nullity that, given his realization of language's inherent undecidability, freights so much modernist thought, his later narratives, which clearly depict women and men trying to come to grips with the uncertainties of their lives and with life itself, rarely fall prey to the nihilism, or solipsism, the sense of unalterable isolation, that also marks modernist writing.[125] While it could be argued that the narrator of *Dom Casmurro* does exemplify this kind of fatal isolation, I would suggest that the predicament he faces is due to his own congenital failure, his inability to prevent the lovable and loving callow young man, "Bentinho," from degenerating into the cruel, twisted, and implacable monster, "Dom Casmurro." And because language is the mechanism by which Machado's characters, including "Dom Casmurro," seek to understand what they are doing and the meaning of what is going on around them, every interpretation begets another; nothing is certain, absolute, or unchanging, though, as we see in novel after novel, this uncertainty does not necessarily lead to fragmentation and a sense of despair. It can, and in many later European modernist narratives it does, but it does not have to. The same condition can manifest itself in different ways, some of which can, in fact, generate "positive difference."

Machado's deeply socialized human creature, always an artistically rendered linguistic construct, muddles on, struggling to make sense of what is happening around her. The society in which Machado's men and women live may be corrupt, debased by slavery, riven with inequities, and, at bottom, a cruel charade, but it is a social structure nevertheless, and his people, his characters, exist in it. Importantly, so do his readers, then as now. And, as we see in the great female character Fidelia of Machado's final novel, *Counselor Ayres' Memorial*, positive change can be brought about, even in such a society as the one depicted here. This outcome is far from a given, however, and the chance, indeed the likelihood, that we will fail, that we will remain isolated, alienated, and alone, haunts modernist literature. But, it is entirely possible to theorize, whether the outcome of the human struggle is positive or negative, for Machado, the artist who would imitate the reality of words by means of words, the epitome of all the controlling but unstable structures that shape our lives, as well as our understanding of them and what they mean, was language. Indeed, it is all but impossible *not* to come to this conclusion. In reading the Brazilian's post-1878 novels, and in comparing them to those he had written before and to each other, one is led to conclude that for Machado, as for Nietzsche and later commentators, the limits of one's world are the limits of one's language, and vice versa.

Indeed, the relationship between Machado and the German philosopher and philologist (the latter fact reminding us of Nietzsche's keen interest in language as a communicative system) is worth considering in the context of my argument here. It is entirely possible that Nietzsche's groundbreaking work between 1872 and 1887 could have influenced Machado's thinking about life, imitation, art, narrative, and language. Certainly, a reader with Machado's catholic tastes would have known about Nietzsche's revolutionary ideas. And, given the new directions in which he himself was already going in terms of his thinking about language, art, imitation, and the novel form, it seems likely that he would have been struck by the German's divagations concerning the "Gefängnis der Sprache,"[126] or the "prison house of language," a concept about language, knowledge, and truth and that was crucial to later structuralist and poststructuralist critics.[127] After Derrida's revival of interest in Nietzsche, in fact, it has even become standard to think of the author of *The Birth of Tragedy* (1872), "Truth and Falsity in an Ultramoral Sense" (1873), *Thus Spoke Zarathustra* (1883–85; Nietzsche's most widely read book), *Beyond Good and Evil* (1886), and *A Genealogy of Morals* (1887) as a kind of proto-deconstructionist.[128] In "Truth and Falsity," which appeared only five years before Machado announced his rejection of Realism, Nietzsche, as Machado would do, had recognized that language was inherently figurative, and not referential, in nature. And, as such, it responded, especially in terms of how it generated meaning, to its own imperatives. "Truth and Falsity," moreover, appeared three years before Machado's novel, *Helena* (1876), which stands out from its predecessors for the elevated level of symbolism it practices.

But, even more interestingly, it is "Truth and Falsity" where Nietzsche declares that the desire to use language to create metaphors is a "fundamental impulse" of the human creature.[129] In this same regard, it is perhaps worth noting that it is at this same time that Machado is beginning to develop what I have noted elsewhere will later become a hallmark of his mature prose—the metaphoric method, his talent for advancing his narratives not by action and narration but, in the manner of poetry, by a series of interlocking images, motifs, symbols, and metaphors, all of which speak to, reinforce, amplify, or complicate each other.[130] In realizing that language is figurative, rhetorical, and metaphorical in nature, and that it must therefore imitate nature and life in the ways that are appropriate for a symbolic system, both Machado and Nietzsche point not just to the power of art but to the unique power of verbal, or language-based, art. As Nietzsche, making a point in 1873 that Machado, who was committed to the novel as an art form, would surely have agreed with, puts it, "That impulse toward the formation of metaphors, that fundamental impulse of man" results in the construction, via language, of "a new world" of order and harmony, one in which this same impulse to create metaphors and linguistic structures "seeks for itself a new realm of action" and imitation "and finds it in *Mythos* and more generally in *Art*."[131] While Nietzsche is considering the philosophical implications of this line of thought, Machado de Assis, laboring away in Brazil but still very much a part of the Western tradition, is beginning to write novels that illustrate it.

This question of "truth" or "falsity" is essential—to the operation of language but also to understanding the "new novels" of Machado de Assis. It is perhaps with Nietzsche in mind that, of this very point, Steiner writes, "The principal division in the history of Western literature occurs between the early 1870s and the turn of the century. It divides a literature essentially housed in language from one for which language has become a prison." After this watershed moment, which basically encompasses Machado's mature period, the same critic is led to this observation, one that makes a point directly applicable to the argument I am making here about Machado's new theory of narrative and the novels he will now write: "The matter of truth has been one of the relations between 'words and words' more often than between 'words and things.'"[132] This is what, by 1878, Machado now realizes ("Eça de Queirós: O Primo Basílio," in *OC*, 3:911 and passim); for human beings, who inhabit the world of words, the concept of truth (like the concept of the "self") reveals itself to be the constant play of language. Truth, for Machado, becomes a matter of narrative form—of words written, read, and spoken (that is, ordered or arranged) in a certain way—and of our always subjective, always evolving response to it. The old Realism, which sustained itself on a close and largely unquestioned identification between words and reality, the things in the world, will, for the Brazilian writer, no longer serve as an adequate means of imitation. Instead, he would need to create a new form of Realism, one inherently and deliberately linguistic in nature and one built around the principle that the words selected by him, as artist, to give his "new novel" a specific and self-interrogating form and structure, relate first of all to other words in the same structure. While Machado's "new narratives" will be eminently readable and full of identifiable characters, conflicts, and social situations, and so valuable as sociopolitical documents, they will, at bottom, be constructed around a radically new theory of narrative, imitation, and narrative art, one now leavened by the techniques of poetry and one based on a new understanding of the semantic uncertainty and mutability that language itself generates. Beginning with *The Posthumous Memoirs of Brás Cubas* and, I maintain, carrying through to *Counselor Ayres' Memorial*, Machado's "new narrative" and "new novel" both stem from this basic premise about language. Truth, Machado's late narratives and narrators will show us, is more a matter of verisimilitude, and therefore of art, than anything else.

Nietzsche, the "decisive forerunner" to many "deconstructionist" critics, "presented a categorical rupture in the theory of language, starting a new historical epoch in which language was first consciously conceived of as always, at once and originally, figural or rhetorical, rather than referential or representational. No primordial unrhetorical language existed. As the distinctive feature of language *rhetoricity* necessarily undermined truth and opened up," in the words (via translation) of Derrida, "'vertiginous possibilities of referential aberration.'"[133] Meaning was now a matter of how different readers respond to a text, a specific verbal structure, and, as I seek to show, Machado's later novels concentrate intensely on precisely this factor. When, in 1878, Machado speaks of the need for a "verdade estética," or "aesthetic truth," in the imitation of reality by language, this, I believe, is what he is talking about ("Eça de Queirós, in *OC*, 3:913).[134] He has now come to grips with the salient fact: when one is dealing with truth as a function of language, it becomes, first and foremost, a matter of form (or structure), of words talking to and with other words and of interpretation, which is itself a matter of words talking with other words. To a degree, we can escape this linguistic prison in the science lab, or in the world of mathematics, but in the human world, where virtually all the institutions we construct and by which we live are functions of language, we cannot. While scientific discoveries are made in the lab, their application to the human experience, their meaning, depends upon language use. Beginning, in the Western tradition, with Nietzsche but also with Machado de Assis, we can now regard "the linguistic sign" not as a stable, unchanging source of knowledge but as "the site of an ambivalent and troubling relation between referential and figural meaning. The problematic of the sign brought into question" not merely the theoretical basis of Realism, the problem Machado was primarily concerned with in 1878 and 1879 and his critiques of Eça de Queirós, but the entire history of "thematic interpretation" while simultaneously encouraging the practice of "rhetorical reading," which, I believe, is why, beginning in 1880, and *The Posthumous Memoirs of Brás Cubas,* Machado works so diligently to create his "new reader."[135]

After 1878, one can reasonably conclude, Machado de Assis was the first writer of prose fiction in the Western tradition to systematically explore this problem, as it relates to narrative art and imitation, and to begin to compose an entire series of "new novels" that exemplified what this new thinking about language, narrative, art, and society might mean. Why, with the advent of world literature, be hesitant any longer to promote a writer from a place called Brazil as occupying a high point of Western literature? Why is this so difficult for us to do? Or to accept? The quality is there, as is the requisite originality of thought, so why not the recognition? The work of European writers had, of course, long circulated in the Americas, North and South. The fact that it was not until the mid-twentieth century that Latin American literature began, seriously, to circulate (via translation) to North America and Europe is more of an indictment of North American and European culture, and its resistance to influences from abroad, than of Latin America, where highly original literature was being produced on a routine basis. We who work on Spanish American and Brazilian literature need to jettison this reluctance to become primary participants in the global circulation of literature, for not to do so only handicaps our efforts to bring our fully deserving authors and texts to the attention of the world audience. Now is the time to do this. As González Echevarría has argued, Latin Americanists must realize that their novels, poems, stories, essays, and dramas are, as works of literary art and critical thought, sometimes superior to those of their European counterparts.[136] An innovator in terms of narrative theory and an acute practitioner of his own, highly distinctive approach to narrative art, Machado de Assis is one such case.

Already in 1880, when Europe is in the grip of a waning Realism and the emergence of a powerful and scientifically based Naturalism, the Brazilian master is showing his readers a startlingly original brand of ironic, self-effacing narrative, one that runs counter to the tenets of both Realism and Naturalism and that anticipates the works of the great European modernists, Proust, Woolf, Joyce, and Mann. The breakthrough for this kind of writing, in theory and in practice, occurs,

I am arguing, not in France, Germany, or England but in Brazil. Latin Americanists (and Americanists generally) must cease being so reluctant to believe that their literary production is eternally inferior to, and mere copies of, the better known paragons of the Western tradition; the "influenced" text is not automatically a lesser thing than the more celebrated "influencing" texts. They can, in point of fact, be more imaginative, more profound, and more stimulating than the works too quickly and too uncritically assumed to be "better." In this revised thinking about the European narrative canon, Machado emerges as the vital link between Flaubert and Proust.

There is, moreover, every reason to believe that, in addition to Flaubert, Sterne, Cervantes, and the other European notables of the time, Machado also knew Nietzsche and his work and that, as he was already thinking along these same lines, he would have seized upon the German intellectual's line of thought, seeing in it an affirmation of his own theorizing.[137] Machado de Assis, we might say, was circulating, widely and deeply, in the European tradition, even if said tradition was not much interested in considering the importance of a little-known writer from Brazil.[138]

As a semantic system, language was separate from what is normally thought of as the realities that surrounded it and that, in some kinds of writing, it seemed to describe and, in its own fashion, imitate. And, as Mallarmé had suggested at about the same time, language use could be said to constitute its own reality, its own system of signification. This was particularly evident in literary language, and most especially in poetry, but, as Machado proves, the same principle applies to narrative as well. The words of a poem mean what they mean overwhelmingly in relation to the other words in the same poem, just as is the case with Machado's post-1878 stories and novels. The theoretical affinities, or points of contact, between the Machado of this period and Nietzsche are many and intriguing. Both were concerned with issues of nihilism and the nature of human conduct in the absence of what Derrida would later term logocentric and phallogocentric belief systems, with doubts about the validity of religious systems, with the figurative nature of language, with the protean nature of meaning, with the concomitant necessity of interpretation (and in all aspects of human life), with the deliberate use of figurative and metaphoric language, and with the concepts of power and strength. While for Nietzsche, this latter line of thought led to his famous notion of the Übermensch, or Superman, for Machado it can be seen in his consistent construction of characters, male and female, who, rejecting passivity and the victim mentality, and putting into practice something akin to Nietzsche's "will to power," actively and aggressively seek better lives for themselves.

This theme, the need to fight if one wished to improved one's lot in life, turns up in *The Posthumous Memoirs of Brás Cubas* when, in chapter 141, the character Quincas Borba declares to his none too skeptical and comfortably upper-middle-class acolyte Brás Cubas, "Fight. You can shatter them or not, the essential thing is for you to fight. Life is a fight. A life without fight is a dead sea in the center of the universal organism" (*BC*, 185). What is interesting here, given the basic argument I am making in this book, is that this perfectly sensible message comes out of the mouth of a madman. Even a deranged person is capable of making sense sometimes, the alert reader realizes (or so she can think), and this fact drives home Machado's core point: in life, it is difficult to discern not just truth from falsity but the reasonable from the unreasonable. And, to further complicate things, sometimes, as in this case, rational pronouncements can come from the mouths of irrational people, thus making it even more difficult to decipher the meaning of all that envelops us. Semantic ambiguity and mutability, we might say, form the narrative sea in which Machado's post-1978 characters swim. As if to provide the reader with a clue as to what she is doing, Machado, making use of his charming (but unreliable) narrator Brás Cubas, as well as a character, the self-proclaimed philosopher Quincas Borba, makes an explicit reference to the "mutability" of meaning in the very next chapter, number 142, in which Brás himself seeks to understand the significance of what Quincas Borba has shown him and told him (*BC*, 186–87).[139] The reader, who is trying to understand the text she is reading, sees the narrator trying to understand what one of his own characters means. To complete the metaphor (which now leads the attentive reader to realize something she has needed to realize), the sea in which these men and women swim is, because it is a sea of language, far from dead; indeed, it is full of life and teeming with infinite possibility and creativity, and the properly engaged reader, fighting (as per Quincas's admonition to Brás) to interpret and create meaning, comes alive in it. Language, in other words, is, for the late Machado de Assis, a sea of eternal semantic life.

Importantly, in terms of their thinking about the nature of language, both Nietzsche and Machado have the German philosopher Arthur Schopenhauer in common, though, arguably, for different reasons.[140] Beyond the question of *Weltanschauung* and the ways language shapes its formulation and expression, one additional sign of this common influence is, in fact, that both Nietzsche and Machado cultivated a witty, self-conscious, and aphoristic style, one full of often mordant word play and puns; the tone and tenor of Brás Cubas's "maxims" (chapter 119, *BC*, 165), in fact, evoke a direct memory of Nietzsche and the sardonic nature of much of his writing. Finally, and pertinent to the argument I am making in these pages, Nietzsche, like Machado, was interested early on in the ability of language to distinguish between truth and falsity ("Truth and Falsity," 1873) and, later in his career (1901 and *Der Wille zur Macht*, the "will to power"), on how it seemed to determine the limits not merely of one's world but of one's ability to think about this world, this being the concept that would later give rise to the image of the "prison house of language."[141] With Nietzsche coming to these conclusions about language and meaning from the perspective of philology and philosophy, and with Mallarmé reaching them from the perspective of poetry, it would not be surprising if Machado found their conclusions not only convincing but fully in line with his own thinking. What remained would be to experiment with the kinds of narrative art that would result from it.

It is a complication of Machado's case that while these other, better known and more widely respected authors can exert these kinds of renovating efforts and be credited, even lauded, for doing so, when a writer—and even a brilliant writer—from a so-called "marginal" or disregarded literary tradition like that of Brazil undertakes the same sorts of experiments, she or he is simply ignored. Or, at best, devalued. This, I believe, has a lot to do with why Machado has for so long been virtually ignored, or misread, by those who operate in the great centers of global literary production and commentary. To be a writer from the periphery is to find it difficult, if not impossible, to get a fair and equal reading. Or, indeed, any reading at all. Though their widely read and very influential book was published in 1966, after the Boom in Latin American literature was well under way in the United States, Scholes and Kellogg's *The Nature of Narrative* contains, for example, not a single reference to a Latin American writer, not to Borges and certainly not to Machado de Assis (who had been available in good English translations since early 1952). The same is true for Jameson's *The Prison-House of Language*, published in 1972. Seeking to overcome or mitigate this egregious omission from the Western canon, I argue here that because our Brazilian writer creates, at the beginning of the penultimate decade of the *nineteenth century*, a startlingly new, pre-Saussure variety of Realism, he must be recognized as ranking among these better known modernist innovators.[142]

But, I stress, and in contrast to them, while these other innovators tend to focus on the "awakening" of "complex correspondences between the psyches" of characters and readers and that "provides a rich and intense 'experience' for the reader," one that "may not only move him but also exercise his perception and sensibility, ultimately assisting him to perceive and comprehend the world of reality more sharply and more sensitively than he otherwise might," Machado achieves all this by concentrating on the fluid, semantically productive nature of language as semiotic system.[143] The uniqueness of Machado's contribution to this tradition is, I believe, of tremendous and far-reaching importance. And, applying it to the writing, reading, and interpreting of literary texts, to the interaction that involves language, a writer, the writer's characters, and the reader, he does it more than two decades before Saussure launches his famous work on linguistics, which, as is well known, becomes the conceptual basis for both structuralism and, more important for Machado's case, poststructuralism. Of the European fiction writers mentioned above, Proust might be the closest to Machado in terms of his understanding of how profoundly language, deeply intertwined with time, memory, and desire, affects not only human thought and expression but also human behavior.

Machado's new Realism also shows us how critical the act of interpretation is, not only in the world of literature, where we expect it, but also in human life generally. To be a good reader, Machado's post-1880 novels imply, is to be a good citizen, and the careful, close reading of novels such as he offers can be good practice for what a good citizen must do with respect to the deciphering of a welter of social, political, and even economic arguments (which are themselves functions of words). This approach to the issue of enlightened social consciousness permeates all of his final novels, up to and including the emergence of the new Brazilian woman and the role she would play in the formation of the new, post-abolition Brazilian Republic. Ironically, then, Machado's new "anti-Realism," or, more properly said, his new and now more linguistically driven Realism, shows itself more realistic, in terms of how accurately or faithfully it imitates our real human experience, both inner and outer, than the old Realism ever did. The arguments put forward by Saussure led the Swiss linguist "to call for a new science of the twentieth century that," based on his discoveries about language and the nature of signification, focus on "the life of signs within society."[144] For Saussure, this new science would be known as "semiology," the study of signs and how they work in human society.[145] I contend that, in the novels he wrote between 1880 and 1908, Machado does precisely this; far more than he had done before, he now begins, as a writer and literary artist, to explore language understood as a system of arbitrary signs and how this new awareness about language as a semantically fluid semiotic system impacts how novels (and short stories) are written, how history is conceived and written, how politics works, and how individual men and woman (the social equivalents of Saussure's concept of the word *parole*) understand themselves, their relations to each other, and the larger social units, or structures, to which they belong. It would thus be a mistake to infer, from my argument as to the nature of Machado's new thinking about language, narrative, and life, that it lacked a social consciousness, for it did not. Indeed, I think the opposite is true, that, aided by his new understanding of what language is and how it works, he was able to comment on his world as a citizen and thinker with an acuity that he had not possessed before.

Literary scholars often say that the difference between nineteenth-century narrative and modern narrative is that while the former tends to concentrate on one's outer life, the world of action, consequences, and things, the latter focuses more on one's inner life, the world of desire, motivation, and interpretation, the attempt to understand. Approached from this perspective, it is not difficult to argue that Brazil's Machado de Assis stands as Western narrative's great transition figure, as the writer who, powerfully drawn to the mysterious and tangled webs that define our inner worlds but also concerned with our outer worlds of history, politics, and society, moves from the one to the other in a seamless web. Machado is, I contend, the missing link, in terms of narrative theory and practice, between, first, Proust and then Woolf, Joyce, Mann, and Kafka. If it is true, as Harry Levin (following Harold Laski and Ernest Renan) has argued, that the French tradition wants its fiction and criticism to be intertwining commentaries on society, then Machado, who was well read in the French literary and intellectual tradition, may well have been influenced not only by Flaubert (whose fiction he knew well) but also by Mallarmé, becoming, in the process, an important but hitherto overlooked precursor not just to Proust but to such other modernist masters as Woolf, Mann, Joyce, and Kafka.[146]

Given all this, one could also argue, as, in fact, I will in the following pages, that Machado de Assis seeks if not to abandon the concept of mimesis (his narratives still imitate the world around them) then to create an entirely new understanding of imitation, and to demonstrate it via his highly distinctive post-1880 "new narrative." What Machado seeks to transform, then, is our sense of what the term "mimesis" could mean for a writer who has discovered a new theory of language. For narrative, which is Machado's concern, this will mean that the people, the things, the character types, and the issues of Brazilian life will now be subsumed by an emphasis not on old visions of theme, form, and characterization but on a carefully constructed and integrated work of narrative art which, within the confines of its own structure, is entirely self-sufficient; it does not depend, for its artistic and intellectual validity, upon anything external to it. Machado's "new narrative," again rather like one of Mallarmé's late poems, stands and functions as an utterly self-sufficient work of art. While in the Americas both Borges and Faulkner will do this in the 1930s (with Borges making more critical statements in favor of it), it is Brazil's Machado de Assis who gets to it first.

1 • THE POSTHUMOUS MEMOIRS OF BRÁS CUBAS

In terms of technical daring and imagination, the gulf that separates *Iaiá Garcia* (1878), usually considered to be the best, the technically most proficient, of Machado's early novels, and a work published just two years later, *The Posthumous Memoirs of Brás Cubas,* is enormous. As critics have long noted, it is with this 1880 novel that Machado clearly enters a new phase of development. Something very new is happening. Reading for the first time in William L Grossman's translation, Susan Sontag pronounced it "thrillingly original," "radically skeptical," and, though it first appeared in 1880, thoroughly "modern."[1] What it is, exactly, has long been a matter of debate and speculation among Machadoan specialists. It is to this discussion that the present book contributes.

Featuring a dead but still very voluble narrator/protagonist and hippos flying through time and space, Machado's first great novel (or, if one prefers, anti-novel) liberates Brazilian narrative from the bonds of traditional Realism. While there are clues in the earlier novels as to where Machado's thinking about how a new and different kind of narrative, and novel, might be written, this 1880 work truly broke new ground, in Brazil, in the Americas, and in terms of the European tradition. It also broke, with clear intent, all the rules about what a good novel should be. And it even had the temerity to poke fun at these same rules, even as it argues that it, too, will continue within the great storytelling tradition of the protean novel form. It will just do so differently, and, I believe, with a new awareness concerning the writer's raw material—language. *The Posthumous Memoirs of Brás Cubas* also demands consideration as Machado's direct artistic response to his own 1879 pronouncement about the uselessness, or falsity, of Realism, as a mode of novel writing, and the value of reality, which, suddenly, is here presented as being much more a function of language than we had seen in his previous novels. The appearance, in 1880, of *The Posthumous Memoirs of Brás Cubas* marks a turning point in the history of the American novel. For those who know this extraordinary Brazilian novel and its place in the comparative Latin American and inter-American perspective, the New World novel has a brilliant new theoretician and a brilliant new practitioner. And for those willing to consider the argument I make here (that while Machado was writing from Brazil, a far-flung outpost of the old European empire, he was also writing from deep within it), so, too, does the European narrative tradition.

In the "Prologue to the Third Edition" of *The Posthumous Memoirs of Brás Cubas*, its real author, Machado de Assis, notes that a real and greatly respected Brazilian intellectual of the time, Capistrano de Abreu, had wondered publicly if Machado's seemingly disorganized and digressive narrative should, in all its rather shocking strangeness, be considered a true novel at all. Rather than reply to this query himself, Machado has his fictional character, Brás Cubas, do so in his stead. This is our first indication that something truly original is about to be experienced. Brás's coy reply to Abreu was that it was and it wasn't, that for some, yes, it could be construed as a novel, whereas for others it would not be so judged. As Brás describes what he has written, "It's a question of a scattered work where I, Brás Cubas, have adopted the free form of a Sterne or a Xavier de Maistre" (*BC*, 3). Then, going a bit further and calling attention to what the reader will soon see to be his improvement over both Sterne and de Maistre, he ventures this: His narrative, he declares, "is a far piece from its models. It's a goblet that may carry a similar design but contains a different wine" (*BC*, 3–4). Recognizing the play of influence and reception that characterizes a living, breathing literary tradition (and Machado claimed the entire Western tradition as his own),[2] Brás Cubas, the putative author of these memoirs, then uses the word "goblet" to stand for, or symbolize, his radically new and innovative novel. He then tells us that while it carries "a similar design," that is, retains at least the outward trappings of the conventional novel form, this "new novel" contains, in truth, "a different wine," which I take to be a direct, if metaphorical, reference to the "new narrative" he is here premiering.

Following this short, cryptic, and quite cunning section, Brás proceeds to give us his "To the Reader" section, wherein he lays out, albeit in oblique form, what he has done in writing this narrative. In other words, Brás Cubas, our deceased and (though we do not yet know this) unreliable narrator/protagonist, feels obliged to tell his reader a little (but only a little) about this unusual text. He says, for example, that it is the "work of a dead man," that he wrote it from the afterlife "with a playful pen and melancholy ink," and that, tantalizingly, "it isn't hard to foresee what can come out of that marriage" (*BC*, 5). Once again, we have lots of words expended, but we still don't know much. Only a close and careful *explication de texte* is going to help us achieve the level of understanding we seek. Quite conscious of how unusual his narrative is and of how it will be received (just as the real author, Machado de Assis, must have been), Brás then allows that while "serious people" (the critics, one could suppose) will find in it "some semblance of a normal novel," "frivolous people" (the reading public?) "won't find their usual one here" (*BC*, 5). In other words, Machado has just told us, through the mouth (or pen) of his acutely self-conscious but also very crafty narrator/protagonist, that he is fully aware of having composed here a very new kind of narrative and novel, that he wants to alert his audience (both sides of it, the "serious" and the "frivolous") to his having done something new and different, and that he is trying to tell us (via his new discursive style) how we need to respond to it.[3]

He then reinforces this position by declaring, as if to set himself apart from his better known New World contemporary, Henry James, who was fond of laying out his narrative theories in elaborate prefaces to his novels, by declaring that the best prologues are either the ones that say "the fewest things" or those that say them in "obscure or truncated" ways (*BC*, 5). I believe that, beginning here, Machado does not explain or elaborate on his theories on narrative and novel writing; instead, he shows them to us by embedding them in the very texts he is writing and that we are reading. Unlike James, an American writer to whom Machado is sometimes compared, Machado prefers to "show us" his new narrative theories rather than "tell us" about them. This is why, I contend, that Brás (or, in this instance, Machado) then writes, "I shall not recount the extraordinary process through which I undertook the composition of these *Memoirs*, put together here in the other world" (*BC*, 5). To do so, he then immodestly avers, would be "interesting" but, in the end, "unnecessary for an understanding of the work" (*BC*, 5).[4] And the alert, engaged reader wonders, why is this? Because, as Brás/Machado, sounding here ever so much like a "New Critic," declares, "The work itself is everything: if it pleases you, dear reader, I shall be well paid for the task; if it doesn't please you, I'll pay you with a snap of the fingers and goodbye" (*BC*, 6).

The business of actually narrating his story then begins in chapter 1, with Brás musing about whether he should begin his memoirs "at the beginning," which would be conventional, or "at the end," when he is dead. In yet another sign that something unusual is afoot here, our narrator chooses the latter. As he (ever thoughtful) puts it, "two considerations led me to adopt a different method: the first is that I am not exactly a writer who is dead but a dead man who is a writer" (*BC*, 7). Although Gregory Rabassa's translation is accurate and deftly captures the key issue (that our novel is going to be narrated by a dead man), the play on words is much more effective in Portuguese,[5] where the reader who knows that particular sign system realizes instantly that the meanings generated here depend not on some inherent quality in the words themselves but on the order—the syntax—in which they occur. In virtually the first sentence, then, of the first novel of Machado's mature period, the reader is given a lesson, a comic one to be sure, in how meaning derives not from words themselves but from the patterns in which they appear and the semantic relationships they have with one another. In Portuguese, the joke here depends entirely on structure and on a curiosity of Portuguese syntax, which is itself an issue of structure. Although the line is funny, and the still uninitiated reader does not think too much of it, Machado and his quite dead narrator manage to make at the outset a serious point about what his "new narrative" is going to be like and how it will have to be read.

Jolted out of her complacency here by some clever word play, the reader is reminded that the text she is reading is not a conventional realistic novel. That same reader is also provided with something of a clue to what is going on when Brás, pretending to clarify his thinking, adds that the point of his second "consideration" is that he wants the writing of his narrative to "be more distinctive and novel," which it certainly is (*BC*, 7). There will be, Brás comically tells us, "a radical difference between this book and the Pentateuch," to which he immodestly compares it (and, both indirectly and ironically emphasizing its supposed truth-telling power), but, for the alert reader (whom he will soon begin to invent), there is also going to be "a radical difference between this book" and the texts of the realistic novel tradition. Already in chapter 1, Machado's "new novel" is coming into existence, and it is going to be profoundly antirealistic. Indeed, this initial anti-Realism is quickly reinforced in chapter 7, with additional commentary by the flying hippo, astride which and sailing backward through time is our narrator/protagonist, Brás Cubas, and by the disquisitions of a mysterious female form that calls herself "Nature or Pandora" (*BC*, 17). While traveling backward toward the beginning of time, Brás and the reader are able to review the endless parade of human endeavor, replete with all the violence, cruelty, and selfishness (a word that, known as egoism, will characterize Brás's own nature) that seem to characterize it. It is in this still hotly debated chapter that Brás (and perhaps Machado himself) introduces the idea of life not as a grand process of constant improvement and progress but as a sorry "spectacle," a dreary repetition of the same crimes and stupidities (*BC*, 18). A continuation of this outlook, we have, in chapter 8, titled "Reason Versus Folly," not recognizable characters discussing the virtues of "Reason" over "Folly," which Machado's reader (believing deeply in the idea of progress) would have been expecting, but "Reason" and "Folly" themselves enjoying a clever but notably inconclusive chat. This is not the stuff of the traditional realistic novel.

Intriguingly, Machado's canny but unreliable narrator/protagonist, the deceased bourgeois Brás Cubas, spends quite a bit of his time telling us about the unusual narrative he is relating, how it compares to earlier novels, and how the reader should learn to respond to it. His disquisitions on these subjects range from the metaphorically oblique to the humorously, and ironically, direct. At the end of chapter 1, for example, Brás is regaling his reader about how he didn't die so much of pneumonia, as he himself has just said, but, ironically enough, because of "a magnificent and useful idea" he had had. He ends by saying that if he had told the reader that, she might not have believed him, and yet, he insists (thus suggesting that we should have confidence in what he says), "it's the truth" (*BC*, 8). Then, speaking directly to his reader, Brás declares, "You can judge for yourself"

(*BC*, 8). This utterance, which quickly becomes a motif in the novel, of requiring the reader to decide things for herself, will now recur throughout the text, becoming, finally, a key characteristic of it. Clearly, Machado understands that he needs to create a "new reader" who can appreciate the "new narrative" that he is also creating. Only a few words later, in fact, as he is relating to his reader how his two uncles, one a military man and the other a canon, felt about his likely future, Brás says, "Let the reader decide" (*BC*, 9). Only a couple of pages later, however, Brás and Machado alert this same reader to the dangers of a single interpretive stance, or, as they put it, comically, from an *idée fixe*, "God save you, dear reader, from an *idée fixe*, better a speck, a mote in the eye" (*BC*, 11). For Machado's "new narrative" and "new novel," the traditional reader, passive and waiting to be told the significance of what is happening, will no longer suffice.

This deliberate construction of the "new reader" that he wants, and, apparently, feels that his "new narrative" and "new novel" demand, continues on until chapter 9, where the reader receives a short lecture of what she has most likely missed or what, still surprised at the oddity of having a dead man as narrator, she has not properly appreciated. Machado opens this decisive chapter with what I propose is a parody of the traditional novel's reliance on the omniscient narrator. Using the comic mode to offset the theoretical seriousness of his endeavor here, Brás, our intrepid narrator, lauds what he takes to be his own great dexterity as a storyteller. "And now watch," he (again, immodestly) tells us, "the skill, the art with which I make the greatest transition in this book" (*BC*, 22). "Watch," he goes on to instruct us, as if to call attention not so much to the transition, the deftness of which he makes much of, but, I would argue, to the unusual and unrealistic nature of the "new novel" he is here writing. But after quickly reviewing what he insouciantly takes to be his cleverness as a narrator, his words (symbols) suddenly take on more serious connotations; not tone, for he is as droll here as ever, but connotations, possible meanings other than the ordinary ones that I believe are now alluding to the "new narrative" he is composing.

Demanding much from his readers, Brás/Machado calls our attention to one thing (his transition) while actually doing something much more significant (showing us her "new narrative" in action, and, in the process, schooling us about what we need to learn to do in order to read it properly). "Seamlessly," Brás brags, his book "goes on like this with all of method's advantages but without method's rigidity" (*BC*, 22). The alert reader, the one who responds to the urgings of both Brás and, I maintain, Machado himself, then begins to consider that the words, "method's advantages," could mean the advantages of the novel form's traditionally flexible definitions (*BC*, 22); that is, a story will be told here, by a storyteller, and for a reader. But it will be told (and read) in a distinctly new way, one that, *arising from out of his own polyvalent words,* does not here suffer from that same "method's rigidity"; that is, it does not suffer from what had become, for Machado, the suffocating confines and conventions of the old realistic novel. The reader is then provided with an additional clue, one that encourages precisely this new line of thinking, or interpretation: "It was about time. Because this business of method, being something indispensable, is better still if it comes without a necktie or suspenders, but, rather, a little cool and loose, like someone who doesn't care about the woman next door or the policeman on the block" (*BC*, 22). If we take the reference to "the woman next door" as his reading public, and "the policeman on the block" as the critical establishment (those who pass judgment on what is, and is not, a good novel), we can also see how the words, "this business of method, being something indispensable," could easily be Machado's recognition of the importance of both tradition and structure in novel writing and, via comic references to neckties and suspenders, how he makes the case for his own "new narrative" and "new novel." Brás/Machado then ends this enigmatic but nevertheless compelling scene by seeming to contrast his new narrative art (which he believes to be superior to the traditional Realism and narration techniques that his readers are used to) with the old: "It's like eloquence, because there's one kind that's genuine and vibrant, with a natural and fascinating art, and another that's stiff, sticky, and stale" (*BC*, 22).

It takes no great leap of imagination to suspect that, in quintessentially Machadoan fashion, Brás and Machado are letting us know that while there was a kind of eloquence to the old Realism (another kind of *idée fixe*), it's manifestly more "genuine," "vibrant," "natural," and "fascinating" when it is expressed by means of his new, language-centric Realism. In other words, Machado is here showing us his respect for the novel's grandly protean tradition while also showing us the invigorating value of his own "new novel" and his new theoretical and practical contribution to the novel form. For the first time in the novel, the reader, now ensconced in a new kind of novel, one made out of new, more language-based thinking about narrative, is being cajoled, in what seems a newly coherent and systematic (if still metaphoric) fashion, to read and think in new, more creative ways.

When she finishes chapter 9, the reader, then and now, must ask herself this question: If Machado did not want his reader to think about the "new novel" he is here offering her, why would he have written this chapter as he has done? For it is not at all "stiff, sticky, and stale," and it is very far from even the best passages of *Iaiá Garcia*, his previous novel. Clearly, some change, radical in nature, has taken place in Machado's thinking about narrative and the novel form. Why would he have taken such pains to call attention to how he, through his unreliable narrator/protagonist, is choosing to compose his "posthumous memoirs" in this fashion? In my judgment, the most plausible explanation is that Machado de Assis puts into practice here a new theory of narrative, one that stems from a radically new conception of how language works, how it produces meaning, and how it relates to reality. In my view, the flesh-and-blood writer, Machado de Assis (speaking, on this point, through the mouth of the fictional character, Brás Cubas), knows perfectly well how extraordinarily different this narrative is (see his "To the Reader" section), from his earlier work and from the Western narrative tradition (and including that of Laurence Sterne, whose *Tristram Shandy* was a clear, and well-known, influence). That Machado assigns such an unreliable narrator/protagonist to present his theory, and then steadfastly refuses to allow him to tell his reader what she needs to know to penetrate this interlocking thicket of metaphors, allusions, symbols, and multiple ironies and interpret it, is, in my view, fully consistent with the demands of the new brand of narrative Realism he is here demonstrating. Or, to put this argument another way, as Machado's thinking about language, reality, and narrative began to change, as I believe it did between 1878 and 1880, so, too, did the nature of his novels. It had to, and his last five novels are, I argue, evidence of this change.

This concern with the creation of a "new reader" to match his "new narrative" continues into chapter 34, "For a Sensitive Soul." The second of Machado's major statements to his reader about how she must respond to the text she is reading, chapter 34 is, surprisingly enough (given the importance Machado gives to the development of his reader), less allusive about doing so. It is, in fact, strikingly more succinct than was the admonition in chapter 9. In the later chapter, Brás is upbraiding the reader for thinking ill of him for seeming to contemplate the seduction of an attractive but lame young woman, Eugênia, who has just entered the story. In particular, Brás, playing the victim, feigns injury, claiming that the reader has come to think of him as a cynic, a charge he vehemently denies. Although this scene is cast, once again, in a comic mode, it deals with interpretation, an issue near and dear to Machado the "new novelist." Specifically, he lets the reader know in no uncertain terms that she had misinterpreted the text she is reading and that she must reconsider it, this time from a different critical perspective, one more in keeping, he implies, with the nature of the new narrative being absorbed. It is clear, in fact, that, in this brilliant first novel of Machado's mature and most experimental period, he utilizes the comic mode to mask his more serious intent—the exploration of what a novel written in accordance with his new thinking about language and narrative art would be like—and what it would demand from his reader! Having chastised the reader for misreading Brás's intentions as far as the fair Eugênia was concerned, he then ends this chapter with a straightforward, if still oblique (with respect to its meaning), statement to his reader: "Take back the expression, then, sensitive soul, control your nerves, clean your glasses—because this is sometimes due to glasses—and let's be done with this flower from the shrubbery" (*BC*, 66). Suggesting that the misreading of a text (the reader's supposedly erroneous conclusion that Brás is a cynic, a conclusion that the engaged reader may well question) is a matter of how one "sees" it (hence, the image of glasses) is more a matter of critical perspective than anything else, Brás and Machado are implying that even the old passive reader can learn to be a better, more involved, more imaginative reader. This charge given to the reader, that she become more involved in the deciphering of the text and its symbols (its words and their shifting meanings), gets ratcheted up in chapter 39. Here, as we have seen, Brás openly challenges the reader in her likely interpretation and ends up suggesting to her that her traditional way of responding to a novel is simply not going to work here; like one's glasses, her reading strategies need also to be changed.

In chapter 42, "What Aristotle Left Out," Brás and Machado, comically invoking the author of *The Poetics* and numerous other influential studies, interject a new element into their narrative, one that, in terms of the argument it makes about how language use produces meaning, eerily presages the linguistics of Saussure. But it also presages the key issue—the power structure has to produce meaning—in a famous Borges "ficción," "Death and the Compass," written during the 1930s. If we know three of a rectangle's points, we believe we can predict the fourth with complete certainty; the laws of geometry (that is, of structure) demand it. No event happens in isolation, this short chapter shows us, just as no word means, or signifies, in isolation. To mean something, it has to connect with other words in their common structure. This is so in language and it is so in literature, or, at least, in the new kind of narrative fiction that Machado is espousing and creating. Echoing, but with a different metaphor and in a different context, the same point they had raised earlier in chapter 9, Brás and Machado call our attention to the importance of systems to our understanding of the world and of the various linguistic systems we use to create, explain, think about, and change it. Some fifty years before the Argentine master does this in "Death and the Compass," Machado, in chapter 42 of *The Posthumous Memoirs of Brás Cubas*, lays it all out in his theory of rolling balls. Just as one rolling ball, when it bumps into another, causes that second ball to roll and, eventually, bump into a third ball, which also begins to roll, and so on, so, too, does a meaning of one word cause another word to have meaning, which then causes other words to have meaning, and so on, without end. Wryly asking himself how Aristotle could have missed such a profound thought as he is sharing with his reader, Brás is really presenting us with a radically new theory about how communication occurs and how the same words can, and do, generate an endless plethora of possible meanings. As a function of language, Machado's seemingly comical theory shows us, when we get past the always droll comments of his glib deceased narrator and think not just about what he is saying but what else it might mean and how differently we might regard it, that meaning is never unchanging and eternal; it changes constantly, depending on which other words are being bumped into, waxing and waning in terms of their significance as the circumstances evolve.

Long before the terms "logocentrism," "phallogocentrism," and "diffèrance" were coined, Brazil's Machado de Assis was showing the world why meaning is not static and stable but relative. And because this is true of each and every word as it relates to other words, it is also true of language, and if it is true of language, then it must also be true of literary texts, which are very carefully crafted verbal structures, each word of which relates to every other word in the same structure. If, as I argue here, Machado had come to this new insight about language, it is all but inconceivable that he would have elected to continue writing novels in the same old ways. I believe that he did come to this realization and that, in doing so, he suddenly saw the kind of "new novel" he would have to write, one that would exemplify, or embody, the new theory of narrative that he had come to hold. It is interesting to note, in this same regard, that while Borges, during the 1950s, became the darling of French structuralists (because his *Ficciones*, published collectively in 1944, were thought to epitomize what the sometimes abstruse theoretical statements about structuralism would actually look like in literary form), we can regard the earlier Machado de Assis, with his emphasis on the semantic slippage and the endless semantic productivity of language, a kind of poststructuralist without portfolio, a writer who put into action, for form, many, if not most, of the basic principles of poststructuralism. Although purporting to tell us about what happens when a ball roles into another, chapter 42 actually shows the reader linguistic structures in action, how one word generates not an end stop or closure but another word, another thought, another line of interpretation. Thus is semantic fluidity built, from the ground up, one might say, into Machado's "new narratives."

This very issue, how, far from stopping the production of ideas, opinions, and responses, the use of a single word actually gives rise to a multitude of other words and thoughts, is actually raised earlier, in chapter 26. Titled "The Author Hesitates" (or, in Grossman's translation, "The Author Is Undecided," a rendering that brings out the undecidability that is at the heart of this text), this chapter purports to explain to us how it was that, urged to marry and go into politics by his father, Brás ends up doodling the name of his eventual lover, Virgília, into the text. More importantly, for my purposes here, Brás and Machado show us exactly how, in the human mind, one word begets not a stop, or a cessation of thought, but more and more words and thoughts. Brás presents himself as writing, randomly (he says), some words *and forms* (a phrase, a line of verse, and a triangle) on a sheet of paper. Alluding, comically, to Virgil, Brás (his unreliability showing) tells the reader that his supposedly idle scribblings are absent minded but, tellingly, I believe, that "there was a logic" to them as well," a logic that could be construed as Machado's new awareness that language produces more language (*BC*, 56). He then goes on to tell us that "it was the *virumque* that made me get to the name of the poet himself, because of the first syllable. I was going to write *virumque*—and *Virgil* came out" (*BC*, 57, emphasis original). He now proceeds to show us how his supposedly thoughtless verbal play finally produces, thanks to his father, who, taking one look at what his son has jotted down, declares (in response to the words he has read): "Virgil! . . . That's it, my boy. Your bride just happens to be named Virgília" (*BC*, 56). Though she laughs at this scene, the reader has been shown Machado's new narrative theory, namely, that language and its structures lead us to see the world in new and hitherto unimagined ways and to speculate on what it might mean.

This same theory of language, reality, and meaning gets a reprise in the very next chapter, "Virgília," in which Brás and Machado, referencing here Pascal, take up the issue of truth and how, in a world where every word leads not to some stable, definable reality beyond it but to other words, a writer (or reader) can every hope to know the truth. This is a critical question, given the theory of narrative that Machado is here advancing, and it must be addressed, whether the reader is aware of it or not. In a direct address, in fact, to his reader, Brás broaches this very issue, saying, "'But,' you're probably saying, 'how can you discern the truth of those times like that and express it after so many years?'" (*BC*, 57). "Ah! So indiscreet! Ah! So ignorant!," Brás replies, chiding us for our old-fashioned expectations about novels and the supposed "truths" about the world they seem to say to us (*BC*, 57). Then, as if reminding us once again about the myriad ways language use determines our sense of self as well as how we claim to know things, and of how an awareness of language forms the basis of his revolutionary "new narrative," he goes on to say, about language and human existence, "But it's precisely that which has made us lords of the earth; it's that power of restoring the past to touch the *instability of our impressions* and the vanity of our affections" (*BC*, 57, emphasis mine). Even as he tells us that we use language to determine our identities, to make sense of things, and to gain dominion over the earth, Machado, through the musings of his deceased and, more and more, unreliable narrator/protagonist, stresses once again the instability of life and of our desire to know. Once again we are given a dose of this narrative's most basic structural motif: what is true of language, must, because the two are so integrally entwined, also be true of human life itself. Machado and Brás then finish this chapter, a short, funny, but ultimately enigmatic disquisition on semantic instability and the elusiveness of absolute meaning, by suggesting that the human creature is (in yet another reference to the acts of writing and reading) a "thinking erratum," someone who, always through language, redefines, or, more accurately, imitates reality according to her linguistically inscribed desires. And, with the inclusion of the phrase "Every season of life is an edition that corrects the one before," it does not strain one's credulity to suspect that Machado is here referring to the ways his "new narrative" "corrects" our previous novelistic editions, that is, the old narrative of traditional Realism (*BC*, 57).

The instability of meaning continues to be demonstrated in chapter 70, "Dona Plácida," in which the complicity of an old, desperately poor, but deeply virtuous woman is bought by the wealthy Brás, who wishes to use the woman to take care of the house in which he and Virgília will conduct their illicit tryst. Because she is in such dire need of money, she accepts Brás's offer of five *contos*. In so doing, of course, she compromises herself, and she knows it. And it pains her. Traditionally, scholars have read this scene, and rightly so, as a demonstration of Brás's selfishness and hypocrisy. What interests me, however, given the thesis I am here advancing, is what comes just before his calculated and self-serving purchase of Dona Plácida's morality. In the chapter's second paragraph, and immediately following the final sentence of the previous paragraph in which Brás, from my perspective, gives us a seemingly whimsical metaphor involving eaves, swallows, and infinity that, by this point in the narrative, simultaneously reminds us that meaning in language is also infinite, he expands, again metaphorically, on this same theme—how it is that the meaning of a place, or a word, is entirely relative. Telling his reader how this same little house in the Gamboa district of Rio is currently occupied by a "virtuous couple," whereas when Brás and Virgília lived there it was occupied by a "sinning couple," he amplifies his point (about how meaning is never stable and unchanging but always dependent on other words and experiences) by noting that the same house will, in the future, gain different meanings by virtue of being lived in by different people, a "churchman," a "murderer," a "blacksmith," or a "poet" (a writer who is acutely aware of language use). This argument presages what Saussure says of the linguistic sign, that, in terms of its meaning and its ability to produce different meanings, it is utterly arbitrary.

In the very next chapter, aptly (given the point it makes about the role Machado's new reader is being called upon to play in the game of fiction) called "The Defect of This Book," Brás openly declares (comically, yes, but also for the enlightenment of the poor reader who has not yet perceived what Machado wants from her) that "the main defect of his book is you, reader" (*BC*, 111). From this rather blunt declaration, Brás then immediately launches into what I take to be not a frivolous digression about style but, instead, another metaphorically charged but, for the engaged reader, deeply serious and revealing (if hilarious) statement of the nature of the "new narrative," the new narrative art, Machado is here creating. Structurally speaking, moreover, this chapter does not stand alone; to the contrary, it links together the same point, though made in different language, in chapters 9 and 34 and sets the stage for the final presentation of this same message in chapter 124. Knowing full well that his reader is accustomed to the reading habits called for, and encouraged by, traditional Realism, Machado, through the mouth of his highly unrealistic narrator, Brás Cubas, tell us, "You're in a hurry to grow old and the book moves slowly. You love direct and continuous narration, a regular and fluid style, and this book and my style are like drunkards, they stagger left and right, they walk and stop, mumble, yell, cackle, shake their fists at the sky, and fall" (*BC*, 111). In my view, this is about as close as Machado will come to nakedly telling his reader how and why his "new narrative" is different from the rote Realism she is accustomed to. His short but theoretically revolutionary disquisition, funny but also quite pithy and to the point, sharply contrasts the conventional realistic novel, which the reader has been reared on, with the "new novel" that he, as iconoclastic author, is determined to produce. And he, Machado, is adamant about doing so because, I maintain, he has come to hold a radically new theory about the nature of language and its ability to reproduce, or imitate, the seen and unseen realities of the human experience.

Machado then follows this key chapter with another one, chapter 72, that basically reiterates the same point, that what the reader has in her hands here is innately different from the kinds of novels she has been reading and, far too often, responding passively to. In this again short, cryptic chapter, titled "The Bibliomaniac," we have yet another allusion to language, writing, reading, and the sundry ways meaning is determined. Here, however, Machado leads his reader away from the nature of the "new narrative" he has put in her hands (this having been the focus on the previous chapter) and, instead, returns her to how she should be reading it and to how she will construct its meaning or meanings. Imagining, for the reader, someone "who loves nothing but books leans over the previous page" to see if she can discern the phrase that, according to our narrator, is close to being "nonsense" (*BC*, 112). If we read "nonsense" as "meaning," as I believe Machado intends us to do (because he is once again trying to train his "new reader" how to participate in his "new narrative"), he is telling his reader that she must read, reread, and then read again, carefully examining the words, the syllables, the letters, and how they all appear in this chapter, and elsewhere, and they relate to each other. Individually and collective, the words must be examined "inside and out" and "from all sides" and "up against the light," a metaphor for reading that, by now, the alert, engaged reader can think of as all the various perspectives from which a word, or a line, might be considered (*BC*, 112). Brás then continues on, providing us with more clues as to "the value of words" and to how we should be reading not the pseudo text being discussed in this chapter but the very text we are reading, the one known as *The Posthumous Memoirs of Brás Cubas* (*BC*, 112). The good reader, the one Machado wants to create, will continue to scrutinize her text, completely given over "to the noble and wearing function of deciphering the absurdity," which, again, we can think of as the possible "meanings" of it (*BC*, 112). Upon reflection, the good reader may well ask: What is the possible error, or "absurdity," that Brás and Machado are referring to here?

Clearly, the question is brought up, but, and just as clearly, it is not explained or resolved. However, the reader who has, by now, decided to involve herself in the narration and who is playing her part in its production of meaning might well conclude this: Is what the unreliable Brás Cubas referring to her as an "absurdity" only so in terms of what it is not, that is, traditional realistic narrative? If we think of it in these terms, the reference put forth here by Brás and Machado eerily parallels Saussure's argument that, in language systems, meaning is always a matter of difference; a word means whatever it means because it is different from other words, or linguistic signs. Is Brás referring here, really, to his own unusual style, which he has been telling us about for many pages to this point? If so, then could we easily read "absurdity" as meaning that the "new narrative" we are reading is "absurd" only because it is different? Either way, the meaning of this chapter becomes "lost in time by reading, rereading, unreading," the very acts, along with writing, that J. Hillis Miller sees as embodying the close analysis he endorses as the essence of deconstruction as a reading strategy.[6] Indeed, it would not be excessive to conclude that the struggle to understand the text the bibliophile is reading and seeking to understand serves as the prototype of Derrida's concept of *différance*. A text written in 1880 Brazil would seem to epitomize what, some eighty years later, the French thinker has in mind. While it is certainly true that, given the nature of language, any text could do this, but, in truth, some do it more intentionally than others, and Machado's does it in about an exemplary manner as can be imagined. Eventually, as is suggested in the closing images of this chapter, what is now judged to be "absurd," or an "error," will have become the norm. And eventually what was the norm will be supplanted by something else. And so on, forever. As in the case of words and meanings, which change through time, so, too, might what is today thought to be "absurd" be tomorrow considered the prototype? I believe that this complicated and elusive chapter allows Machado to show us how his new theory of narrative art actually works and how it must be read.

In chapter 124, "As an Interlude," the reader is treated to yet another telling but unexpected lesson in comparative aesthetics and the problem of verisimilitude. The chapter's very first line, in fact, suggests (if we substitute the word "art" for "death") the connection between life and artistic imitation that Machado wants us to think about. The justification for doing so stems from the fact that this same, short chapter then ends with a much more direct statement of the same issue—the connection between life and art and, moreover, the connection between this venerable question and the nature of the very text we are here reading. I believe, in other words, that the very structuring of this chapter (its beginning and its end) demands that we read it in accordance with the new theory of narrative art that Machado is here propounding. We are presented here with two kinds of artistic representation, both of the same character, a loathsome but superficially respectable man named Cotrim. Demonstrably cruel and avaricious, and a financially successful smuggler in the now banned slave trade, Cotrim likes to present himself as a pious and upright pillar of the community, a good father who loves his children and a citizen seemingly to be admired and emulated (*BC*, 171). Although she is not immediately aware of it, the reader is led, by the structuring of the narration, to make a determination about which of the two imitations of him, one a painting, the other the text that we are reading, is the more truthful. Though not so obviously stated, then, the essential theoretical question posed here is this: Which form of imitation, the portrait of Cotrim (which one of the brotherhoods he was a member of ordered painted to honor him) or the narrative characterization he gets thanks to the less compromised Brás Cubas, is the most verisimilar? In terms of Cotrim's double representation here, one, which is a portrait that, though spoken of, we do not see (and which we have to imagine via the words used to describe it) comes across to us as superficial, misleading, and, ultimately, false. The other one, what we learn of Cotrim through what he says and what others say about him, involves language and is the one that structures our appraisal of the other, imagined manner of imitation.

Whereas this chapter purports, on the surface, to present the complicated nature of Cotrim's character, to show us what kind of man he was, underneath it sets up a structure in which painting and specifically portraiture are implicitly compared with literary representation. In both cases, however, the reader's response, or reaction, to an art form is required. Two forms of verisimilitude (painting versus literature) are here being compared. Where does the truth lie? Which form of artistic representation best captures it, and why? Which is the most verisimilar? A closely related question, and one that speaks to Machado's well-known and long-standing interest in the inner world of human motivation and desire, is how does the concept of "truth" relate to questions of art and to the imitation of nature, here extended to two depictions, or artistic renderings, of the same man, Cotrim?

As is so typical with the kind of linked narrative structuring that we associate with the mature Machado, he brings the reader into the debate by posing, at the beginning of the very next chapter, 124, what seems to be an innocuous enough question, one that, upon a second (or third) reading reveals itself to also be a kind of dual inquiry, one, into the difference between art (representation and verisimilitude) and life, and the other into the reader's response (to art and to life): "If I hadn't put this chapter together the reader would have suffered a strong shock, quite harmful to the effect of the book. Jumping from a portrait to an epitaph can be a real and common act. The reader, however, is only taking refuge in the book," that is, art, "to escape life" (*BC*, 171).[7] In my reading of it, and given the argument I am advancing here, this line evokes a key part of Aristotle's defense of poetry, which argued, in effect, that art actually improves life, or reality, by perfecting it, something that does not and cannot occur in "real" life, that is, in reality itself. Examples of this type, where art and reality are explored, contrasted, and compared, abound in Machado's later novels, becoming, finally, a distinguishing motif of them.

And while the response of our narrator to the questions being posed here, all of which, for Brás, center on how we should think about the complex and controversial character, or identity, of Cotrim, is one thing, the response of the reader to them requires a more serious and larger consideration—can truth ever be a "realistic" goal of artistic representation? Or, to come at this question from another perspective, when we seek to evaluate a piece of art in terms of its "truth," its verisimilitude, its faithfulness of the reality it claims to represent (in this case, Cotrim), what, really, are we evaluating? The reality itself, or the rendering of it? And with respect to the comparison being offered here, does language have an advantage in the artistic representation of sentient beings, and, more specifically, human beings? The question, I think, is central to Machado's theory of narrative art as this manifests itself in his late novels. And I believe it gets at the very problem that, eighty-three years later, led René Wellek to his famous observation that the "theory of realism is ultimately bad aesthetics all art is 'making'" and, as we see so powerfully expressed in The *Posthumous Memoirs of Brás Cubas,* "a world in itself of illusion and symbolic forms," which, according to my lights and adding the additionally destabilizing elements of self-referentiality and unreliability, is precisely what Machado's groundbreaking 1880 narrative is.[8]

Indeed, the signal importance of this very question is, I contend, established by Machado in the previous chapter, titled (as if to prepare the reader for the consideration of the two forms of imitation that compose chapter 124) "The Real Cotrim" (*BC*, 169). In the kind of one-two punch so often utilized by Machado in the structuring of the scenes of theoretical importance in his novels, chapter 123 provides the alert reader with a solid clue as to what the following chapter is really about, and especially so its theoretical importance to the linked questions of artistic imitation and verisimilitude. Beyond the more obvious issue about the true nature of Brazilian society during this turbulent era, that it is a culture that, though beautiful and (as with Cotrim) seemingly progressive and forward looking on the outside, it is, again as with Cotrim, rotten on the inside, built as it was on the institution of slavery, the other, more theoretical question that Machado is exploring here in the nature of artistic representation.

Machado's assault on the outlooks, assumptions, and methods of traditional Realism continues in chapter 55, in which we are treated with a new spin on "The Old Dialogue of Adam and Eve." Recalling Laurence Sterne's *Tristram Shandy,* Machado goes further here to involve his reader more directly than ever. Although the title of this chapter clearly speaks of a "dialogue," the speakers here, not Adam and Eve but two other progenitors of a new society, our indefatigable (he is dead, after all) narrator/protagonist, Brás Cubas and his paramour, Virgília, who reveals herself to be, in effect, the female version of all that Brás is—otiose, self-centered, wealthy, and socially privileged. They are a perfect match for each other. Indeed, in the previous chapter, 54, what appear, drolly, to be the respective Ids of Brás and Virgília, have, on the window sill of Virgília's bedroom, a little chat, about what the perhaps now overly lascivious reader can only imagine. The scene, cast in language and nuance that would make Freud proud, is very funny. What catches the reader's attention in chapter 55, however, is that there are no words to this dialogue; neither interlocutor speaks, although their *potential* comments, which the reader, called upon now to ponder their respective characterizations to this point, is left to imagine, are suggested by means of their constructed personalities to this point, by a series of dots (we might think of them as super ellipses) of varying length and by differing punctuation marks. Thus, Brás opens the "discussion" by asking Virgília this question: ". . . ?," to which Virgília then replies, ". . ." (*BC*, 90). And on it goes, back and forth, with, seemingly, ideas being proposed, debated, and rejected, until, finally, both Brás and Virgília come, rather emphatically, it would seem, to an identical conclusion, or agreement: ". . . !" (*BC*, 91). Guided by what she already knows about these two characters (if, as Brás Cubas and Machado have assiduously urged her to be, she is paying close attention to what she is reading), by the number of dots in the "sentence," and by the punctuation marks utilized, the reader is literally forced into making a decision here: either she can ignore this chapter as some sort of unrealistic nonsense and skip over it, or she can recommit to reading this narrative in an attentive and engaged fashion. In this remarkable chapter, Machado's "new narrative" openly (and comically) demands a "new reader" for it; the narrative itself makes this demand. Ever voluble and loquacious, Brás could have provided the words for this "Old Dialogue" (a reference that invokes, albeit ironically, the Bible and its creation story), but he does not. It is entirely up to the reader, who must decide whether she will buy into Machado's "new narrative" or, in the realistic tradition, elect to remain a passive, unthinking consumer of the story being told, a reader seeking mere entertainment rather than active engagement in the generation of the text's many possible meanings.

Chapter 127, famous as a lacerating parody of Comte's positivism and as a withering critique of capitalism as a system that organizes human activity and that establishes not the real, human worth of things within that system but their superficial and inhuman, nonhuman, or antihuman market values, can also be read as another of Machado's demonstrations of how meaning in language, and therefore in life, is a function of a system. The word "system" in fact stands out in this chapter and, I believe, is crucial to it. Here, as in his other late novels, Machado's "aim . . . is a critique of all representations of power in which systems, ideas, and emotions become dependent on power and wealth."[9] Just as global capitalism is (already in 1880) an operating, worldwide system (one that connects Brás Cubas and his hunger, which he satiates by chewing on a chicken wing, to agriculture in Africa and slavery, both of which are interlocking systems themselves), so, too, are the languages we use to understand all these other systems. For the modern reader, who knows Saussure's linguistics, the parallels that exist between what is discussed in this chapter (how a series of seemingly disparate, but, in truth, closely interconnected global events allowed Brás to dine, in Brazil, on chicken nurtured by grain and slave labor from Africa) and how meaning is produce in Saussure's new linguistics, are compelling. Whether a piece of chicken or a word, a thing means something, or has value, only in relation to other things. In reading this chapter, the reader sees immediately the power of systems, whether economic or linguistic, to produce the different (but always connected) things they produce and the values, or meanings (always relative), that are assigned to them.

By chapter 138, "To a Critic," Machado and Brás are (almost) done berating the hitherto docile and lethargic reader and, taking a slightly different line of attack, now take on those who, in the literary world, like to stand in judgment of others.

But upon close reading, and a more open-minded consideration, what Brás and Machado are going after here is not so much the traditional gripe of authors—that critics misinterpret what they were trying to do—as it is the more serious question of how they can, or cannot, deal with work that is genuinely original, that is, with work (a different kind of novel, for example) that flouts the conventions that have long prevailed and that have allowed critical judgments to form and grow both rigid and stale, thus rendering them (the critics) able to deal with something that is truly, and, in this case, radically new.

In this sense, Machado here presages T. S. Eliot's 1920 essay "Tradition and the Individual Talent," except in reverse; here, Machado is saying, it is the tradition (Realism) that has become arid, inflexible, and stifling, and it is the renovating inspiration that comes from individual talent (like his own) that must revive it. Published as part of *The Sacred Wood*, Eliot's essay makes an argument with which Machado would surely have agreed, that the modern writer cannot and should not seek a definitive break with tradition but, instead, should make use of the best of the past in creating something new. This is, I maintain, precisely what Brás and Machado advocated in chapter 9, when they clearly militated in favor of both method and artistic integrity (two very traditional items) and of the importance of artistic innovation so that a new age could have its own artistic eloquence. And when an exasperated Brás adds, toward the end of this chapter, that "I do mean that in each phase of the narration of my life I experience the corresponding sensation," he sounds very much like Eliot seeking to explain his "Objective Correlative" (*BC*, 183).

More, even, than this, both Eliot and Machado (the latter some forty years before former) emphasize the need of criticism to take issues of language, the generation of meaning, and structure more seriously than it had the traditional issues of biographical and historical concerns. Machado, however, goes much further with this than Eliot, for whom style was more a matter of its status as a force external to the text rather than a feature of the text (an artistically rendered but still linguistic construct) itself. When one recalls that it is the Eliot of this famous essay who begat the "New Criticism," it suddenly does not seem so surprising that, in the "To The Reader" section of *The Posthumous Memoirs of Brás Cubas*, Brás/Machado comes across as sounding very much like a "New Critic." In chapter 138, however, the "tradition" that is coming under attack is, I contend, conventional Realism, which, as defended by its critical establishment, cannot accommodate Machado's new narrative art. It has become sclerotic and brittle in its theoretical underpinnings; it cannot deal with change. For a literary historian, it is intriguing to think that Brás and Machado have concocted the kind of semantically opaque and, for some, pessimistic "new narrative" that so upset Auerbach. The concluding line of this key chapter sums up Brás's, and, we can think, Machado's, frustration at not being understood: "Good Lord! Do I have to explain everything?" (*BC*, 183).

Having shown us here a bit of the trepidation Machado must have felt as, with this revolutionary 1880 novel, he began to give form to his new and quite audacious theory of narrative, his "new novel," and his new reader, chapter 142, "The Secret Request," shows him retreating back into his narrative, disappearing from it, as it were, behind the first of his great unreliable narrator/protagonists, Brás Cubas. As if a kind of summary, or coda, of all that has preceded this moment, this chapter draws together key references to the issues that have borne the text forward to this point: how a single event is always open to multiple interpretations (even in this case, where a fight between starving dogs over a meatless bone is pronounced a "beautiful" thing by the insane but very articulate Quincas Borba, chapter 141, *BC*, 185); how doubt abounds concerning all the interpretive lines taken about any issue or pronouncement; how change is a constant force in terms of how we feel about life;[10] how even a letter (a specific form of language use that, here, intends to impart a bit of information from the writer to the reader) from a loved one (in this case, Virgília) resists full and complete understanding; and how desire inevitably skews even our own ability to comprehend what we do and say. This latter point is driven home in comic fashion, with the ultra-vain Quincas declaring that while Pascal,[11] to whom he, Quincas, is now positively comparing himself as a philosopher, was "a great man," his (Quincas's) seemingly absurd philosophy of Humanitism was both "worth more than" Pascal's and "more profound," the profundity being, the reader surmises, that in the world of language, any system of thought, no matter how contradictory or counterfactual, can be argued to be valid (*BC*, 187). Tragically, some of human history's most violent, bloody, and stupid experiences, from Nazism to "Birtherism," are products of these kinds of misguided or deliberately deceitful and malignant intellectual systems.[12]

After chapter 142, the novel draws to a rapid close. Images of madness, death, and folly mix with more subtle images of translation, interpretation, reflection, comprehension, and difference (the latter images antedating later occurring theory of how, by means of difference, linguistic signs produce meaning. By the penultimate chapter 159, which continues to work the issue of difference while also referencing the additional issues of truth versus falsity, reason versus madness, and illusion versus both reality and representation (here the point of departure for the reader is Brás's sly suggestion that Pangloss may not have been quite the fool that Voltaire thought he was) the reader has been prepared to contemplate the most powerful image in the book's closing pages: Quincas Borba, the deranged philosopher, as the epitome of the human condition. As Brás now tells us, "Quincas Borba was not only mad, but he knew that he was mad, and that remnant of awareness, like a dim lamp in the midst of shadows, greatly complicated the horror of the situation" (*BC*, 203). This, I believe, sums up Machado's post-1878 view of life, with "that remnant of awareness" being delivered unto us, in a way that anticipates Woolf's "luminous halo," by and through language. And, again paralleling the condition of Quincas Borba, we are painfully aware of knowing the true nature of our "madness," our predicament as human beings, the animal that, using language, can contemplate its own existence, its own confusion and frustration, and its own demise. As a philosopher, Quincas uses language to try to explain the mysteries and ambiguities of life, and, echoing Nietzsche, his own great philosophic system, Humanitism, vividly (and parodically) demonstrates how our ability to understand is linked to the system of language we use to explore it, to ask the questions, and to frame the answers.

But Machado pushes the equating of Quincas Borba and human existence even further, explaining that not only could Quincas recite long passages from his treatise (yet another Machadoan example of words talking not to reality and facts but to other words), he has also devised a macabre dance that represents, or imitates, the various ways the human creature deals with the vicissitudes of life, a life she realizes she can neither understand nor control (see *BC*, 202). With all this happening within artistically rendered structures of language, with words being used to try to understand the meanings of other words, which are themselves struggling to discern (or create) the meaning of still other words, actions, and events, it is not difficult to read this extraordinary scene as a metaphor for the painfully self-aware, anxiety plagued modern malaise (*BC*, 202). We humans exist, Machado here suggests, in language, and the only tool we have at our disposal to deal with this illusion-like situation is interpretation, and it is subject, as we know, to both error and change.

With this ending to chapter 159, the reader (or, rather, the reader Machado wants) is now set up to interpret the famous final chapter of *The Posthumous Memoirs of Brás Cubas*, the one in which the argument for Machado's supposed pessimism is, for many, most tellingly presented. Very short, and titled "On Negatives," chapter 160 does seem bleak. Yet it also scans, for the reader's parting consideration, the issues that, I believe, reveal the first full exposition of Machado's new theory of narrative and his new novel: the nature of narration not as the simple telling of a story but as a manifestation of how language, understood as an endlessly productive semiotic system, generates meaning; how this kind of narration is an exercise in artistic creation and imitation; how desire (that of Brás and his own ego or that of the reader and her own inclination) affects and effects one's response to (most especially) the literary text; and, most important of all, how Machado's "new narrative" demands a new, higher, and more active level of readerly participation.

It is, in my reading of this landmark novel, this latter point that dominates this final chapter and that reminds the reader, albeit obliquely and for one final time, that while interpretation is essential, in novels and in life, it is never perfect and it is never unchanging. It is, like meaning, always in flux. And, like the language that allows interpretation to take place, and like life itself, it is inherently, inescapably unstable, indeterminate, and ambiguous. "Putting one and another thing together," Brás tells us, as he himself ponders the meaning of his own life, "any person will probably imagine that there was neither a lack or a surfeit," at the moment of his death (which, the alert reader remembers, opened the novel), "and, consequently, that I went off squared with life. *And he imagines wrong*" (*BC*, 203, emphasis mine). In other words, and for the final time in this novel (which, as I posit, is built, as per the image of the dim lamp enveloped in shadows, around the imprecision of language and the vague, relativity of meaning), the reader is reminded, bluntly but also rather comically, of the importance of (but also of the uncertainty in) that same essential process, interpretation.[13] Human existence involves our efforts to interpret all that is around us, and this requires the use of language, but we also know that even as we try to do our best to understand, we are prone to error; we often get things wrong and misinterpret (as Brás quite pointedly says we do here), and, like Quincas Borba in his madness, we know it. At every step, and in anticipation of Kafka, we are acutely aware of reading incorrectly the avalanche of signs that engulfs us. And we fear doing so. "Because," Brás rather blithely informs us about his own experience with this, for us, disturbing aspect of the human condition (our inability to know with certainty and to be with satisfaction and confidence), "on arriving at this other side of the mystery" (Brás, we remember, is writing to us from the grave), "I found myself with a small balance, which is the final negative in this chapter of negatives—I had no children, I haven't transmitted the legacy of our misery to any creature" (*BC*, 203). What is often taken as a negative sign, not having children, is here presented by our narrator/protagonist as a positive. The impact on the surprised reader is disturbing and dislocating.

Understandably, this last line (which, in the original Portuguese, ends with the words, "nossa miséria," or "our misery," in *OC*, 3:637) has long been interpreted as an expression of what many critics regard as Machado's fundamental pessimism about life. And while this may or may not be true, I believe another take on it (another interpretation) is possible, one generated by the semantic self-referentiality of the text, or structure, in which this utterance occurs. I refer here to the possibility, advanced in this study, that the wellspring of "our misery" as human beings is that, like Quincas Borba, we know we are mad with our endless and, in the main, fruitless quest, expressed through language, for perfect knowledge and understanding. But we also know, as perhaps Quincas did not, that, as language creatures, we are forever lost in the "prison-house" of language, and that we cannot escape it. Our use *of* language to think *about* language precludes it. This makes the anguish of our situation, our awareness of it, even greater. We are all too painfully conscious of being able to ask the great, defining questions about life (Who are we? Where do we come from? Where do we go after death? What is the meaning of it all?, and so forth) but also of not being able to answer them. Or to answer them in any satisfying fashion. We yearn to know and understand, but we cannot; we crave constancy and clarity in meaning (we seek what George Steiner terms the "Ur-Sprache," the original, pre–Tower of Babel language of God and the language of perfect communication),[14] but we can never attain these things, we can never grasp them, and we can never fulfill or even quell our desire for them. The "Ur-Sprache" forever eludes us. But we can never slake our thirst for it and for the perfect knowledge and being it promises. And, like Quincas Borba, we know it. We are limited by, or, to continue with the Nietzschean metaphor, incarcerated by, the limits of our language, and so rendered unable to comprehend life. Prisoners of the very system we rely upon to think about life, identity, and the nature, or purpose, of our being, we are condemned to have to deal with the misery of eternally wanting more understanding than we can ever attain.

This is where Machado's first "new novel" leaves us. For as funny as much of *The Posthumous Memoirs of Brás Cubas* is, it ends on a sober, if not necessarily chilling, note. At the same time, it is worth considering that while Machado does seem here, in the first of his experiments with his new theory of language and the actual writing of the kind of novel that illustrates it, determined to confront this distressing and eminently human dilemma but without having a response to it, by 1908, and *Counselor Ayres' Memorial,* he does. The answer, which will come from the mouth of a progressive and spirited young woman, is that rather than allow ourselves to fall prey to, or be paralyzed by, the endless indeterminacies of language, we must stress instead its potent ability to create, to improve, to liberate, and to inspire us to more productive action. To wallow in confusion and frustration does not have to be our fate. The same language system that can lead to nihilism, despair, and solipsism can also, if utilized differently and for different purposes, lead to more rewarding lives and a more just society, to better laws, more equality of opportunity, and more egalitarian outlooks, codes of conduct, and social structures. In short, Machado's final "new novel" implies, we must learn (as we were told by Brás Cubas in chapter 34 of the first of his "new novels") to discipline our nerves, clean our glasses, and make our own meanings, our own decisions, and our own determinations, whether in the act of reading novels or in choosing which candidate to vote for. And, as the female protagonist of *Counselor Ayres' Memorial* does, once we formulate these decisions, we must then act on them. To do this is within our power as human beings, and while it must all take place within the limits of the "prison-house" of language, we have the capacity to be prisoners with some degree of agency, some measure of control over our destinies, as individuals and as societies. As Fidelia's complex story unfolds, the reader sees change, the great concern of Aristotle with respect to artistic imitation, being dealt with by means of change in the language used to both initiate it and shape its course. So while Machado begins his "new narrative" theory and novel with what seems to be a negative, he ends it, in 1908, with a positive, though by no means perfect (and by no means closed), interpretive path. In rereading both novels, however, and in comparison to each other as structures of verbal imitation, the outcome remains a function of language and its visceral, perhaps genetic connection to the human experience.[15]

First appearing, in serial form, in 1880, *The Posthumous Memoirs of Brás Cubas* offers the reader nothing less, I believe, than an entirely new "poetics of the novel," one in which constant semantic play lies, restively but, in terms of the true human experience, also realistically, at the heart of it all.[16] And, I propose, this was done entirely by intention on Machado's part; this was the gist of his new narrative theory, and it directly determines the nature of the "new novel" that he now wanted to write. Machado shows his reader of the time, just as he shows us now, that this basic uncertainty about how to interpret life is true for language but is also true for human existence, which is, here and in his later novels, Machado will more and more suggest, overwhelmingly a function of language and how we use it.

2 • THE PSYCHIATRIST

Written at about the same time as *The Posthumous Memoirs of Brás Cubas*, the novella *The Psychiatrist* (1881–82) offers both a different take on the "new narrative" that Machado, armed, now, with his new thinking about language and its unique ability to imitate the world of human action and motivation, was now committed to writing and a more concise theoretical grounding for it. Written largely in the third person, *The Psychiatrist* is commonly, and accurately, read as a satire of two things: an unwarranted belief in the ability of science to eliminate all of humankind's woes and of the ability of revolutionary politics to achieve a just and fair government (see Barbieri). While the first can be appreciated as another of Machado's critiques of positivism, the second can be read as a critique of global political systems that, always in the name of what's right, merely replace one form of tyranny with another. Indeed, the chapter divisions of *The Psychiatrist* parody the historical development of the French Revolution of 1789. Here, Machado steps away from the flagrantly antirealistic techniques that so spectacularly give form to Brás Cubas's story to one that, more tightly constructed, appeals to what he knows is his reader's desire for, if not a truly verisimilar text, then one that seems to be such. The very nature, or meaning, of verisimilitude itself thus comes into question here. This explains why, in contrast to the tale that a dead and unreliable narrator spins out for us, *The Psychiatrist* tempts us with the illusion of a text, like the old Realism, that purports to tell us the truth and in a way that allows us to know it.

Machado's narrator makes this clear in the text's very first sentence: "The chronicles of Itaguai relate that in remote times a certain physician of noble birth, Simão Bacamarte, lived there and that he was one of the greatest doctors in all Brazil, Portugal and Coimbra" (*Psy*, 1). References to the these chronicles and what they say dot the entire text of *The Psychiatrist*, and always to the same end: to play to the reader's long cultivated desire to find truth and knowledge in what she reads against the inherent falsity, or fictionality, of the very text she is reading. The idea of this text being a "chronicle," a particular brand of historical writing, underscores its supposed truthfulness, its reliability, its status as a historical, and therefore reliable, text. But it is not. As Machado will demonstrate, even the kind of writing we commonly think of as "nonfiction" is, in fact, a "fiction." History itself is a fiction, though both kinds of writing (the historical and the fictional) have much in common, often (though perhaps more so in fiction) making use of the other's assumptions and techniques.[1] This is certainly true of Machado de Assis, and we can see it in his novels and stories as well as in his crônicas and criticism. Even the idea of fiction is a fiction. Indeed, all language use, Machado suggests, is fiction, and the fact that we like to think that there is a difference between "fiction" and "nonfiction" does not change this basic truth.

In a general sense, then, the central conflict in *The Psychiatrist* is between certainty and uncertainty; in a more textually specific sense, it is about the appearance of things (in this case a text that, purporting to be "realistic," wants us to think it speaks the truth to us) and their reality (their existence, in this case, as verbal constructs, systems of signs and structures of words that, for their meaning or meanings, refer more to themselves than to any reality outside of the structure in which they appear). But while this accurately describes Machado's new thinking about what language is and how it works, it does not in any way eliminate the ability of these same texts to lead their readers to think hard about the nature of the social, intellectual, and political institutions that shape their lives. This is a big part of Machado's genius as a theoretician and practitioner of his "new narrative"; he now knows perfectly what the consequences of this view of language could be on human society, but he also knows perfectly well that human beings do, in fact, live in and deal with this semantically unstable, uncertain environment. This very situation, I believe Machado would say, is the real truth of the human condition, and, as a "new narrativist," he is leading us to learn to deal with it.

And it is the process of interpretation that is at the heart of it all, as we read literary texts and as we perform our civic duties, which include interpreting all sorts of political discourses and texts. The skills that Machado insists that his new reader develop will serve her well as a good citizen as well. Machado's new thinking about language, imitation, and life does not in any way cancel out his importance as an astute social critic; indeed, it enhances it, for it makes us more aware of how language use affects our lives and the decisions we make, as readers and as citizens. As our active, engaged consumption of the funny but, in terms of the meaning it generates, elusive text that calls itself *The Psychiatrist* shows us, Machado and his narrator lead us to consider how all the consequences that derive from his new thinking about language and its peculiar relationship with both being and knowing speak to our public and private lives, to how we think about ourselves and our societies.

Far from being nihilistic in its view of life and what it means, this language-centric approach to novel writing is both more honest and realistic, in Machado's new understanding of the terms, and positive. In observing and thinking about a fictional character like Dr. Simão Bacamarte, who is so confident in what he believes (the absolute supremacy of science) that, in the final chapter, he ends up fatally deluding himself, the reader and citizen can, if she is inclined to do so, learn to do better in her own life. Life is not art, but the latter can, if done well, teach us something about the former. In this respect, *The Psychiatrist* represents a major step forward in the development of Machado as a writer, as a public intellectual, and as a theoretician of the "new novel" form.

It is not too much to conclude, in fact, that Bacamarte is the quintessence, simultaneously, of what we would call today both logocentric and phallogocentric thinking. And it is on him that the text of *The Psychiatrist* focuses. It is his text, for he is the psychiatrist of the title. Less affable and less self-interrogating than his immediate predecessor, Brás Cubas, Dr. Bacamarte is a darker, more sinister kind of character, one who feels he has the force of truth behind him but one whose logic and whose methods are wholly out of step with the human condition and its attempt to understand, at any given moment, what is happening around it. And yet, for all the certainty of his outlook, Bacamarte does not lack for comedic aspects as well, aspects of his being that the alert reader can laugh at. The good doctor's relationship with his wife, Dona Evarista da Costa e Mascarenhas, allows us to see how twisted his ideas really are, and especially when he moves them from the theoretical realm to that of actual implementation. "Science," Bacamarte declares, "is my only office; Itaguai," a real place, located some seventy-five miles west of Rio de Janeiro, "my universe" (*Psy*, 1). When Bacamarte reaches his fortieth year, he elects to marry. But the doctor, a man of science and therefore one guided not by passion but by reason and logic, is no love-smitten swain. His bride, a widow, Dona Evarista da Costa e Mascarenhas, was, the narrator reports (with an aura of objectivity and veracity), "neither beautiful nor charming" (*Psy*, 1). On the other hand, she did, as Bacamarte himself had noted, enjoy "perfect digestion, excellent eyesight, and normal blood pressure; she had no serious illnesses and her urinalysis was negative. It was likely she would give him healthy, robust children" (*Psy*, 1). And, as a kind of bonus, since Dona Evarista was not "pretty," "he would not be tempted to sacrifice his scientific pursuits to the contemplation of his wife's attractions" (*Psy*, 1). Clearly, the reader is led to feel, the good doctor has his personal priorities straight, though another reader might well wonder if he is not evaluating his wife as one would the purchase of a breeding mare, a thought that could give one pause to think about the value systems in play here.

Set in the eighteenth century, when Brazil was still a Portuguese colony, *The Psychiatrist* is marked by several interconnecting motifs: change, meaning, interpretation (both in terms of what history seeks to do and of meaning produced by language use), difference (as well as *différance*), and our human desire to know and understand. In chapter 1, Dr. Bacamarte makes a proposal to the town council that, if enacted, would change forever the ways Itaguai treats its mentally ill citizens. "The proposal," the text (based on official chronicles) tells us, "aroused excitement and curiosity throughout the town" (*Psy*, 2). But there was also "considerable opposition, for it is always difficult to uproot the established way of doing things, however absurd or evil it may be" (*Psy*, 2–3). Given the fact that this line was written in 1881 or 1882, at exactly the time Machado was breaking away from the old Realism and embracing a new kind of writing (one that he felt was closer to the uncertainty inherent in the real human experience), I believe we are here being invited to read this line in at least two different ways: One, the obvious one, relates to the emerging conflict in the story being told; Itaguai is going to have to deal with change, and while the good doctor argues for it, most people oppose it. An alternative reading, and one consistent with the line of interpretation already set in motion by Brás Cubas a year or two before, leads the reader to suspect that Machado and his narrator are talking to us about the "new narrative" Machado is writing and how it is disrupting "the established way" of writing and reading novels, "however absurd" (that is, unrealistic) "it may be" (*Psy*, 2–3). In other words, I believe that here, in chapter 1 of *The Psychiatrist*, Machado is once again calling our attention to his new thinking about language and its imitative powers and to how his new reader must respond to it.

After a comedic interlude in which Bacamarte's wife says she will eat whatever her husband thinks is necessary for her to attain "a certain objective" (that is, pregnancy), the narrator tells us, in what seems to be a sign pointed at the problematic reception Machado's "new narrative" was going to have in Brazil's intellectual community, that Bacamarte "then went to the town hall" (which the reader can take as the reading public), "where the Council" (Brazil's critical establishment, a reiteration of Brás Cubas's reference, in chapter 9 of his novel, to "the policeman on the block") "was debating his proposal" (Machado's new theory of narrative) (*Psy*, 3).

This line of reading seems to gain credibility when, as this paragraph ends and then flows into the next one, we learn that "one of the Councilmen" (one of the critics), "who was opposed to the doctor's" (or Machado's) "undertaking," declares, as if in a summary dismissal of Machado's "new narrative," that "Bacamarte's project will never be executed. Who ever heard of putting a lot of crazy people together in one house?" (*Psy*, 3). It does not strain credibility to imagine reading this line, as Machado and his narrator seem to hope his new reader will, as a critic's rejection of precisely the kind of novel that is being presented here, that is, one that comes alive for the reader as a lot of "crazy" (that is, different and nontraditional) elements being brought together in a single narrative structure. To the traditional critic, reared on traditional ways of viewing the novel form, the text that we are reading as *The Psychiatrist*, like *The Posthumous Memoirs of Brás Cubas* before it, would, indeed, seem to be a truly "crazy" undertaking. But, at the same time, for the reader who understands where Machado is now coming from as a writer, who understands the premises about language, imitation, and meaning that are driving Machado, the text that is *The Psychiatrist* would not seem crazy at all. To the contrary, it would seem entirely realistic, albeit in a different sort of way.

Either way, the first sentence of the very next paragraph suggests that Machado's critics were wrong, because "Bacamarte," read Machado, "built his madhouse," his "new narrative," on, appropriately enough, "New Street" (*Psy*, 3). However we read it, this line epitomizes the new kind of writing that Machado is now cultivating. It fits perfectly into two very distinct modes of reading; one, arguably more superficial and passive, makes sense within the context of the story itself, how the officials of Itaguai respond to Bacamarte's new and very disruptive proposal about how to treat mentally ill people, while the other makes perfect sense when read as a defense of Machado's new thinking about language, how it imitates human life and how it generates both meaning and ambiguity simultaneously. While this same force animates *The Posthumous Memoirs of Brás Cubas*, I believe that here, in *The Psychiatrist*, we are seeing a more distilled version of it. It is almost as if Machado, having finished the 1880 text, has almost immediately written another text, denser and more tightly structured, that approaches the same problem—the nature of his "new narrative" and how it would have to be read—but from another perspective, and under the guise of a text that purports to be both nonfiction (the chronicle) and truthful (the very quality that the text itself undermines and that the alert, engaged reader observes doing so).

The first chapter then draws itself to a conclusion with a comic commentary on Dona Evarista, who, a delightful and very humane character, loved both fine clothes and the adulation of people around her, people who, the text implies, laud and celebrate her with what they hope will be taken as the selfish and destructive form of envy (the most common form) but "the noble and blessed envy of admiration" (*Psy*, 4). In responding to this language use and the ironies it sets up, the good reader now picks up on the fact that the same words can and do mean different and even contradictory things. Meaning is relative and, like Ferdinand de Saussure's linguistic sign, utterly arbitrary.

That same thoughtful, discerning reader, the kind of reader that J. Hillis Miller wants to encourage, will also play a key role in chapter 2, where, once again, we are treated to a scene in which the same words are shown to mean very different things.[2] In chapter 2, however, the change of meaning is less pointedly a function of how each reader responds to the same text (though this is clearly a part of it) than it is a function of how the interpretational demands and expectations of different disciplines (here, religion and science) determine the meanings of the words we use to discuss them. Viewed from beginning to end, chapter 2 thus shows us how it is that, in our human quest to discover or determine the meaning of things, words talk more with other words than anything else, including external realities. Even scientific facts require that language be used to determine their meaning.

Machado's narrator begins chapter 2, humorously titled "A Torrent of Madmen," by offering us a comparison of the role reading and interpretation play in the worlds of science and religion. Speaking to another character, one Crispim Soares, who is a druggist and thus sort of a scientist himself, though a much less fanaticized one, Bacamarte, in a rather imperious fashion, says this: "Charity, Soares, definitely enters into my method. It is the seasoning in the recipe, *for thus I interpret the words* of St. Paul to the Corinthians: 'Though *I understand* all mysteries and all knowledge . . . and have not charity, I am nothing'" (*Psy*, 4, emphasis mine). The issues of careful reading (preceded, of course, by careful writing on Machado's part) and interpretation thus rise up from out of the text itself, and, as always now, illustrating how the same words mean a variety of things, with none entirely canceling out any others. What we have here, in the words of Barbara Johnson (writing of the play that is inherent in deconstructive reading and writing), is "nothing less than a revolution in the very logic of meaning. . . . Instead of 'A is opposed to B' we have 'B is both added to and replaces A.' A and B are no longer opposed, nor are they equivalent. Indeed, they are no longer even equivalent to themselves."[3] The narrative that Machado is cultivating now contains "within itself a trace of the other" so that "reading and writing now emerge as supplements of each other (*supplément*, signifying both 'addition' and 'substitution' or 'replacement.'"[4]

At issue in chapter 2 is the language use of a particular young man, one who, "every day after lunch," gives a public speech in a very "academic discourse," one filled with elaborate metaphors, conceits, and quotes from a variety of classical figures (*Psy*, 5). More pertinent to the story the narrator is spinning out about Dr. Bacamarte and the impact his own new theories (on madness) had on Itaguai, the young man's supposed dementia will be comically attributed to the inflated and pretentious words he uses. The incongruity of a "coarse, ignorant young man" giving such a rhetorically fancy speech, one full of words that have no grounding in the lived reality of his modest life, leads the psychiatrist to interpret the fellow as insane. The village priest, who also finds the man's language use to be strange, says that the only reason he can think of for such strange behavior "is the confusion of languages on the Tower of Babel. They were so completely mixed together that now, probably when a man loses his reason, he easily slips from one into another" (*Psy*, 5). Bacamarte, however, seeks a "purely scientific" explanation for the man's actions, and he believes there is one. And that he will find it, such is the conviction of his own line of interpretation. In what would seem to be a foreshadowing of Machado's next novel, *Quincas Borba*, the text tells us that, in addition to the young man who gives florid public speeches every day after lunch, there were, running around the streets of Itaguai, "some noteworthy cases of megalomania," including some in which people began to equate themselves with divinities (*Psy*, 5).

The narrator, relying on the chronicles that are thought to explain what happened in Itaguai, then offers up a parallel between what is happening in his story about the asylum, the Green House, and the doubts Machado had about how prepared Brazil was, in terms of its cultural institutions, to move ahead as its leaders moved toward the establishment of its Republic. Bringing this to a head, the narrator has Bacamarte declare, to the priest, that the "Green Housenow has its temporal government," that is, a government that showed the harsh realities of its true predicament as a slave-owning society with such weak social institutions such as public education, an adequate transportation system, and a solid public health structure, "and its spiritual government," the vision of Brazil as the land of the future and as a true and exemplary Republic, an ideal which Machado believed Brazil could not, given its structural weaknesses as a modern society, attain (*Psy*, 6). This is a reading that one might well associate with John Gledson and his take on Machado, and yet it does not cancel out the argument I propose here; indeed, it enriches it by showing how, in Machado's "new narrative," multiple lines are simultaneously possible. Machado's narrator takes pains to reinforce what Bacamarte says by having the priest, Father Lopes, respond by laughing and declaring that it was "a delightful novelty . . . to find a society" (*Psy*, 6), one the reader takes to be the Brazil of the early 1880s, "in which the spiritual," that is, its vision of itself as about to become the ideal Republic, one built on the best, most noble words, "dominates" social and political discourse so utterly—so much so that other, perhaps more sober interpretations of the same social, political, and economic facts were drowned out. This play on words involving the difference between the real and the ideal, a pun noted both in the original text and in the English translation, would not have been lost on readers in Machado's time. But neither it is lost on readers today who, more sensitive to the vagaries of language, see in it the difference between hard reality and the use of language to make things seem other than they really are.

Chapter 3, the title of which, "God Knows What He Is Doing," comically evokes for the modern reader what we mean with the terms "logocentrism" and "phallogocentrism," returns the reader to the problem of how words, even the exact, same words, mean different things. But it also brings up, for the first time in this text, the key problem of Machado's "new narrative": verisimilitude, and how it is achieved by language.[5] As Bacamarte, the man of science, becomes more and more obsessed by what he is certain is the correctness of his point of view (one produced by his own use of language), he begins to segregate himself from other people, and even his wife, Dona Evarista, who now begins "to complain a little" about her abandonment (*Psy*, 7). "Who would ever have thought," she muses, sadly, "that a bunch of lunatics . . . ," which, given its context, the reader takes to mean that Dona Evarista blames the "lunatics" for her unhappy lot in life (*Psy*, 7). The ellipsis (so common in the late writing of Machado de Assis) that marks the end of this sentence also serves as an invitation to the reader to ponder a bit more just what she means here. Her words, the reader feels, are negative, in the sense that Dona Evarista seems to feel that her present unhappiness is being caused by "a bunch of lunatics" who, even though they do not relate directly to her personal experience, do, in fact, affect her quality of life because they are isolating both her and her husband. That words and actions mean different things to different people and in different circumstances is quickly reiterated in the text, as if Machado did not want his reader to miss it, in the narrator's humorous observation that Dona Evarista, who had just cast her lovely black eyes to the ceiling in frustration over her husband's disregard for her, now uses those same eyes "in much the same way when trying to get Simão Bacamarte to propose. Now she was brandishing her weapon," her eyes, "again, this time for the apparent purpose of cutting science's throat" (*Psy*, 7).

Later in this same chapter, the very same words uttered by Dona Evarista as she complained about having become, because of her husband's commitment to his work, a widow for the second time, but now mouthed by her husband and in reference to how wealthy that same "bunch of lunatics" have made them, come to have a completely different meaning, one that speaks positively and approvingly of all the money they have made through his practice. As he shows an amazed Dona Evarista (who, we are told, "was not quite sure what" the numbers "signified") the figures in the hospital's account books—figures that show, that "prove," how much money they now had, "mountains of gold, thousands upon thousands of cruzados and doubloons. A fortune!," Bacamarte then whispers, "mischievously," in her ear, "Who would ever have thought that a bunch of lunatics" (*Psy*, 8, 9). Still more than a little mystified by what she is seeing, and reading, Dona Evarista does what people often do when confronted by things they do not understand—she appeals to God, the presumed ultimate authority and giver of all meaning. "God knows what he is doing," she declares, feeling now more content by appealing to God and to the kind of confidence people had in what they believed to be language's ability to demonstrate stable, knowable meaning before the advent of Saussure, structuralism, and, most especially, poststructuralism (*Psy*, 8). What impresses Machado's reader of 1881 is that, now, in Machado's new theory of language, narrative, and imitation, words do not have solid, reliable meanings in them; rather, their meanings are fluid and vary according to the circumstances in which they are being written and read. The relativity of meaning, Machado shows us, is a fact of life, one with which we must learn to contend, as readers and as citizens.

Chapter 4, titled, as if to call attention to Machado's own new theory, "A New Theory," depicts Bacamarte being seized by "a new and daring hypothesis," one that "was so daring, indeed, that, if substantiated, it would revolutionize the bases of psychopathology," just as Machado's new theory of narrative changes how we think about language and the nature of the modern novel form (*Psy*, 8). Once again, words determine, and then change, how we view and understand reality. Yet again, Machado makes use of the comedic mode to disguise a very serious point—how language generates multiple meanings and thus destabilizes our desire to create, or invent, single, stable, and unchanging meanings for words (which is the very definition of logocentrism). Frantic with worry, and expecting the worst, the druggist rushes to Bacamarte's house to learn what has happened.

"Some news of our wives?," he asks, "in a tremulous voice. The psychiatrist made a magnificent gesture and replied: 'It is something much more important—a scientific experiment'" (*Psy*, 9). The contrast between the realm in which the great doctor resides, the theoretical, and the world of the druggist, that of human reality, could not be made, more seriously or more comically. Whether the one or the other, it is a vivid contrast, one that subtly underscores the point that I believe Machado is making in his late narratives—that we live both in the world of reality and in the world of language, and that, confusedly, we use the latter to try to deal with the former.

But in such an uncertain situation, misinterpretation is bound to creep into our efforts to understand who and what we are and what it all means. And so it is that, one morning, the good doctor, energized by his new and different theory, sends a message to the druggist, Soares, telling him that he, the psychiatrist, "wished to see him" (*Psy*, 9). Immediately fearful, as a decent and caring human being would be, that something bad has happened to his wife (who is accompanying Dona Evarista in her visit to Rio de Janeiro), Soares misinterprets the meaning of Bacamarte's message. "'Some news of our wives?,' asked the druggist in a tremulous voice" (*Psy*, 9).

But the doctor, working with a more ethereal value system, has other issues on his mind. Making a "magnificent gesture" to his colleague, Bacamarte then replies, "It is something much more important—a scientific experiment. I say 'experiment,' for I do not yet venture to affirm the correctness of my theory," a comment that, at this point, can easily be taken as a wry comment from Machado about his own new theory (*Psy*, 9). "Till now," the doctor continues, "madness has been thought a small island in an ocean of sanity. I am beginning to suspect that it is not an island at all but a continent" (*Psy*, 9). He enjoys the druggist's "amazement" at this new notion and then goes on to explain that "the number of persons suffering from insanity . . . was far greater than commonly supposed" (*Psy*, 9). While, in terms of the larger narrative in which it occurs, this line is very funny, the reader also suspects that it could be another iteration of Machado's new thinking about language and meaning; just as Bacamarte now believes that there are many more insane people running around than he had previously thought, so, too, are there many possible meanings generated by a single word, or sign, many more, in fact, than readers before this time may have suspected. For the reader, the parallels between Bacamarte's new theory and Machado's new theory are there to be seen. While Father Lopes, who, like the reader, is "not quite sure" what the doctor's new theory means, he wonders this: "Under the present definition of insanity," the "fence around the area," that is, the thinking that has long sought to separate the sane from the insane, has been "perfectly clear and satisfactory. Why not stay within it?" (*Psy*, 11). In considering this argument, the modern reader will see the old seductiveness of what we now speak of as binary thinking, which itself depends on difference; for those enamored of binary thinking, a thing either is or is not, though we know that in real life, that it is rarely that simple to distinguish between people, ideas, actions, and events. Although the reliabilities of Bacamarte's theories have, up to this point, been presented by the chronicles (and by the text we are reading) as being beyond suspicion, he now presents a new theory, one that, for the judicious reader, will call that same perspicacity into question. The text of *The Psychiatrist* thus begins to call itself into question, and the alert reader begins to pick up on it and observe it happening.

With the motif of insanity foreshadowing Machado's next novel, *Quincas Borba, The Psychiatrist* then closes this chapter with what can easily be taken as a thinly veiled reference to the theoretical decision I believe Machado himself made a couple of years earlier about how he would write his "new narrative" and his "new novel." Citing "our century's contempt" for "the institutions of the old regime," and thus seeming to reference chapter 7 of *The Posthumous Memoirs of Brás Cubas*, the section in which the narrator tells us that every generation is contemptuous of those that preceded it, the chronicles that, supposedly, give substance and the appearance of truth to the fiction that is *The Psychiatrist* now depict the good doctor saying this: "No, I won't announce my theory to the public," "I'll do something better: I'll act on it" (*Psy*, 10). It does not tax the reader's imagination to feel that Machado may here be referring to his own situation as the owner of his own new theory and how, instead of discussing it publicly, deciding simply to "act on it," to begin writing it, as he does, I contend, first in *The Posthumous Memoirs of Brás Cubas* and then, immediately afterward, but in a different way, *The Psychiatrist*. What Bacamarte says here is exactly what Machado himself does; he puts his new theory about language and narrative into action. It is at this point that people begin to be hurt. Bad theory produces bad results, real damage, just as bad ideas produce bad legislation, which also hurts real people. This is the problem with conservatism, the ideas of which are better in theory than in actual practice. The chapter then ends with a once again humorous take on the problem of new theories and their understanding by the people most affected by them. "Itaguai," like the old Realism that had dominated narrative theory and practice for so long, "were on the brink of a revolution" (*Psy*, 11).

Chapter 5 is built around the uncertain nature of interpretation and the elusiveness, or, one could argue, the multiplicity of meaning. Several separate but interconnected examples mentioned in the text bear this out. And in each case, the text itself alludes, figuratively, of course (since all language is figurative in nature, a point the consequences of which I believe Machado was now exploring), to this very concern when, in reference to widespread debate among the characters as to the meaning of the doctor's actions and of his explanations of them, the narrator tells his reader that these interlocking issues were "gossiped about on street corners and in barber shops. Within a short time it developed into *a full-scale novel*," that is, not the truth but an illusion of it (*Psy*, 13, emphasis mine). By referencing a literary form, the "full-scale novel," that Machado knew his readers would associate with fiction, he underscores what I believe is his new contention, that all writing is (as Borges will declare in the 1930s) a fiction, even the ostensibly "nonfiction" chronicle that this text purports to be. With *The Psychiatrist,* the distinction between fiction and nonfiction, so often thought to come with the Barthes between 1968 and 1975, is already effaced by Brazil's Machado de Assis in 1881–82.

Responding to the uncertainty that all this puzzling about the meaning of Bacamarte's words and deeds (which generate even more words of discussion), the narrator then proceeds to advise his reader that something indeed was going on here, but they, the actors in the drama (or farce), did not know what it was. "All this," suggests the narrator, and calling her attention to the confusion that now reigns supreme among the text's characters, "*could be read* in the druggist's jocund expression and discreet smile—and in his silence, for he made no reply" (*Psy,* 14, emphasis mine). The role of interpretation, in this text and in real human life, is made quite apparent here, this being a point then underscored by the narrator who, speaking of "the townspeople" as if they were serving here as his Greek chorus, declare, sagely but confusedly, "'There's something very strange going on,' thought the townspeople" (*Psy,* 14). Nevertheless, we learn, some of them, wanting to understand, were speculating in earnest about the mysterious events and words that had engulfed them. Inferences were drawn and "communicated to Bacamarte," whose eyes, always on the lookout for the presence of people he, and he alone, could judge to be "insane," "lighted up with scientific voluptuousness" (*Psy,* 15).

Meaning and interpretation, whether from the townspeople (whom we may fairly think of as citizens seeking to understand their civic and political circumstances) or from the person (Bacamarte) who takes himself to be the supreme interpreter, the one, unimpeachable reader who can divine the author's intended meaning in the old realistic "work," continue to dominate Machado's very open text. As K. David Jackson notes, the case of the character, Costa, both illustrates this problem and, in his great generosity (which, with pungent irony, Bacamarte will deduce as a sure sign of insanity), anticipates "the fate of Rubião in *Quincas Borba.*"[6] Panicking, because they do not understand what is going on and sense, therefore, that they are in danger of agreeing to something (a political discourse or ideology) that could harm them, the people of Itaguai turn to the doctor's wife, Dona Evarista, for help. She and she alone, it is now thought, could "alleviate" what was now taken to be (interpreted as) the "scourge" that was sweeping over their town (*Psy,* 16). A comically humane figure, and a woman who, though she tried always to be strong and smart and to do the right thing (if it could be determined just what that was), regularly fell prey to the allure of good food, fine clothes, and precious jewels, "Dona Evarista found it strange indeed that all those people should have gone mad" (*Psy,* 17). Sounding a note of rational thought in the midst of great confusion (and thus functioning just as Machado wanted his new reader to do), Dona Evarista mused to herself (and, of course, to the reader), "It might easily happen to one or another—but to *all* of them?" (*Psy*, 17). But, on the other hand, and considering now the power of her husband's scientific stance (which parallels the old confidence in the author's intention in a work of literature, the meaning that was there and that the reader needed to find and embrace), she also knows that "she could hardly doubt the fact" that all these people had been judged, by a supposed authority figure, to be insane (*Psy*, 17). How dare she doubt that? How dare she doubt such authority (her husband, a character we can easily read as the author, understood in the old sense of the stable, knowable "work")? The meaning of the "facts" that are there must be the meaning we are to take from them.

But, no; Machado's "text" undercuts this very certainty, or desire for certainty. Unchecked, the "terror grew in intensity. One no longer knew who was sane and who was insane," just as the reader cannot tell what is true here and what is not (*Psy*, 19). The words used in the text to summarize and describe what was happening do not offer a single, clear, and reliable explanation, and neither do the words used by the reader who, responding to the carefully structured words in Machado's text, is trying to figure it all out. What emerges from *The Psychiatrist*, the text being read, is that it steps off its passive status on the page and enters the reader's mind as a self-conscious and ironic parody of how we handle the fact that, in life as in language and literature, meaning changes constantly. To believe otherwise, Machado insists, is to maintain an unjustified faith in the unrealistic illusion perpetrated by the old realistic novel.

Chapter 5 then comes to its conclusion by making, in rapid succession, two decisive points, both dealing with the inescapably pluralistic nature of language's production of meaning. In the first one, the narrator points out that, in the name of trying to clarify the struggle over who is sane and who is insane, and to clarify who has the right and the ability to determine this, a lawsuit (itself a function of words) is brought against one of the participants. This legal action, we are told, "grew not out of hatred or spite but *out of the obscure wording of a deed*," a distinction that clearly illustrates, for the reader receptive to the issue, how the real problem here is not "hatred or spite" but the uncertain nature of language itself (*Psy*, 20, emphasis mine). What appears, at first glance, to be the case, in other words, turns out, on closer inspection, not to be the case, and the careful reader, the very kind Machado is calling for, does not fail to pick this up. Coelho, the barber in question here, preferred people who, like him, "also liked to talk," that is, to converse, to communicate, to use words and exchange opinions, and this leads another character, Father Lopes, who did not care for Coelho's loquaciousness, to quote Dante, but, crucially for the meaning of the reference, "with a minor change" (*Psy*, 20). "'La bocca sollevò dal fiero pasto / Quel seccatore,'" which the note, translating the Italian (and once again demonstrating how language always "translates," interprets, and inevitably changes, other language use), explains this way: "'The pest raised his mouth from his savage repast.' Father Lopes substituted *seccatore,* 'pest,' for Dante's *peccatore,* 'sinner.' Count Ugolino, the sinner, was gnawing the head of another sinner. *Inferno,* Canto XXXIII" (*Psy* 20).

With this deliberate change (the product of desire larded by interpretation), which foreshadows what Bento Santiago will do to his unfinished sonnet in *Dom Casmurro,* Machado is showing his reader how the change of a single word ineluctably changes the meaning of the entire structure, just as a change in the structure (the novella that is *The Psychiatrist,* for example) changes the meaning of every word, or sign, in it. Giving the last line of this chapter over to Coelho the barber and how his cohorts, and fellow citizens, regarded him and the quote from Dante, the narrator comically informs us that "the priest's remark did not affect the general esteem in which Coelho was held, for some attributed the remark to mere personal animosity and others thought," in yet another humorous reference to the perils of interpretation, "it was a prayer in Latin" (*Psy,* 20). Clearly, Machado's text shows us, in life as in literature, interpretation is never far from misinterpretation, but it is all part of the same fluid and ever-changing linguistic game—how words signify.

Chapter 6, "The Rebellion," concentrates, parodically, on how words can lead not only to other words but to action, and virtually always with unintended consequences. In what rapidly escalates (as clashing theories often do) into a full-scale dispute over what is "true" or "correct" interpretation of what is happening or being said, the narrator reports to us that "about thirty people allied themselves with the barber. They prepared a formal complaint and took it to the Town Council, which rejected it on the ground that scientific research must be hampered neither by hostile legislation nor by the misconceptions and prejudices of the mob" (*Psy,* 20–21). Words, or lines of interpretation, are warring with other words and lines of interpretation in a scene that very realistically imitates how human efforts at self-government work. After meditating on this turn of events, the barber "then declared that . . . he would give Itaguai no peace until the final destruction of the Green House, 'that Bastille of human reason'" (*Psy,* 21). In a deliciously comic comparison with the French Revolution, the "revolution" engulfing Itaguai is seen to lack, in its conflicted verbal presentation here, the harmony that Machado will, beginning in his next novel and continuing on to the end of his career, associate with music as an artistic form. Itaguai will know no peace until the Green House, which is equated to the famous French prison, is destroyed, and probably not even then, the engaged reader suspects. Even more intriguingly, however, the idea of "human reason," a function of language use, as being its own kind of prison is also floated by the reader for her consideration. It is as if Machado is speculating about how, as humans, we use language to think ourselves out of one prison and into another, hitherto unforeseen one.

Bringing once again to the reader's attention the destabilizing force of language in human affairs, the narrator then tells us that "the figure of speech, 'Bastille of the human reason,'" has so impressed people that many of them change their opinions and actually change sides in the revolution (*Psy*, 21). This powerful and affecting "figure of speech," he and Machado tell us a second time (in case we missed it the first time), "counterbalanced to some extent the one about the Bastille," the real one in Paris in 1789 (*Psy*, 22). In putting it as he does, the narrator seems here to be arguing for a quality of this particular figure of speech, employed, as it is, in this place and time and by this particular character, that recalls the notion of supplement, the process of "addition," "substitution," or "replacement" that one word, or sign, brings to its relationships with other words, the "traces" each word carries in itself of all the other words it contacts and interacts with.[7] And the repletion of the term "figure of speech" a third time suggests that Machado wants to drive home for the reader this one key point: all language use is, in the sense that all language is figurative, a fiction, a function of writing, structure, and reading. And it elicits a response, an interpretation. The problem is that we who live and labor in the world of language (which is to say, most all of us) never know for certain if we are producing a good, reasonable interpretation, one consistent with the facts, or whether we are producing a misinterpretation, one based on erroneous facts, "alternative facts," or no facts at all.[8]

This scene comes, comically, to a head when Dona Evarista, who, as she is "trying on" one of the thirty-seven silk dresses she had bought in Rio and brought home to Itaguai, is led to comment on the meaning of, or interpret, the bloodthirsty riot that is taking place outside her window. "'It's probably just a bunch of drunks,' she said as she changed the location of a pin" (*Psy*, 22). Much to the reader's delight, poor Dona Evarista, so preoccupied with her fancy dress, fails, as humans so often do, to correctly assess the meaning of what is happening all around her. Interestingly, it is Dona Evarista's black female slave who does read the situation correctly, pointing out to her otherwise preoccupied master that the mob is calling for the death of her husband, to which the good lady says, sharply: "Be quiet! Benedita, look over here on the left side. Don't you think the seam is a little crooked? We'll have to rip it up and sew it again. Try to make it nice and even this time" (*Psy*, 22). Meanwhile, outside her window, "'Death to Dr. Bacamarte! Death to the tyrant!' howled three hundred voices in the street" (*Psy*, 21). The problem of misinterpretation, of doing so carelessly, or of refusing to interpret carefully, has rarely, if ever, been presented so humorously or so tellingly.

Nevertheless, Dona Evarista is eventually roused from the ardor her new dresses cause her and, finally understanding the urgency of the situation, she rushes to her husband's side to warn him and stand by him in the impending crisis. Normally "an easy prey to emotions of pleasure," Dona Evarista, the narrator tells us, manages, in this case, to be "reasonably steadfast" in the face of "adversity" (*Psy*, 23). Her husband, however, lost once again in the reverie of theory, "was examining a passage," that is, certain words, "in Averroës," the latter being an Arabian scholar and interpreter of Aristotle, a figure whose importance to Machado's new theory of language, imitation, and verisimilitude I have already alluded to (*Psy*, 23). Why, I conjecture, as per my argument here, would Machado have taken pains to build into his narrative a reference to a celebrated Arabian scholar of Aristotle if he did not want his careful reader to take note of it and thus be led to consider how it fits into his new thinking about language, reality, and imitation? It is possible, of course, that the reference to Averroës is innocent and entirely gratuitous, though to me this seems, given Machado's vast knowledge and craftsmanship, highly unlikely. But Machado's narrator carries on, working the same issue, how we use language to think about language, and creating a marvelous metaphor to encapsulate it all. "His eyes," the narrator tells us, of Bacamarte's reception of the news from his wife, "blind to external reality but highly perceptive in the realm of the inner life, rose from the book," the language structure (about Aristotle, we can suppose, knowing what we know about the Arabian scholar) at hand, "to the ceiling and returned to the book," the repository of all the knowledge that Bacamarte held dear (*Psy*, 23). After calling to him a third time, and just as "the shouts were coming closer and closer, threatening, terrifying," Bacamarte finally responded (*Psy*, 23). "He understood," the text tells us (*Psy*, 23). But then, in a grand symbol of how we humans, lost in our illusions of certainty, the good doctor rises up "from the armchair," shuts the book, "and, with firm, calm step," walks "over to the bookcase and" puts "the volume back in its place" (*Psy*, 23). If the reader did not quite grasp the symbolism of this action, Machado and his narrator give her one additional prodding to do so: "The insertion of the volume," they tell us, "caused the books on either side of it to be slightly out of line. Simão Bacamarte carefully straightened them" (*Psy*, 23).

Given my thesis here, I find this scene an extraordinary foreshadowing of Saussure's later theory of how language works, of how each word, or sign, in a system cannot be altered without causing a corresponding change to other words and signs in the same system. Just as the books here are being jostled by the removal of one of them from their collective structure (their position on the bookshelf), so, too, are the meanings of words jostled by their rearrangement as per the other words in their own collective structure. And, once again, I find it scarcely credible to believe that Machado would have constructed such an elaborate metaphor had he not been thinking about how words change their meanings not on their own but in accordance with the positions and relationships of other words to them.

When Bacamarte faces the crowd and insists on the integrity of science and free, innovative thought (a point on which Machado himself might well have agree with in 1881), the barber, sensing a shift in mood, "waved his hat as a signal" to the crowd, an act the modern reader will likely read as an expression of what Saussure himself called for as a new form of scientific inquiry—semiotics. The problem of what this sign means, and what its accompanying signs mean, continues on as the barber demands that "the Green House be destroyed or at least that all the prisoners," the same people who had earlier been happily considered patients being cured of their illnesses, "in it be freed," a demand to which Bacamarte, now himself illustrating the connection between human existence and what philosophers term ontology, responds, "I don't understand" (*Psy*, 24). They then go back and forth about who understands what and, finally, the psychiatrist smiles, but, the text tells us pointedly, it was not one the crown could perceive, much less understand.

Then, Bacamarte speaks, and "the people were astounded at *his words*" (*Psy*, 24, emphasis mine). More words are then employed, by the barber, hoping to rally his troops, and by Bacamarte, who sought only that the integrity of science and the right of free and unfettered inquiry (again, something Machado would likely have wanted for himself and for the reception of his "new narrative"). But it is the words of the barber that win out, and the crowd, swayed by the vehemence of the barber and "emerging from its stupor," once again threatens to move on the Green House and destroy it (*Psy*, 25).

At this point, the unexpected happens. Chapter 7 opens with the arrival of "a corps of dragoons" whose job it is to quell the riot and establish order once again (*Psy*, 25). It is not too hard to think of these dragoons and their official duty as the analogs of the "policeman on the block" from chapter 9 of *The Posthumous Memoirs of Brás Cubas* who, as I have already suggested, seemed to serve as an ironic reference to Brazil's critical establishment, which, as Machado must have suspected, was not likely to view favorably the arrival of his irreverent and profoundly iconoclastic "new narrative." Change, the very thing Aristotle's *The Poetics* mentions as a key element in any form of imitation but does not actually discuss in any detail, is what Machado's "new narrative" excels at representing for us. And we see it here very clearly, albeit with the same kinds of problems with understanding, or interpretation, that come with all language use. We see change, and we see its effects, but we have great difficulty understanding what it means, much less what it will mean in the future. Our lot, as human beings, is simply to deal with it as best we can, and this is what Machado shows us doing, in all our glorious confusion and misunderstanding but also in our sincere, if frustrated, desire to know.

Emphasizing the aleatory nature of life, an aspect of its imitation that language handles conspicuously well, chapter 7, "The Unexpected," emphasizes how the situation changes when the troops arrive. The narrator himself tells us that "what followed is indescribable. The mob howled its fury. Some managed to escape by climbing into windows or running down the street, but the majority, inspired by the barber's words, snorted with anger and stood their ground" (*Psy*, 25). Though their defeat now "appeared imminent," the protestors, "inspired by the words" of their leader, suddenly and unexpectedly become the winners in this confrontation when "one third of the dragoons, for reasons not set forth in the chronicles, went over to the side of the rebels" (*Psy*, 25). This scene is a succinct example of how language can accommodate change in its imitation of life, change being, as we have seen, an aspect of imitation that Aristotle, though aware of its complicating force in the artistic reproduction of human activity, does not elaborate. Machado does, and, in the process, he demonstrates the unique power of narrative as an imitative mode.

While the phrase "what followed is indescribable" is so commonplace as to be a cliché, here I believe it has a quite different and much more significant function. For Machado the "new narrativist," the meaning of this utterance has more to do with the ability of language to imitate reality and to do so in a particularly verisimilar way, one that features the core role language plays in the human experience itself. While it is very successful in most instances, its ability to capture the physical details of the outer world as well as the vagaries of our inner world, for example, it is not, however, perfect in its ability to do so. There is still a divide between language and the things it points to. Words are not, and cannot be, the actions, thoughts, motivations, and emotions they seek to re-present. There is a gap between language and reality and we must understand this, as readers and as citizens. Machado's great breakthrough as an artist and theoretician of the novel form was to realize this and then to write a series of narratives that demonstrate the consequences, aesthetic, intellectual, and civic, that stem from it.

With this unexpected turn of events, the rebels are heartened, and the narrator's words allow the reader to appreciate, if, perhaps, not fully to understand, this dramatic change in the nature of the situation. "The loyal soldiers refused to attack their comrades and," in point of observable "fact," "one by one, joined them," with the again unexpected result that "the people and the troops fraternized" together (*Psy*, 26). Harmony, though not likely to last as long as that achieved by music, prevails, at least for the moment.

An immediate consequence of this newly and surprisingly achieved harmony between the rebels and the officials of law and order is that the town council, which has misinterpreted what was going to happen when its forces, the dragoons, arrived on the scene, suddenly finds itself the beleaguered faction. Again, it is change, set in motion and kept in motion by the use of words, that emerges as the crucial factor in human events. Sensing that he and his colleagues have lost the ability to control things, the President of the council "held his head high" and delivered an inspiring speech (more words) to his cohorts urging them to stand fast in their allegiance to "His Majesty" and to "the people of Itaguai" and that they serve them until the end (*Psy*, 26). Upon hearing these fine words, and interpreting them and the parlous situation in which they now found themselves, in a quite different way, one of the councilmen then "suggested that perhaps they could best serve the Crown and the town by sneaking out the back door" (*Psy*, 26).

Now the apparent winner in this confrontation, Porfirio, the barber, declares himself (as if he were Cromwell) "Town Protector" and proceeds to write an official and inflated edict that, as the reader clearly understands, is not connected in any meaningful way to reality. "Fellow Itaguaians," he begins, in an obvious effort to sway the thinking of his fellow citizens, "A corrupt and irresponsible Town Council was conspiring ignominiously against His Majesty and against the people" (*Psy*, 27). The reader, interpreting these words as well as the series of events that has led to their being uttered, understands that they are a deliberate distortion of the facts. These words make sense, as Machado's reader now realizes, not in terms of reality but only in terms of how they relate to the other words employed by Porfirio to define what he judges to be his newly found power and to those that form the entire narrative that we are reading.

The issue of interpretation, and misinterpretation, continues on, with the narrator then telling us that, as they contemplated the meaning of the barber's words and of the actions of Bacamarte that followed in their wake (the doctor admits even more people into his asylum/prison, depending on how one views, or interprets, it), "Everybody erroneously interpreted" everything (*Psy*, 27). Not even the chroniclers, whom we may think of as the historians, understood this correctly.

The "day ended happily," however (and in yet another unexpected turn of events), for the people were now "confident" that their government would raze the Green House and wipe their town clean of what they now believed was its pernicious influence (*Psy*, 27). In what seems to be a nod to Brazil's pre-Republic struggles, the narrator, employing the same pun he had employed before in chapter 2, avers that there was now "an alliance between the temporal power," Brazil as it really was, "and the spiritual power," or Brazil as it hoped to be when, as if words alone could change its flawed realities, it declared itself a Republic (*Psy*, 27). Few scenes in Machado's post-1880 narratives capture the fusion of Brazilian social, political, and economic reality and the author's new theorizing about language, imitation, and the "new narrative" he was now writing as tightly and as convincingly as this one does. The people now "blessed the name of the man who would finally free Itaguai from the Green House and from the terrible Simão Bacamarte," the very same man whom these same people had earlier, when they had been under the spell of different words and interpretations, hailed as their savior (*Psy*, 28).

In chapters 8 and 9, which can again be read together as forming a single discourse, with one (chapter 9) commenting on the other, we see changing the name of something can, in fact, change its perceived reality. But we also see how, via the process of reading and thinking, "one idea" leads "to another," just as, in Saussure's new linguistics, one word, or sign, leads not to any external reality but to another word, or sign, in the same structure. This, I believe, is the point Machado and his narrator are seeking to impress upon their reader in these two chapters. Resorting once again to the supposed truth-telling authority of the kind of writing known, then and now, as nonfiction, the narrator informs us that "the chroniclers all agree that Mrs. Soares," the druggist's wife, "found great comfort in" what she thought was "the nobility of her husband, who, she assumed, was going to the defense of his friend," Dr. Bacamarte, "and they note with perspicacity the immense power of a thought, even if untrue" (*Psy*, 29).[9] The chronicles themselves are not reliable; they, too, are subject to misinterpretation, just as any other form of language use is. History can be wrong, just as fiction can. Verisimilitude, the appearance of truth, is as elusive for nonfiction as it is for fiction.

Chapter 9 is a kind of elaboration of chapter 8, yet one that makes its case by leading the reader to further contemplate the nature of language and its ability to signify, to imitate human behavior, and to accommodate change, both in the world of human action and the unexpected and in terms of meaning. Building on a discussion between Porfirio, Itaguai's new, albeit self-proclaimed "Protector," and Bacamarte, the resolutely scientific doctor who is committed to putting his theories of madness into action, no matter the consequences or the costs in human suffering, chapter 9, "Two Beautiful Cases," demonstrates to the reader that the two problems of polysemy and (mis)interpretation are inherent in language itself. Since, as the narrator and Machado remind us, the town government "lacks the ability to distinguish between the sane from the insane," this being a matter for science and not politics, the problem of how we can know things in life looms large in the text itself (*Psy*, 30). This same statement about not knowing who is sane and who is insane has, of course, a parallel in the world of language, where it is similarly impossible to know with any degree of precision what words mean. This issue has for many years been a problem for modern philosophers. In the twentieth century, for example, the Logical Positivists, Rudolph Carnap, Moritz Schlick, A. J. Ayer, and others, sought to create a "verification principle," a more objective way to distinguish between utterances whose meaning could be proven and those in which it could not. Admirers of science, as was Bacamarte, the Logical Positivists found it difficult, as Machado shows us in *The Psychiatrist*, to speak about verifying the meaning of linguistic usages while using language itself to do the verifying. It is difficult, if not impossible, to escape from what Nietzsche and others would later term the "prison house" of language, a point Machado makes, albeit figuratively, already in 1881 and 1882.

Misapprehensions, or misinterpretations, Machado's narrator warns us, must be laid aside or avoided in our quests to know who is sane and who is not and in our quest to know what words and events in life mean. The problem with this very sage advice is that, living and existing in the world of language as we do, we humans cannot lay this problem aside or avoid it; we are stuck with it, for it defines who and what we are. In words that seem to speak directly to our human dilemma as it relates to this point, the narrator and Machado tell us that we, like Porfirio and Bacamarte, "must therefore find a compromise that will both permit" the "continued operation" of the Green House "and placate the public" (*Psy*, 29). It seems to me that Machado is here saying that, yes, language is perhaps infinitely changeable and relative in terms of what it means, but that it nevertheless is a huge part of the world in which we humans live, think, and try to understand. Machado's "new narrative" has, and simultaneously, both an aesthetic and theoretical grounding and a political grounding, with neither canceling out the other.

Like Saussure's linguistic sign, Machado's new thinking about language, narrative, and imitation has two sides to it, and he seems acutely aware of this. The "compromise" that the barber suggests is, obviously (in the context of the story being told here), very political in nature, but it also sets out what I think Machado's new theory of narrative entails: while the semantic mutability of language, all language, appears to be a simple, undeniable fact (as Saussure would later argue), and while it is also empirically true, seemingly, that this destabilizes nearly all of human existence and the various institutions and disciplines we create to deal with life, it is also true that we must learn to accept this situation and deal with it. We must, in short, learn to "placate" ourselves, just as the fluid nature of language will have its "continued operation" (*Psy*, 29). These, I believe Machado is showing us, are the facts of life as they pertain to the human condition, and, unless we wish always to live an illusion and suffer for it, we must come to grips with the reality of our situation. This word, "compromise," comes up late in the chapter when Porfirio, highlighting the power of language to change our understanding of reality, reminds Bacamarte (and, through him, the reader and Brazil's reading public) that even though we lack "the ability to distinguish the sane from the insane," or, we might conclude, by extension, the "true" meaning of one word from another, we can propose compromises that allow us to "accept" and work with our situation (*Psy*, 30).

Thus, I believe, does Machado span what one might conclude was an unbridgeable chasm between the uncertainties of language and reality, and, moreover, thus does Machado establish the utility of his "new narrative" to the domains of both literary art and philosophy and both history and social science. It is language that binds all these disciplines together, and whatever is true of language must affect them. Chapter 9 then comes to an end with more words from the barber: "For order, my friends, is the foundation on which government," and, the good reader will now add, language, understood, of course, as a linguistic system, "must rest" (*Psy*, 31). Structure, whether in language, government, or society (as Claude Lévi-Strauss famously demonstrated), is what generates meaning.[10]

Chapters 10 through 12 can also be read as a unit. In a comment that Machado's readers would have found very funny, a new pretender to the throne of political power in Itaguai, one João Pina, avers that the town council, a body the reader would have taken to be Brazilian culture itself in the early 1880s, is "a body contaminated by French doctrines wholly contrary to the sacrosanct interests of His Majesty" (*Psy*, 32). And because of the compromise struck by the barber and Bacamarte, "the population of the asylum increased even more rapidly than before" (*Psy*, 33). No one could say or do any of the things that normal people say or do without fear of being locked up as insane. This led the people of Itaguai to conclude that "the psychiatrist's concept of madness" now "included practically everybody" (*Psy*, 33). Again, the problem of interpretation and misinterpretation. These same people are then shocked when they learn that Bacamarte has "sent his own wife to the asylum," the reason being that her love of fine clothes and fondness for jewels were "symptoms" of "a serious condition" (*Psy*, 34). The townspeople interpret this deed as a sign that the doctor truly had not motives other than "those of science itself" and that he, therefore, had to be a man "of integrity and profound objectivity, a combination of Cato and Hippocrates" (*Psy*, 35).

Chapter 11 opens with a new and, once again, startling revelation: all of the supposed insane people locked in/committed to the Green House "had been released," by order of Dr. Bacamarte, who had become enamored of yet a new theory of insanity. From now on, in his revised view, "normality lay in a lack of equilibrium," whereas, in his new view of things, the "abnormal, the really sick, were the well balanced, the thoroughly rational" (*Psy*, 35). The text, itself a function of language, gives us more change, but, as Machado's narrative also makes clear, it is change brought about because of the fluid, ever evolving nature of language and interpretation. The consternation that follows in the wake of this new theory, judged by its author to be as absolutely true as every other theory he has spouted before, centers on Porfirio, the barber, who, "having been locked up in the Green House" for his rational approach to what was happening around him, now declares, in the kind of exasperation that most of us feel at times about the confusion of life and our struggles to make sense of it all, "You're damned if you do and you're damned if you don't" (*Psy*, 40). For all of its exploration of language's protean nature and its semantic slipperiness, Machado ends this chapter on a very realistic, if wryly comic, note, one that shows both how language forms the heart of our human vision of the world and how it constantly frustrates us.

Chapter 12, the final chapter, opens with another act of interpretation. "All the chroniclers agree," we are told, that Bacamarte "brought about the most amazing recoveries," a conclusion that itself invites further interpretation (*Psy*, 41). "By the end of five months all the patients" of the Green House, which is now once again regarded as a hospital and not a prison, "had been cured. Councilman Galvão, so cruelly afflicted with fairness and moderation, had the good fortune to lose an uncle" (*Psy*, 42). Dripping in irony, the narrator adds that he says "good fortune" because "the uncle's will was ambiguous and Galvão obtained a favorable interpretation of it by bribing two judges" (*Psy*, 42). Clearly, Machado implies, the process of interpretation is rarely, if ever, an act of objectivity or neutrality; agendas are often involved, here and in life.

Then, and speaking directly to his reader and her interpretive skills, the narrator says this: "If you think the psychiatrist was radiant with happiness on seeing the last guest leave the Green House, you apparently do not yet understand the man. *Plus ultra* was his motto," and so "something told him that his new theory bore within itself a better, newer theory," just as every word carries within it some "better, newer" meaning (*Psy*, 42). Still, Bacamarte believes there is an "ultimate, underlying truth" to life and that he can discover it (*Psy*, 42). It is not difficult to see how this belief parallels the belief of the reader of the old Realism that the author had built a knowable truth into the text and that it could be discovered. The text of *The Psychiatrist*, like Machado's other late novels, refutes this readerly attitude and shows instead that the process of reading always produces multiple, often conflicting interpretations about the multiple meanings that are generated by the act of responding to a text or to any system of signs. The structuralists and, more pointedly, the poststructuralists (like Machado de Assis) argue that there is no "ultimate truth" to be found in a text; instead, there are many possible meanings, with all being more or less plausible. To think otherwise is to commit what some describe as the mistake of logocentrism. As Machado shows us so brilliantly here in *The Psychiatrist*, our ideas about "truth" are relative and temporary, subject at all times to different readings, changing circumstances, and our also changing points of view and systems of valuation.

The chapter's supreme irony surfaces in the text's final lines, when we learn from the narrator that what "Bacamarte meant," in his final attempt to establish the theory for which he was searching (the one that would explain everything in perfect, immutable, and eternal fashion), "was that he had found in himself the perfect, undeniable case of insanity. He possessed," in his impeccable personal qualities (his "wisdom, patience, tolerance, truthfulness, loyalty, and moral fortitude") and in his belief that he would one day find perfect understanding, "all the qualities that go to make an utter madman" (*Psy*, 43–44). As a reader of his own life and his quest, Dr. Bacamarte is not unlike the reader of the old realistic novel, except in the latter case there was, built in by the author, a message to be received and understood. In Machado's "new narrative," there is not; there are multiple and sometimes quite different messages, all of which are gleaned by the attentive, engaged reader and reformulated by her into structures that seem to make more sense to her personally and that respond to her readings of the text.

The doctor, "his eyes alight with scientific conviction . . . , entered the Green House, shut the door, and set about the business of curing himself. The chroniclers," speaking of an external fact they could, unlike the reader, have seen and verified, "state . . . that he died seventeen months later as insane as ever" (*Psy*, 44). "Some," however, and in a reference that refers to both the citizens of Itaguai and the readers of this narrative, "venture the opinion that he was the only madman (in the vulgar or non-Bacamartian sense) ever committed to the asylum" (*Psy*, 44). The narrator then proceeds to disparage this notion, since, as he says, it was based on comments made by Father Lopes, "doubtless erroneously, for, as everybody knew, the priest liked and admired the psychiatrist," a point the careful reader may well doubt (*Psy*, 44–45). The chapter, and the entire narrative, then ends—but, as we can see, on yet another demonstration of the importance of interpretation, in life and in literature, as well as the ever-present danger of misinterpretation.

In terms of Machado's development of his new theory of language and his own "new novel," *The Psychiatrist,* though short and tightly structured, marks a new level of sophistication in terms of narrative technique and control. In reading it against its immediate predecessor, *The Posthumous Memoirs of Brás Cubas, The Psychiatrist* comes off as considerably more focused and organized. By contrast, *The Posthumous Memoirs of Brás Cubas,* although stunningly iconoclastic, seems now to be too loose. The reader gets the impression that while with the earlier work Machado wants to see just what kind of text could result from his new theory of language and narrative art, he himself immediately recognizes that he should now seek to see what he could achieve with a more tightly controlled and structured version of the same theory. Thus it is that *The Psychiatrist* deals with the same set of questions and problems as did *The Posthumous Memoirs of Brás Cubas,* in a different way. What seems incontrovertible, however, is that in making this very decision, Machado is now concentrating not merely on telling stories or writing more novels; he is engaged in an exploration of what his new thinking about language and narrative art might mean and how this could be best applied to the actual writing of his "new narrative" and his "new novel."

3 • QUINCAS BORBA

Published eleven years after its immediate predecessor appeared, *Quincas Borba*, the second lengthy novel of Machado's mature period, moves more resolutely into considerations of narrative, imitation, symbolism, and verisimilitude. In this, *Quincas Borba* achieves a new level of sophistication over both *The Posthumous Memoirs of Brás Cubas* and *The Psychiatrist*, though its technical and theoretical links to them remain clear. It is clear that Machado, as both a theoretician and a practitioner of his "new narrative," is developing rapidly. *Quincas Borba* also continues to pound away at the job of the reader, who is here forced as never before to contemplate the unstable nature of a literary text that is structured according to how language functions. What was once considered the least experimental of Machado's three best known novels,[1] *The Posthumous Memoirs of Brás Cubas, Quincas Borba*, and *Dom Casmurro*, his 1891 offering is now, and rightly, judged to be one of his most accomplished efforts. But, as a text that exudes the essential *Angst* of modernity (that of uncertainty, our inability to know), *Quincas Borba* is also one of Machado's most powerful and disturbing efforts.

In terms of its theoretical concerns with genre (specifically narrative), imitation, and verisimilitude, it reveals itself to be a significant, and more confident, step forward from his more famous 1880 novel. As Celso Favaretto notes, *Quincas Borba* "dramatizes the inadequacy of the historical novel, the naturalist novel, and the bildungsroman in the face of the loss of existential unity which is so obvious in the modern experience. . . . This is the modern effect of the novel; going far beyond its portrait of the elites of the Brazilian Second Empire, it dramatizes the limitations of the human condition through the crisis of the novel itself as a genre."[2] As John Gledson has pointed out in *Machado de Assis:Ficção e História*, Machado here examines the concept of verisimilitude from a perspective that links it to another of Machado's great strengths as a novelist, his skill at characterization.[3] Building on the work of Gledson, Favaretto concurs, arguing that "cleverly and with great irony," Machado "demands from the reader a different sort of reading, a reading of what is hidden in the narrative—a narrative in which his characters' lack of consistency is the objective correlative of his critique of verisimilitude.[4] Interrupting the narrative flow, reshuffling the chronology, and changing the focus of the text from one character to another, he makes it impossible for the reader to simply follow the plot: reading, as a result, is no longer an automatic process."[5] For Gledson and for Favaretto, the fragmentation, or loss of unity, that bedevils the novel's protagonist, a man named Rubião, is directly connected to Machado's new sense of how narrative can achieve a special and (in its own, unique fashion) powerfully realistic sense of verisimilitude. For my purposes, I believe that, in its theoretical sophistication, what Machado achieves in *Quincas Borba* goes beyond what he did in *The Posthumous Memoirs of Brás Cubas*. In terms of making a more coherent and concise theoretical statement, the 1891 narrative is superior to the earlier, 1880 one. This is what makes it a more focused and unified work of art. But what they have in common, the thread that connects them, is a new understanding of how the nature of language, and especially in its production of multiple and often conflicting meanings, affects the nature of narrative representation and the structurings that stem from this realization.

Like *The Posthumous Memoirs of Brás Cubas* before it, *Quincas Borba* can be thought of as an "antinovel," though its "singularity" as a text "lies," as David T. Haberly argues, "in its denial of the text as" a "created" and "knowable" "version of reality."[6] While its predecessor showed us this, *Quincas Borba* drives home the point that while the "ultimate example of" our "human quest for order is the created, knowable reality of the literary text," the second novel of Machado's mature period systematically denies us the very thing we seek—the order that art gives us.[7] In Quincas Borba, Machado is taking on the question of imitation by means of language, specifically narrative and, even more specifically, the novel form. Theoretically speaking, the step from *The Posthumous Memoirs of Brás Cubas* to *Quincas Borba* mirrors the move from Machado's speculations about what kind of novel would result from his new thinking about language and artistic imitation to a clearer, more decisive decision about what the novelistic consequences of such thinking would necessarily be. For me, the fragmentary and intensely self-undercutting nature of the 1891 novel are the logical and necessary consequences of the experiments initially undertaken, in a less focused way, in the 1880 text. *Quincas Borba*, then, is where Machado's theorizing about language and the novel form must take him.

Arguing that Machado's narrator in *Quincas Borba* works intentionally to betray the reader's expectations (about finding unity and a knowable reality in the text she is reading), or, at least, to deny her these, Machado "demands the unexpected of us."[8] "He presents us," Haberly contends, not with the order and unity of the traditional realistic novel but "the 'tatters of reality' his narrator has stitched together into an ordered sequence."[9] But, in my view, the "ordered sequence" that Machado and his narrator give us is not that of the old realistic novel but the one that derives from his new understanding about language, structure, imitation, and meaning, and this changes everything. Apropos of this, I believe, "the narrator's evident unreliability invalidates that order and forces us to create our own reality from those tatters. A unitary explanation of events, imposed by a narrator or an author, gives way to chaos—a potentially infinite number of possible readers and of possible readings."[10] This is, in a nutshell, the reality Saussure will lay out some fifteen years later in his lectures on linguistics, the nature of the linguistic sign, and the fluidity of meaning that derives from it. The ultimate irony of *Quincas Borba*, then, is that it uses form (albeit the protean form of language in action and, thinking again of Saussure, through time) to represent, or imitate, what Machado now sees as the inherent falsity of artistic form, and most specifically that of the realistic novel. While, in *The Poetics*, Aristotle posited that art was actually superior to reality because it completed it and gave it a unity that did not exist in nature,[11] Machado now believes that the true reality of language involves a ceaseless process of making and unmaking, of establishing order and meaning and then undercutting these. *Quincas Borba* shows us what kind of novel must result from this kind of thinking.

While the modern problem of fragmentation, or as, more pointedly, is the case in this novel, is introduced in *Quincas Borba* as early as the first two chapters, it is another problem, one more aesthetic in nature, that occupies my attention here. Two characters, one named Quincas Borba (who, in a bit of auto-intertextuality, is a holdover from the previous novel) and the other named Rubião, are introduced, and they, in chapter 4, will show us the novel's basic structural motif: the difference between art and reality, presented to us once again in a wry and allusive fashion. We learn that while "philosophy is one thing," "dying is another" (*QB*, 9). Already in the novel the reader is led to think of philosophy as art, or more commonly as a system of words, which take shape and generate meaning through interlocking systems of words, while "dying" is very much life or reality. And while this oblique but funny reference makes it clear that philosophy and dying are two very different things, it is the former, which is a function of language, that seeks to make sense of the latter, which we can think of as reality. Machado's second great novel will replay this same basic motif, in different contexts and involving different issues, time after time to the very end. Indeed, it is only a slight exaggeration to say that the novel's entire structure is based on an exploration of this same problem—the difference between reality and language's ability to depict, or imitate, it. Machado was not entirely certain, I believe, in *The Posthumous Memoirs of Brás Cubas* of what the consequences of his new thinking about language, imitation, verisimilitude, and narrative art would be for the novel form, but in *Quincas Borba* he shows us just what they are.[12]

Machado returns us to this same problem in chapter 18. Although they are, the text tells us, "confused and frayed," Rubião begins to give "careful consideration" to the "allegory of the starving tribes," this being a tale told him two chapters earlier but which, at that point, he did not understand. Now, however, Rubião thinks he does understand, that he has finally interpreted the allegory's true meaning. In this chapter, the word "allegory" appears twice, as if to give the alert reader a hint of what I believe its special importance is. In the Western literary tradition, which Machado knew intimately, an allegory involves an issue of genre. Specifically, it is a kind of extended metaphor in which the people, objects, and actions of a narrative take on, or are imbued with, meanings both inside the narrative and outside it. Thus, the characters, their actions, and the narrative world they inhabit in the story that involves them and that the reader absorbs also generate meaning when considered in their social, religious, or political contexts. In the case of *Quincas Borba*, as a number of Machado's most astute scholars have suggested, the novel itself seems to cry out for being read, or interpreted, as presenting (in Gledson's view) Rubião as "an allegorical representation of Pedro II, ruler of Brazil from 1831 to 1889," or that Machado's allegory (a term, as we have seen, turns up twice in chapter 18, *QB*, 26–27) actually "extends beyond the person of the Emperor to include the Empire itself."[13] Modern critics, from Edwin Honig to Walter Benjamin and Paul de Man, have argued positions that concentrate on the processes of artistic representation and, in so doing, make the politically charged interpretive stances offered by Araripe Júnior, John Gledson, and David Haberly seem quite viable, even compelling.

For Favaretto, too, the emphasis Machado puts here on the genre of allegory has great significance for our response to the narrative. Terming it "an allegory of bourgeois modernization in late nineteenth-century Brazil," he goes on to argue that *Quincas Borba*'s "method of composition" constitutes a "displacement that implies a critique of literature, of mimetic Naturalism," and "of the novels then in fashion," including, I would add, the would-be realistic ones.[14] While I certainly agree with Favaretto, and others, on this point, I also believe that the crux of the matter, the source of the "displacement" that occurs in this text, is essentially linguistic in nature. Machado is here pushing "language, our 'poor human tongue,'" which, as we shall see, he expands upon in chapter 28, "to its limits, intensifying and transforming both symbolic structures and the fixed discourse of social life. . . . He explodes the use of language as a mere representation of reality," and in so doing "displaces both plot elements and metaphors, emphasizing their articulation; by creating a gap between sign and significance, he produces a vacuum of meaning which must be filled in by the reader. . . . Machado thus redefines realism through a new balance between content and expression."[15]

In a near perfect display of mirroring that also exemplifies this sense of displacement, Machado shows one of his characters, Rubião, doing to a form of language use (a story he was told) exactly what the reader is doing to the text, the narrative art form known as the novel, *Quincas Borba*, that she is reading. Both subjects are struggling to interpret the interlocking and self-referential set of signs they have been given. The problem in this is that, as the reader of the novel will soon discover, Rubião misinterprets the meaning of what he has been told; he gets it wrong. Moreover, this failure to interpret signs correctly will, from this point on in the narrative, grow, evolve, and become, finally, one of the text's most basic motifs.

In the very next chapter, 29, in fact, the narrator makes clear that Rubião's struggle to understand what is going on around him and to respond correctly is not abating; indeed, it is growing worse. More and more, Rubião, the prototypical modern hero (or, read from another perspective, the modern comic, or perhaps tragicomic, hero) is becoming engulfed in a sea of signs he can neither interpret correctly nor respond to in positive, productive ways. His inability to understand what is happening around him begins to emerge as his fatal flaw. And by chapter 32, the same problem, the misinterpretation of signs, will emerge in the text as a turning point in Rubião's mental disintegration. But in chapter 18, Rubião is confident that he understands the meaning of the concluding words of his friend's allegory: "To the victor, the potatoes!" (*QB*, 27). He is so confident, in fact, that he decides to place these same words on a seal he will use to identify himself. Exemplary of Machado's new sense of language's core importance as a determining factor in our very human desire to give ourselves a stable, coherent identity, his character, Rubião, first misunderstands what these words meant for his philosopher friend, Quincas Borba, and then misunderstands how far they will be from misrepresenting who and what he truly is. The reader, however, eventually will see this—and wonder if the problem from which Rubião suffers does not apply to all of us. Providing us with a clue as to how to read the narrative art form known as Quincas Borba, Machado has his narrator then write, "He forgot about the seal," which we can think of as reality, "but the formula," inscribed in language and now a living part of his identity, "lived on in Rubião's spirit" (*QB*, 27). After a few more words that could be regarded as additional clues to the reader who has not yet caught on to the real allegory that is being spun out here (not the one about "starving tribes" laid out in chapter 6 but the one about how language both makes and unmakes identity and a good portion of what we think of as our human realities), we are told, by the narrator, that "it's so true that the landscape," like the narrative structure we have in our hands and that we are reading, "depends on the point of view" of the person interpreting it (*QB*, 27). The narrator then brings this decisive chapter to a close, again enigmatically, by offering us one of Machado's greatest metaphors, one that melds the theoretical question of how a person reads a literary text (but, in truth, any text or set of signs) with the all-too-real issues of slavery, power, and violence: "the best way to appreciate a whip is to have its handle in your hand" (*QB*, 27).

Setting up an implicit comparison between the possible thoughts of a dog (also named Quincas Borba, to further complicate our various streams of interpretation) and those of a human being (and in the process building into the text yet another instance of mirroring and readerly displacement), Machado's narrator suggests that the dog is to the world of his masters (the people around him) as the reader is to the very text she is reading and to the world around her, a reality that is, for her, more often than not a jumble of signs to be interpreted. Rubião then tells us how his thoughts, also a function of words, are now blurring into a single, now composite vision of his two friends, the deceased one (the man, Quincas Borba) and the living one (the dog, also bearing the name Quincas Borba). Considering the entire tangle of words and meanings that are now in play in this scene, our narrator avers that "there are a lot of ideas, now," "too many," even, and different, to be organized into the making of a single point or argument (*QB*, 36). We are, at this moment, awash in a sea of signs, each one slightly different from the others but, at the same time, clearly relating to them. Then, reflecting on what is going on inside his head, as he, too, struggles to decipher this plethora of signs, the narrator, fusing the two Quincas Borbas that the text has offered up, declares that what is being mulled over here is not a coherent thought (as the traditional reader would be expecting from the traditional realistic novel) but "a jumble of ideas" (*QB*, 36). Instead, and cueing up the reader's task in this novel, what is being sought here, by, through, and in language (understanding), amounts to something "even less than a jumble, *the reader is probably explaining to himself*" (*QB*, 36–37, emphasis mine). As if to underscore Machado's desire here for the reader to confront the babble of possible interpretations that are now in front of her, the chapter then concludes with an amusing discussion of how a dog thinks, a series of comments that, I believe, should also be read as showing us something very different: how meaning, in any semiotic system, changes in accordance with circumstance, place, and time.

As is so often the case in reading the fiction of the mature Machado de Assis, the reader must regularly ask herself: Why is this scene here? What does it have to do with the rest of the book? In this case, I believe that Machado's real point is less what Quincas Borba the dog, Quincas Borba the dead man, and Rubião the living character think than how language use gives rise not to absolute understanding or the discovery of a knowable, immutable meaning but to more language use, and that it does so ad infinitum. This is where the worlds of science and the language-based humanities part company, though, in the human experience, it is the difficult task of the latter to determine and explain the significance of the former. What Machado wants this final discussion of how a dog interprets the universe to show us is not the simple fact of confusion or confusion but how we, as readers and as citizens, use language to describe and then to ascribe meaning to what is going on around us. For some, to return to Machado's allusion to power, violence, and slavery, the whip is a symbol of pain and suffering, while for others (those who hold its handle) it is a symbol of law and order. The same semiotic sign, Machado now understands, means different things to different people, including the reader, who seeks to understand the text (the structure of narrative art) she is reading, and the citizen, who seeks to understand a still different structure of signs, one known as political discourse, but a structure made of language and interpreted by language nevertheless.

The problem of how language imitates nature, and specifically the actions and thoughts of women and men, continues in chapters 65, 66, and 67. Interlocking, as they so often do in Machado's post-1880 novels, to form smaller structures within larger structures (but with all tying together to form the macro unit that is the novel itself, from its first page to the last), these chapters can be read as a short but insightful discourse of the nature of what we today would call semiotics. Discussing the nature of "signals" being sent and received in a conversation between the increasingly befuddled Rubião, the self-possessed Sofia, and another of her suitors, the (superficially) attractive but, in truth, deeply cynical Carlos Maria, Machado's narrator has the latter initiate an exchange between he and Sofia that involves what he is praising as her natural beauty as compared to that captured by a portrait of her that hangs on the wall (*QB*, 94). Creating a scene in which reality and another (nonlinguistic) kind of imitative art (painting) are evaluated in terms of each other, Carlos Maria, pointing to the portrait, says to Sofia, "You're much more beautiful, infinitely more beautiful than the painting. Just make a comparison, ladies" (*QB*, 94). To judge from what he actually says, his position is the rather routine one, that art (the portrait, no matter the level of its verisimilitude, which we will soon learn is quite high) is inferior to reality. But before considering what else Carlos Maria means here (and seduction does seem to figure into his plans), the reader must, of course, also consider his unstated motivations, which the reader has to extrapolate from the ways he has so far been presented to the reader in the text and including what other characters say and think about him. Again, ambiguity reigns supreme. But beyond that, the lesson we learn here is that it is for us, the involved, engaged readers, to make the comparison and to consider what it means, how valid it is, and not, or not really, for the "ladies" to whom he is talking in the scene itself. It is with this thought that chapter 65 ends.

Following hard on its heels, chapter 66 begins with both the reader and Rubião pondering the possible meaning of Carlos Maria's words. Subtly calling the reader's attention to the relationship of art and reality, and to how the former imitates the latter, Rubião leads us to focus on the core issue, the nature, or quality, of the imitation: "Negating the portrait" (art) "in order to praise the person!" (reality), he declares, then adding, "The portrait is obviously a good likeness," which suggests that its level of verisimilitude is quite high (*QB*, 95). Increasingly unable to deal with reality, Rubião, the thoughtful reader sees, is beginning to be seduced by if not art then at least imitation, and, as we see played out in chapters 145 through 149, the potential change in identity that the latter involves.

Coming at the same problem but from a different perspective, chapter 67 moves us from portraiture to literature, that is, from painting as imitation to imitation by language. In this chapter, Rubião, while reading a newspaper story involving his name, ponders both the style the author of the piece uses and the propriety of his having made public, in florid and dramatic prose, what Rubião had supposed a private matter. From the perspective I promote in this study, however, these very same words, entirely appropriate for the story line being advanced in the novel, lend themselves to a very different line of interpretation, one that comes to life as a criticism of Realism as a literary mode. Implying that events are one thing while their descriptions, re-creations, or imitations by means of language are quite another, Rubião's discontent with the story he has just read, a story in which he himself had been the principal actor, leads the reader to ask the following questions: How does an artist depict, or imitate, the actions of human beings via language? How does one achieve verisimilitude? And, finally, how verisimilar is the imitation, the art object? How does it compare in this respect to painting, sculpture, and music, an issue Aristotle touched on in *The Poetics* but did not explore in detail? In my estimation, Machado de Assis is picking up where Aristotle left off; that is, the Brazilian writer is here asking whether imitation by language could be somehow more intrinsically involved in determining the nature of the human condition than are these other modes of imitation. If human beings are at least partially defined by their ability to create and use language, then it would follow that to imitate them by means of language could be expected to achieve a greater level of truth, or verisimilitude, and this, I believe, is what Machado wants to explore. If this is correct, or if one considers it possible, then it would add a new, more language-based dimension to our understanding of Machado's famous ambiguity and to the discussion John C. Kinnear has offered as to how Machado's narrator has both led and mislead us.[16] By the end of the chapter, however, Rubião's unhappiness with the piece was quickly vanishing, and, in fact, we learn that he comes to rather like it, ordering it reprinted, in "boldface type," in the "letters to the editor" section of another paper, the *Jornal do Comércio* (*QB*, 97). Not merely uncertain but also fickle and quicksilver are our responses to the "tatters of reality" we read and hear in the worlds of language and literature!

Machado continues to wrestle with this same problem, the nature of imitation as it manifests itself in narrative art, in chapter 110, where, behind a series of Latin phrases dropped into the text, one presumes, to give it the patina of veracity, the issue of truth is entered into the commentary. Yet after giving the next chapter, 111, over to a fascinating and only partially misleading discussion of language, writing, sound, and meaning, Machado's narrator then embarks, in what seems a comic aside dealing with intertextuality and some of the prototypical novels of European Realism, on what can be taken as one of *Quincas Borba*'s primary demonstrations of how and why, like *The Posthumous Memoirs of Brás Cubas* before it, also parts company from the traditional realistic novel form. This disarmingly funny digression, crucial, I believe, in terms of his new theory of narrative, allows Machado and his still unreliable narrator to contrast his antirealistic "new narrative" against the old standard, realistic novel of tradition. In discussing his own novel and its methods of composition and structuring, Machado's narrator openly declares, in chapter 112, "Here's where I would have liked to have followed the method used in so many other books—all of them old—where the subject matter of the chapter is summed up: 'How this came about and more to that effect'" (*QB*, 159). How, according to the norms of traditional Realism, we are told what we need to know, and so we read these texts with confidence and certainty about what is meant. Referencing such European masters as Bernardim Ribeiro, Cervantes, Rabelais, Fielding, and Smollet, our narrator argues his case. Then, citing one very specific case (*Tom Jones*, book 4, chapter 1, where the title reads "Containing Five Pages of Paper"), our narrator prepares to make his own case. Of this section of Fielding's novel, he says, "It's clear, it's simple, it deceives no one.[17] They're five sheets of paper, that's all. Anyone who doesn't want to read it doesn't, and for the one who does read it, the author concludes obsequiously: 'And now, without any further preface, I proceed to our next chapter'" (*QB*, 160).

And, indeed, in the very first sentence of the very next chapter, the narrator and Machado show us (but do not explain to us) what makes their approach superior to that, as far as the realism of real human life is concerned, of Fielding and all the others: "If such were the method of this book, there would be a title here explaining everything: 'How Rubião, satisfied with the correction made in the article, composed and pondered so many phrases that he ended up writing all the books he'd ever read'" (*QB*, 160).[18] Sounding here more than a bit like the later Borges, Machado's 1891 narrator then says, involving his reader in the discussion, "There is probably some reader for whom this alone is not sufficient. He will naturally want the complete analysis of our man's mental operations, *not noticing that Fielding's five pages*" will not achieve a complete imitation of his state, either; to think that it will is to fall prey to an illusion, the illusion, Machado would say, of orthodox Realism (*QB*, 160, emphasis mine). "There's a gap," our narrator tells us, between language and reality that makes perfect understanding impossible (*QB*, 160). "The best thing," our narrator says, finally, is "to leave it" just as Machado has written it, with all the uncertainties, ambiguities, and dislocations intact. Why? Because, I think the post-1880 Machado would say, that is a more realistic portrayal of, or imitation of, real human life than is the way Fielding and the other champions of the old Realism do it. And, finally, because to argue this case further would involve an "analysis," or defense, that would of necessity "be long and tedious," Machado and his narrator now drop it, preferring to show us rather than tell us what his "new narrative" is like.

Following hard on the heels of chapter 112 (and, in fact, chapter 114 as well), this discussion of semiotics and how the science of signs affects human life continues on in chapter 119, where, evoking Saussure, the discussion centers on the semantic difference between "*doubt*" and "*debt*," with the difference turning, as we are told in no uncertain terms, on "the substitution of an *e* for an *ou*" (*QB*, 174–75, emphasis original). If this sounds like Saussure, it should. The only difference, the Swiss linguist would later argue, between the word/sign "hire" and the word/sign "fire" is one letter. It is on a thread this tenuous and arbitrary that the whole of human communication (or lack thereof) depends, this being a realization that, I contend, the post-1880 Machado had become acutely aware of as a novelist and as a commentator on the social and political scene. Why, one might fairly ask, does

Machado put this scene here if not to lead us to think about this very issue—semantic fluidity, how switching the letters of the same word, or linguistic sign, results in a concomitant change of meaning? What kind of reading results from this understanding about language? What kind of society? The issue touched on by Machado here goes beyond a simple fussing over what some might think of as mere semantics; it speaks, I contend, to how language creates much of our human reality, how arbitrary constructions (and their resulting de-constructions)[19] end up actually becoming the structures that rule our lives and that determine how we think about such fundamental, but language-based, subjects as religion, justice, freedom, honor, courage, identity, integrity, truth, knowledge, and love.[20] It also determines, I believe, the very distinctive ways Machado's last five novels are structured.

In chapter 123, Machado continues to explore this same question, how, from literature to politics, language affects how the structures that define so much of our human experience are organized and understood. Here, Machado's narrator is musing over how an idea, a mental image (albeit one once again formed in, by, and through language), can have the same force in human affairs as an actual painting. We learn, moreover, this this same idea, or mental "picture," as the narrator calls it, is itself "being reproduced," or imitated, in the mind of another character, a young bride, one Maria Benedita, who uses someone else's idea, or "picture," to conjure up her own version of reality (*QB*, 182). Imitation, Machado seems to conclude, is not limited to the physical world; it exists internally as well. Yet even there, it lives, and even thrives (as the case of Maria Benedita shows), as a function of language.

As chapter 123 gives way to chapter 124, so, too, does the discussion of imitation in this chapter sequence move to a consideration of how language, and specifically narrative, effects its own form of reproduction. Music, too, enters this chapter and, aside from the details of the banal little domestic episode being related here by our narrator, the alert reader—the one who has elected to perform the kind of close, productive reading that Machado's narrator has insisted upon—can find herself thinking here about how ideas, words, and music (here, the aria from "*Lucia: O bell'alma inamorata*" [Lucia: Oh, beautiful soul in love], and a "bit from the *Barber. Ecco ridente in cielo / Spunta la bella aurora*" [Here, in heaven laughing / emerges the beautiful dawn]; *QB*, 182, emphasis original).

And, in turn, chapter 124 produces chapter 125, where the entire issue gets not only a thorough going over but, at the very end, another example of mirroring and readerly displacement as well as a reminder of the role that imagination plays in artistic imitation. At the beginning of this chapter, the focus moves to Sofia, a major character in the novel (and arguably Machado's greatest female character).[21] Frustrated at trying to understand her changing situation, she idly picks up a novel to peruse. It reminds her, we learn, of Rubião, whose adoring presence in her life has complicated things for her. Specifically, she is mulling over what Rubião, her increasingly mad suitor, meant when he told her she was going to be his "empress" (*QB*, 183). "What did the phrase mean?," she asks herself, partially flattered by the thought and pleased to be so ardently desired (*QB*, 183). At the chapter's end, Sophia reads from the novel's first page a line about a person deserving to be loved, a not innocent reference that obviously ties together the narrative she is reading and the narrative we are reading about her. As if lost in contemplation, or, perhaps, self-reverential reverie, she then closes her eyes and becomes "lost in herself" (*QB*, 183).

Clearly, what Sofia is seen here to be doing, trying to interpret both a piece of narrative art (the novel she is reading) and the new directions her life is taking (in her own novel), mirrors and also amplifies what the reader is doing to the piece of narrative art (and another novel) that bears the title *Quincas Borba*. And in both cases it is the problem of interpretation that dominates. And in neither case can we see things clearly; all is in doubt. We learn, for example, that Sofia did not "understand" the "enigmatic" words of Rubião, but, we begin to realize, neither do we, as readers of this novel. Like Sofia, we, the readers of the narrative structure called *Quincas Borba*, do not ever really "know" reality; instead, we have, even in art, which seeks, as Aristotle held, to complete or perfect nature, little more than the "tatters of reality" that Machado de Assis and his narrator have assembled here, in a very deliberate act of artistic imitation, for our contemplation (chapter 106). And as we contemplate the text that is *Quincas Borba*, we come to realize that it is a structure of fragments, of bits and pieces, shards of a reality that can never be completely known. As humans, we try to deal with this situation by seeking to understand the basic ambiguities of existence, and the mechanism by which we do this is language.

Machado's probing of the issue of imitation continues in chapters 145 through 149. Here, however, he comes at it from the perspective of how, sometimes, life seeks to imitate art. As Rubião's mind continues to degenerate, his fall into megalomania and schizophrenia is paralleled by his increasing identification with Napoleon III, the ruler of France's Second Empire (1852–70), which, as we have already seen, Haberly, Araripe Júnior, and Schwarz believe is a parallel to, and, with all due irony, reflects Dom Pedro II's Empire in Brazil, from 1831 to 1839.[22] In chapter 145, we have, once again, the key of motif of Machado the "new novelist" stitching together here not the aforementioned "tatters of reality" but the supposed realities of "a placid life," with its salient aspects, or characteristics, "sewn together with pleasure and," in what appears to be a wry reference to the ways language can make reality more pleasant and attractive than it really is, "with an excess of lace" (*QB*, 204). While the part about how narrative can, indeed, sew disparate elements together into a single entity (one with or without organic order), how real the effect is, how convincing is its level of verisimilitude, is, however, quite another question. And this, I believe, is what Machado wants us to think about, as his narrator explains how an increasingly deluded Rubião one day came to enter a barbershop (run by a French barber, one Lucien) not, we find out, merely for a shave and haircut but for a complete makeover, one that will transform him, as art does reality, into the figure of Napoleon III. To help guide his reader to consider the role that imitation continues to play in this novel, Machado's narrator informs the reader that, to further stimulate Rubião and provide a clue to the reader, there is a bust of Napoleon (along with one of Louis Napoleon, the lesser of the two historical figures and, one supposes, a lesser piece of art as well) on a desk. But this is not all; on the wall, there hangs "an engraving or lithograph showing the Battle of Solferino and a portrait of the Empress Eugénie" (*QB*, 204). The scene is set for Rubião to cross into madness, and, as the next chapter clearly shows, the mechanism by which he will make this crossing is imitation.

Thus it is that Rubião, who, in a lovely but sad detail, thinks that he is now speaking French rather than Portuguese as he gazes, entranced, at the bust of Napoleon III, orders Lucien to "restore" his face to that likeness. As he transforms Rubião into Napoleon III, Lucien, whom we may here, in a comic moment, think of as the barber who is an artist, is said by the narrator to declare that "it was difficult to make one thing," real life, "match the other," art (the bust), "exactly," with this final word reminding us once again of the importance that verisimilitude, the semblance of truth, the appearance of reality, has in this novel. Of this issue, and praising his own artistic work, Lucien calms an anxious Rubião by saying that "you'll see how close the resemblance will turn out" (*QB*, 206). Then, and continuing to play the artist but in a comic mode, the French barber adds, of his own artistry, "Oh, I'd rather do ten original pieces of work than just one copy" (*QB*, 206). Ten minutes later, "he," Rubião, "was the other one," Napoleon III (*QB*, 206). "In a word," the narrator assures us, "they were the same" (*QB*, 206).

In chapter 147, we see Rubião totally at home in his new identity; art, and most particularly narrative art, has imitated not just his outer life, his physical aspect, but the desires of his inner life as well. What could not be discerned by someone watching this process of artistic transformation that was being performed by the barber was what we get partially in the language of chapter 146, as Rubião begins to respond to the changes in his face that he sees being done but totally in the language of chapters 147 and 148, where, with another ironic turn, the artistically transformed reality of Rubião was now being judged by onlookers as even "better than the previous one," that is, the Rubião of the pre–artistic makeover. Art, in other words, is here shown to be superior to nature, and, I believe, by means of the same justification of art that Aristotle had utilized in his famous defense of it—that art is superior to nature because it alone can complete it and thus perfect it. Nature simply "is"; art must have form. As Machado shows us with the transformed Rubião, art succeeds when, as an analogue of life and reality that works in accordance with ordered principles, it reshapes reality, or life, in a way that manifests the principles that define it. Art, according to Aristotle, makes manifest, or brings to life, those principles of ordering, perspective, and proportion that are not present in nature itself but that constitute the basis for all artistic imitation. In Machado's novel, where the medium of imitation is language, we see why it is that narrative art can succeed so brilliantly in showing us, or making manifest to us, not merely the external features that demonstrate verisimilitude but the inner desires that, unseen to the naked eye of the beholder of a portrait or a statue, can be made to come alive, in language, for the reader, and engaging her in endless, sometimes contradictory ways. And while, for Aristotle as for Machado, form, or structure, is the decisive element in the process of artistic creation, the Brazilian innovator knows that, in the world of language, structure carries some additional qualities that will have a direct effect on the nature of the narrative that is created from it. This is why, in showing us Rubião's inner world, Machado's narrator tells us that, following his artistic transformation in the barber's chair, art had, indeed, been imitated by life, but with the unseen result that "Rubião was" now "two. There was the mixture in him of his own persona and the Emperor of the French. They took turns. They grew to forget each other.... They were in equal balance, one without the other, both integral," none of which anyone except the reader of this narrative could possibly know (*QB*, 208). Art and reality have become one; the imitation has achieved perfection.[23]

As Machado winds his narrative down, his narrator once again reminds the reader of the relationship between his text and the idea of "allegory," that is, of a text that, in a quite deliberate fashion, has a significance that goes well beyond the text itself and that has something to say about the larger world around it. The reader thus gets another opportunity to consider this term critically, as a problem in genre (a topic of keen interest to Machado) that piques the reader's attention on several levels, one of which (and this being in addition to the narrative's clear sociopolitical ramifications) is linguistic in nature. But in Machado's late world, the reader is frustrated in her quest to find the order and meaning typical of the traditional realistic novel. And of these late novels, *Quincas Borba* stands out for systematically denying the reader this satisfaction. Here, much information, the realistic novel's connective tissue, is missing, and what is present is often misleading, erroneous, or simply a matter of incorrect interpretation. The latter case, in fact, plagues Rubião from beginning to end; time after time, he is simply unable to properly read the signs around him and so ends up making disastrous decisions as to what he thinks, says, and does. This is the fount of his ill-starred relationship with Sofia, for example. In terms of the argument that I am making in this book, this is the element that, still grounded in language's role in how we humans determine the meaning and value of all that happens around us, gains for Machado the social, political, economic, and ethical resonance that his novels so powerfully generate.

And it is why the reader's role in this novel, as in Machado's other post-1880 novels, is so important. As Favaretto sees it, the reader's role in the narrative imitation of human life that is *Quincas Borba* is to "find meaning in a constellation of scattered signs" and to try to assemble the "fragments" of meaning that are discerned in these into some kind of coherent, cohesive form. Reading the later Machado makes one think that, perhaps, the structuralists were correct; perhaps the human creature does, in fact, crave order and structure, of only to try to stave off what seems to be the dangerous chaos of the universe. But then one can also come to suspect (as I do) that, going beyond the structuralists, Machado is most interested in the inherent instability of all systems, whether these be political, religious, economic, or linguistic in nature. In the narrative world of Machado de Assis, all is fluid, evolving, and uncertain, and, with respect to his last five novels, this quality is most evident in *Quincas Borba,* where indeterminacy is woven into the warp and woof of the narrative itself. Here, the "representation the reader confronts is one ordered not by reason, but by delirium, by madness, by the imagination," and, I would argue, by the reader's desire to see order where there is none.[24]

In the penultimate chapter, 200, Rubião dies, totally engulfed in his madness—and in his inability to navigate the signs that still determine his life, his identity, and his ability to understand. As he enters into the final seconds of his life, Rubião, lost in illusions of grandeur and certainty, tries to put a crown on his head, "a crown," the narrator tells us, "that wasn't even an old hat or a basin, where the spectators could touch the illusion. No, sir. He took hold of nothing, lifted up nothing, and put nothing on his head. Only he saw the imperial insignia" (*QB*, 270). "To the victor . . . ," he says, calling attention one final time to the allegorical nature of his life, of the society in which he lived, and of the text we are reading, and then he dies.

At this point, the narrator reenters the narrative to have the last word. "It's possible," he says, anticipating how the reader interprets all of this and reminding us of the decentering roles mirroring and displacement have played in this narrative, "that you will ask me whether it is he or his late namesake," the dog, Rubião, "who gives the book its title and why one instead of the other—a question pregnant with questions that would take us far along" (*QB*, 271). "Come now!," he then adds, as if in a rejoinder to the reader, who, perhaps innately (as the structuralists contend) or by dint of reading too many exemplars of the old realistic novel, needs to find, or to be given, the kind of solid, knowable meaning she has come to expect in proper novels (*QB*, 271). But for the "new reader" that Machado insists on creating, or training, *Quincas Borba,* like the novel that came before it and like those that will follow it, is, I believe, simply "not written for those who seek not verisimilitude," at least of the traditional kind, but "a mental shock, a liberation of the imagination, the surprise and laughter that derive from unconscious motivations. . . . Machado speaks to the reader, saying: do not seek the truth in my plot; it is hard enough to 'mend the tatters of reality'; nor should you seek an easy ending to the spectacle of humanity, since the only finality is that of nature."[25]

While I believe Favaretto is on the right track here, with these very perceptive comments, I also believe that we must go further. The key question, I maintain, is how, exactly, does Machado achieve the singular, highly distinctive effects of which Favaretto speaks here? What mechanism allows him to produce this odd kind of verisimilitude, this openness of form, this constant self-interrogation and destabilizing, this elusiveness of meaning? I believe it is language. In a certain sense, *Quincas Borba* and its post-1880 mates are, in effect, language novels, that is, narratives that are about, and that reflect, how language works and, with all of its semantic fluidity, how it structures much of human existence and human social structures, from religions to political structures and from ideologies to personal relationships. Here and elsewhere, Machado de Assis has hit upon one of the most terrifying aspects to the modern view of life, its aleatory nature. The traditional realistic novel imposed order on this randomness and so led its readers to expect that in their novels, to become dependent upon it. Seeing human reality different, and through a more linguistic lens, Machado forces his reader to wean herself from this false dependence and, instead, to confront the reality of winding up "confused and lost" and charged with trying to learn to deal with the "chance" and indeterminacy of life.[26] For me, this explains what I take Machado to be suggesting when, as Favaretto writes and as Machado warns us, "The most to which one can aspire . . . , is 'for the colors not to contradict each other—when they are unable to follow symmetry and regularity.'"[27] For me, the Brazilian critic is citing Machado as he theorizes for our benefit what he, as a literary artist, a practitioner of a new and (in his view) much more "realistic" brand of Realism, is seeking to do here. It is not so much that Machado explores the idea of a "lost unity of life" as it is that, anticipating Saussure, he posits a human world in which even the concept of unity is a false one and that human reality is, as Saussure might say, a system (or a system of interlocking systems) ruled by differences that exist without positive values. I believe, in other words, that Machado's new Realism is as it is because it was created to reflect what language itself does as it seeks to imitate the complex and ever changing world of human beings and, at the same time, to highlight the peculiar nature of its own unique form of verisimilitude.

4 • DOM CASMURRO

In *Dom Casmurro*, the entire plot hangs on the question of verisimilitude. Indeed, the entire novel, published in France late in 1899 and distributed in Brazil early in 1900, is built around appearances, similarities, differences, and the uncertain process of interpretation. It is permeated by these and related issues, all of which relate, in one way or another, to artistic imitation (including the literary) and to our responses to them.[1] This is one reason why, in Portuguese, the verb *parecer* (to look like, to seem), and its variants, appears so often in the text, as do comparisons between various forms of imitation and their varying levels of verisimilitude. And it is why Fábio Lucas credits this third of Machado's mature novels (and the one most often cited as his masterpiece) as a text that exalts art as an illusion, yes, but an illusion that, as an artistic creation, is superior to the treacheries, snares, deceptions, and extraneousness of real life.[2] While the force of this is sometimes lost in the novel's various English translations, it nevertheless has a powerful presence in these texts, too, as do the nouns "illusion," "verisimilitude," and "imitation."

These issues come up, albeit obliquely, as early as chapter 1, when we see the narrator being compared to a younger man and when we learn the story of his nickname, "Dom Casmurro," the one that, in another example of mirroring and displacement, also gives title to the novel we are reading. The act of writing, presented as a creative force that does more than imitate, then opens chapter 2, where we learn that our again self-conscious and (though we do not yet understand this) unreliable narrator/protagonist desires "to reproduce," in his old age, the house in Rio de Janeiro that he had grown up in as a child (*DC*, 4). This house, which we are led to think of as art, was "to have the same appearance" as the original one, which, of course, we conceive of here as reality, the one that is going, here, to be imitated. The new house, the artistic imitation, was to be "more or less identical," that is, its level of verisimilitude was to be as high as possible. What the nature of this verisimilitude is, where it lies, how it is achieved, and whether it is a matter of external appearances alone or something else as well are all questions relating to this most fundamental of aesthetic problems that will be taken up time after time as the narrative progresses.

We learn later in the same chapter that, as if establishing a parallel between what an artist does and what our now aged narrator is doing here, the intention, "the purpose," behind this plan "was to tie together the two ends of" his "life, to restore adolescence in old age" (*DC*, 5). But, much to the narrator's surprise, this does not happen; instead, as he tells us, in a key line, "If the face," or reality, "is the same," that is, if the level of verisimilitude is high, "the expression," the art, "is different" (*DC*, 5). Something, as yet unknown to the reader (but, we will later come to feel, perhaps not to old "Dom Casmurro" himself), is wrong, something is missing. Intriguingly, our canny narrator then tells us, as he ponders those he has lost, "I myself am missing, and this lack is essential" (*DC*, 5). What we do not know is what he, as the artist who is creating this narrative, means by this, again enigmatic and ambiguous, phrase. Via a verbal comparison with the process of applying dye to one's hair and beard (yet another kind of artistic creation), we are told that while the house he had ordered built was accurate in its *external* aspects, its "inner structures," the realities that could not be seen but that truly defined its nature and being, did not take the dye, that is, they defied the desired imitation. We are not told why, though we are (as in the presence of all great art) both tantalized and left wondering.

Keying, I believe, precisely on this particular readerly response, Machado's narrator then concludes the chapter with a *seemingly* innocuous (but I believe very strategic) reference to narrative and to what I see as Machado's belief in the special power of narrative imitation. In noting the several busts (all of tyrants, a point that goes uncommented on and that the engaged reader must take note of) that, as objects of art themselves, adorn his desk, the narrator tells us, again privileging the act of writing, that perhaps "the act of narration would summon the" desired "illusion," that of a lost childhood and the presumed innocence that went with it, for him and for the reader, who is, of course, devouring this very "act of narration," the one that is already taking shape (and being quite deliberately structured) as the very novel, the narrative art form, that she is reading (*DC*, 6). In this marvelously interwoven opening scene, the reader is suddenly thrust into a situation in which several forms of artistic imitation are shown to be communicating with the reader in the context of each other and which must all be interpreted, individually and as they speak to each other as parts of the same artistic and (thinking specifically of narrative imitation) self-referential semantic system.[3]

The issues of life, art, mimesis, and verisimilitude continue on in chapter 7, where, once again, Machado and his narrator invoke painting as the basis for a comparison with narrative as contrasting forms of imitation. In the second half of this short chapter, the words "portrait" and "portraits" are used no fewer than five times, and, in each case, the context is how true to life they are, this in spite of the effects wrought by the passage of time (this being one of the mature Machado's essential, and pre-Proust, themes). While the realistic aspects of the portraits (of the narrator's mother and father) are such that they "could pass for" the "originals," verisimilitude is not the only aesthetic issue here under examination, however. Crucially, and toward the end of the chapter, the narrator says not just once but twice to the reader that he knows "nothing of them, just as" he "knows nothing of their sorrows" (*DC*, 16). As far as the process of imitation is concerned, the problem is twofold: Where does the truth about one's identity lie, and how can the artist capture, or represent, it? Clearly, the portraits, which, we are told in the chapter's final line, "are like snapshots of felicity," the lives of their subjects were much more than superficial in nature. Their inner lives must have been immensely complex, evolving, and had, at times, perhaps even contradictory aspects to them. But none of this could have been shown by the painting, no matter how verisimilar they were. Narrative, on the other hand, could get closer to the tangle of emotions, thoughts, and desires that constitute their inner worlds, and by the end of the novel that is *Dom Casmurro,* the reader will have, in her mind, a portrait—a verbal portrait—of the novel's deeply flawed narrator/protagonist that, in terms of its veracity, far exceeds anything that, Machado will show us, could be achieved in oils, stone, or sounds. In the new Realism being propounded by the Brazilian author, we, the readers of his tragic narrative, become progressively more aware of how much, of life and of reality, that we do not know or understand. Little by little, the narrative told by the narrator, "Dom Casmurro," and that we are reading, and responding to, in the form of the novel, *Dom Casmurro*, makes us more and more aware of the gaps, the moments of semantic uncertainty, that are present in the narrator's tightly and purposefully structured tale and that slowly but surely reveal, in ways he does not intend, his true intent in telling us this story. By the end, the reader sees that the very language he depends upon to make his case is the same language that undoes his argument.

Only a few pages later, in chapter 9 (which presents life as an opera, yet another form of artistic representation, and once involving music, costumes, and spectacle), the words "imitation" and "appearance" actually present themselves in the text, and in a way that suggests to the reader that the underlying issue being dealt with here is not the comical one of life as an opera, where God is the poet/author while the Devil scores the music, but the problem of how effective artistic imitation is in revealing to us the truth of the thing imitated. The chapter then closes with a wonderful suggestion that human life is more a function of our love of imitation than it is our ability to reason logically.[4] Put another way, it is this: we humans love the opera (with its distinctive fusion of music and language), and all artistic imitation, more than we care to deal truthfully, or factually, with reality. The latter simply interests us less.

As is so typical of Machado the mature artist, chapter 9 then morphs into the very short, but crucial, chapter 10. Here, our narrator, agreeing with the argument just advanced by the old Italian tenor that "All is music," that is, the temptations of art, how it lures us into its structures, modes, and expressiveness, also uses a key word, "verisimilitude," and in a way that links it to what he will very soon tell us is the "truth" of the narrative he is spinning out for us (*DC*, 21).[5] "I, friend reader, accept the theory of my old Marcolini, not only because of its verisimilitude—which is usually all that truth is—but also because my life fits his definition" (*DC*, 21). With these two key words now fixed in the reader's mind, the rest of "Dom Casmurro's" narration will be a demonstration of the case the narrator/protagonist wishes to advance. For Michael Wood, what our narrator means here is that "appearance is often all we've got and that things sometimes just are what they seem. . . . But since this proposition comes from a man" "Dom Casmurro," "who has wrecked several lives, including his own, on the basis of his reading of the looks in people's eyes, notably those of Capitu, and of little more than what seemed to him an undeniable resemblance his child and his friend, we may reach a different conclusion."[6] While the discourse laid down by the narrator takes us in one direction, the very words the narrator uses to make his point lead the careful reader to suspect something else. The text of *Dom Casmurro* undoes itself, and the reader witnesses this undoing. Although she does not yet know it, the reader will, in the novel's famous conclusion, be called upon to make a decision about the truth or falsity of the argument so artfully advanced by our narrator, an argument that, as a verbal structure itself (and one with a very specific intent), will be interpreted, and resolved, only through more language use, that is, the response, or responses, of the engaged reader.

This problem of veracity, in art and in language, continues in chapter 45, where, quite deliberately, one suspects, the actual word "veracity" is employed. But while its use here does relate, and directly, to the believability of what the narrator is telling us (this to emerge later as the text's crucial question), there is, more in play, another, less obvious question about veracity—that of words themselves, a point our narrator, "Dom Casmurro," himself brings up, although (ironically enough, given his intentions) with respect to the character who is by now beginning to take shape in the narrative structure he builds as his antagonist, his beloved wife, Capitú. As if to win over the reader and to convince her of the truthfulness of his version of all that happens in his narrative, "Dom Casmurro" tells us, once again utilizing the comic mode to make, and perhaps mask, a very serious point, "I trust you will pick . . . up again" the novel you are reading (one that he has just told us, playfully, that may be too "tedious" for the reader to enjoy) "and open" it "to the same page, without necessarily believing in the veracity of the author. And yet there is nothing more exact" (*DC*, 96). By bringing up the question of his own reliability as a storyteller, and then humorously displacing it, our wily narrator ends up firmly establishing his credibility in the mind of his reader. "It was just so," the narrator then tells us, "that Capitú spoke, *and in those very words*" (*DC*, 96, emphasis mine). In my reading of this novel, this is a critical scene because it marks, for the first time, the narrator's efforts to undercut, or call into question, all that Capitú says. From this point on, the narrator calls into question, in the reader's mind, Capitú's words, words that "Dom Casmurro" himself, as narrator of this entire story, puts into her mouth. The same words, in other words (so to speak), mean something different to different people. Meaning is not stable; it is highly unstable, and it is precisely this "truth" about language use that complicates so many human relationships, decisions, and institutions.

The real "veracity" of this chapter, however, is not what the narrator, "Dom Casmurro," says it is; rather, it is in the ways he manipulates language as a communicative system, one that he bends to his point of view and one that he very judiciously uses to seem to uphold the argument he is slowly building. His carefully chosen and carefully structured words seem to have about them the patina of truth—the truth, that is, that he wants his reader to believe and accept! Yet at this point in the narration, the reader is, as yet, not aware of being so skillfully maneuvered as to how she responds to the text. As with much conservative political discourse of the present time (2016), "Dom Casmurro" uses language not to tell the truth but to hide it, to deceive and misread his reader.[7] In Machado's previous novel, *Quincas Borba*, the narrative told by his also unreliable narrator shows us clearly what an authentically rendered Realism would be like in a literary work of art. Although this is disconcerting to those readers who need, or expect, order, clarity, and semantic certainty, the text of *Quincas Borba* shows Machado not offering us the same, old Realism of the traditional realistic novel but a new kind of Realism, one that imitates nature, or reality, in a way that shows us just how profoundly language determines our sense of being and our sense of knowing. In *Dom Casmurro*, however, Machado's experimentations with narrative art take a different turn, one that focuses more tightly on the inescapable mutability of language produce meaning and on how a single person can manipulate this quality for his or her own benefit.

A captivating example of this, chapter 55, which deals with the partial writing of a sonnet, can be read as a humorous and metaphorical exploration of the twin problems of interpretation and meaning. The narrator here tells us of how he wrote the first line of a sonnet and then the last, and how he then struggled to determine the meaning of the first and last lines of his very formal literary creation. He determines, finally, that by simply changing the order in which certain words are used in certain lines, he can radically change the meaning of his putative poem. After transposing the order in which the words of his sonnet line occur, he allows them to produce a meaning that is "exactly the opposite" of their earlier meaning and surmises that this move on his part would "coax inspiration" from him and allow him to complete the poem (*DC*, 112). "Perhaps in writing," he muses, "the verses would flock to me" (*DC*, 112). In speculating that using words produces more words, the narrator, "Dom Casmurro," is broaching an effect that Ferdinand de Saussure would expound upon some fifteen years later in his theory of how language works and how it produces meaning.

The transformative power of syntax, in any language system, is thus shown to have tremendous influence on meaning. Meaning, as Machado shows, is less an inherent quality of words than it is a matter of where they appear relative to the other words in the same text or verbal structure. In terms of the argument I am making here, the importance of this entirely metaphorical chapter is that it shows us, once again, something fundamental to Saussure's linguistics: how a change in the location, or placement, of a work (a verbal sign) within its structure results in a change of meaning. Meaning, here and elsewhere in *Dom Casmurro*, reveals itself to be not constant but relative, and mutable, in nature. This is true at the level of the individual line and its guiding syntax and, in this case, at the narrative's larger structures (chapter sequences and plot structures, for example) as well. And this is exactly what we have here, in microcosm, in the discussion of the possible meanings of an unfinished sonnet. Chapter 55 not only makes manifest Machado's realization that meaning in language is never stable but forever changing, it also links, self-referentially, to chapter 2, in which the mysterious problem of the "Dom Casmurro's" missing self is first mentioned. Having written one sonorous final line, "*Life is lost, the battle still is won!*," our narrator, recalling, at this point, a moment from his youth, then says, "Worn out with waiting, I decided to alter the meaning of the final verse by the simple transposition of two words, thus: *Life is won, the battle still is lost!*" (*DC*, 112, emphasis original). Referencing the "missing middle" of chapter 2, and speaking, already in 1900, to "hollow" men and women everywhere, the narrator's comments, of his little alteration, "the meaning turns out to be exactly the opposite," but, he then adds, as if in an invitation to the reader to do her interpretive job, "perhaps this in itself would coax inspiration" (*DC*, 112). Thus does the scouring of "elusive verses" for their "proper consonances and meanings" proceed (*DC*, 113). This key chapter then comes to a close with the narrator gently admonishing the reader and telling her to do with her sonnet exactly what is not being done here—filling in (with creativity, truthfulness, and interpretation) the missing middle.

As *Dom Casmurro* slides into the novel's second half, and especially as it moves, inexorably, toward its tragic conclusion, the roles that narrative art, mimesis, and verisimilitude play in it gain force. As noted earlier, in fact, they are instrumental in its plot structuring, plot being the characteristic that Aristotle designated as the most important element in a literary construct. But in Machado's novel, the conflicts that drive the plot are entirely a matter of narrative structure, imitation, and the appearance of things. In chapter 59, a chapter Jacques Derrida himself would have adored, his concept of *différance* becomes textually epitomized, and at both the lexical level and the structural level. The chapter opens with "Dom Casmurro" telling us this: "There are remembrances that do not rest until the pen or the tongue publishes them" (*DC*, 119). The suggestion made here, that a "remembrance," memory, or even a thought about the past (and the text of the novel, *Dom Casmurro*, is all concerned with something that, allegedly, happened in the narrator's past) cannot come into existence until it is narrated, or put into words as a story (or narrative art), which we remember is what our narrator said he wanted to do back in chapter 2. So this basic theme of the novel, how narrative (language) makes, or creates, the reality that we think of as "the past," is reiterated here at the same time that it is given a new level of importance to the plot structure; Capitú's guilt or innocence will be a matter not of fact but of speculation, and speculation, like interpretation, is a function of language. More specifically, Machado's novel demonstrates the inherent instability of language and its production of meaning. The novel itself, in other words, represents the true nature of language. With this in mind, I believe, Machado's narrator then works the reader's sympathy by seeming to want to explain himself and the narrative he is here so craftily structuring as a verbal indictment of his spouse (whom he suspects of infidelity): "There is no way of emending a confused book," he says, referring deliberately and, I think, both strategically and ironically, to his own discourse, which he (believing that it is not) presents as being faulty, the work of an innocent, naïve man (*DC*, 119).

Then, speaking once again to the reader and advising her about how to read, and (by agreeing with what he insists is its abundantly clear truth) improve, this narrative, he says, "but everything may be supplied," by the reader who is being won over by the narrator's point of view, "in the case of books with omissions," the latter word being one that, for the modern reader, cannot fail to remind her of the concept of "aporia," a kind of irony in which, for post-Derrida theoreticians, a text demonstrates its inherent undecidability. The point I am making here, however, is a bit different; I believe that Machado de Assis is, in 1899, already exploring this same aspect of language and writing entire novels based on the consequences of this kind of thinking. As a form of narrative art, *Dom Casmurro* imitates both language and life in a way that epitomizes both Derrida's concept of *différance* and its spinoff critical term, "aporia." How, Machado asks us, can we make decisions in a world where language, our primary mechanism for determining who and what we are, is so riven with semantic fluidity and uncertainty? How can we ever know anything, with certainty, and, in such a condition, how should we live our lives? How should we regard the social, political, philosophical, and religious institutions (all functions of the same language that bedevils us) that (like novels) we create to try to order the chaos of life? These are the questions that Machado the egregiously unacknowledged theoretician of the new narrative and the new novel leads us to consider.

Having led his reader, increasingly seduced by his words, to consider the nature of the story he is telling, and, at the same time, the novel we are reading, "Dom Casmurro" ends this chapter by giving us one final bit of advice about how to respond to this text: "The fact is, everything is to be found outside a book that has gaps, gentle reader. This is the way I fill in other men's lacunae; in the same way you may fill in mine" (*DC*, 120). Language and interpretation, in other words, are how we must read this novel, but they are also how we must deal with life. In my view, this is a brilliant demonstration of how one word, or thought (a series of words tied, one hopes, together), leads not to a stop or certitude, but to more words and thoughts. As in *Quincas Borba*, but from a different creative perspective, the text is here continuing to explore how language "fills in" the spaces, or "gaps," that exist between words, and between our various human identities and realities, that a writer seeks to stitch together for a reader. Interestingly, Machado comes right back to this same issue in chapter 77, when, having just told us something, he then adds, "This is not clear—but not everything is clear in life or in books," this being a self-conscious that establishes a structural parallel with both chapters 2 and 59. Interpretation is never certain, but it is an unavoidable part of human life. In artistic creation, as Aristotle might say and as Machado shows us, it is the nature and mode of the imitation that counts. And if language is the medium of imitation, then uncertainty and undecidability are, inescapably, involved. The reader, like the citizen, must learn to take them into account and to deal with them. The verisimilitude produced by language is, therefore, of a very special sort, and it must be both recognized and dealt with. Certainty is an illusion of the old Realism; uncertainty, Machado shows us, is the new Realism, the Realism of modernity.[8]

The reader's role in interpreting the text continues in chapter 73, where the reader witnesses the narrator himself makes a critical error of interpretation, one that shows the alert reader his underlying motive not merely in telling this story but in telling it as he does. In so doing, our narrator undercuts his presentation of himself as the teller of a tale (his own life story) in which the reader can have total confidence. The issue has to do with something to which he, as a young swain, was an eyewitness, and thus, in conventional terms, an utterly reliable commentator. One day, Bento (as "Dom Casmurro" was known as a youth) observes another young man, a "dandy," he says, riding under the window of Capitú, the girl he loves. In his version of the events, the anonymous rider "was not content to pass on, but turned his head in our direction, the direction of Capitú, and looked at Capitú, and Capitú looked at him" (*DC*, 147). The reader, who tends to accept this without hesitation, cannot know if this is a true, or verisimilar, rendering of events or not. And even if the events did happen more or less as laid out here, she could not know what was going on the mind of the rider or in that of Capitú. We cannot know if they looked at each other or not. The text itself stresses this key point; yet upon careful reconsideration, it clearly tells us only that they looked in the direction of each other, with the word "direction" appearing twice, in rapid succession, as if to clue the reader in to this salient and totally destabilizing fact. In terms of the macro-structuring of the text, this chapter, as important as it is, also presages a later, and even more important, chapter, 118, in which the same point (about the essential undecidability of our linguistically inscribed world) is driven home even harder.

The intensity by which the vagaries of imitation come to control the final chapters of *Dom Casmurro* increases dramatically in chapter 83, "The Portrait." A true turning point in the novel's plot structure, chapter 83 also brings the problems of artistic imitation and interpretation to the surface of his narrative. Linking two key earlier chapters (10 and 31) with the several later chapters (99, 112, 131, 132, and 138) that, upon reflection, as a closely integrated unit, will bring the novel to its tragic conclusion, chapter 83 once again centers on the question of artistic verisimilitude and how we humans respond to it, our tendency to mistake the semblance of truth for actual truth. Again involving a portrait, a character, one Gurgel, asks our narrator (again, in this scene, a young man) if "Capitú was not like the portrait" (*DC*, 160). After carefully explaining to us why he would respond to this question as he was going to do (when it is not inconvenient for him to do so, he always agrees with whatever people say to him, a point riven with both political and intellectual problems), our narrator answers, "yes," the portrait and Capitú were very much alike, as if, in fact, the one was an accurate imitation of the other. Much to the reader's surprise, however, Gurgel then says that the portrait was not of Capitú but of his wife. In this case (which centers on painting), not even a verisimilar imitation is entirely faithful in terms of its object; its "realism" does not, as artistic representation, correspond perfectly to its external reality, its referent in the outside world. The chapter then ends with more words from Gurgel, words that, in this context, are innocent enough but that, in the larger context of the motive behind the structuring of the story "Dom Casmurro" is advancing here in the text that is the novel *Dom Casmurro*, have sinister implications, for art and for life. "Sometimes," Gurgel avers, "in life, there are these strange resemblances" (*DC*, 162). Strange indeed. So strange, in fact, that the modern reader especially will wonder if these "resemblances" (this being a word that will reappear multiple times in the closing chapters) are more than that, if they are not really illusions, the artifices produced by the peculiarities of linguistic imitation.

The full meaning of Gurgel's words will not become clear, however, until the very end of the narrative, when, much to the horror of the reader, their relationship to other words in other scenes will become abundantly clear. In terms of plot structure, this line serves as one of the novel's most important in that it both prepares the reader for the fateful moment ahead (when she will be asked to agree with the interpretation, or judgment, that "Dom Casmurro" asks from her) and, upon reflection (more language use, more interpretation), undercuts the decision it so openly elicits.

In chapter 92, this same problem, the nature of imitation by language, is contrasted, implicitly, by Gurgel's ensuing discussion of mathematics, a system, he correctly notes, that is, like language, made up of symbols. On this point, the comparison is quite explicit, and the engaged reader cannot miss it (*DC*, 178). "Arithmetical ideas," in other words, have a linguistic parallel; indeed, the former are here elaborated by means of language (*DC*, 178). The same character then carries on this same comparison (mathematics being presented as yet another symbolic manner of imitating reality) to make his point: "Look at the digits: there are no two which perform the same function: 4 is 4, and 7 is 7" (*DC*, 178). Confident of the precision of mathematics and comparing it to what he sets up as the imprecision of language, Gurgel then opines, "Thus I was not able to resolve, then and there, a philosophic or linguistic problem, whereas he could add up, in three minutes, *any* amounts" (*DC*, 179). Language use, Machado reminds us, leads us not to the kind of finality that we have in the "4 is 4" equation but, inevitably and always, to more language use. As Gurgel himself notes, his inability to solve, or finalize, "philosophic or linguistic" problems once again call our attention not merely to language as a system that constantly generates meaning but, once again, to the linguistics of Saussure. Just as no two digits can "perform the same function" (4 must always be 4 and 7 must always be 7), so can no two words perform—exactly (as in the cases of the digits)—the same function; in the linguistic system known as English, only one letter differentiates art from fart. In very fundamental ways, Machado shows us, in this chapter, a radically new theory of imitation, one similar not only to painting, sculpture, and music but also to mathematics and one based on language and its semantic fluidity.

The same issue, the fluidity or mutability of meaning, turns up again in chapter 96, "A Substitute." Here, however, the text actually presents not one but two kinds of substitution; the first one involves the substitution of one plan for another (which is what the more casual or conventional reader would likely respond to), while the second one, much more subtle and hidden in a web of irony and intertextuality, and presented, as is so often the case with Machado, under a comic veneer, has to do with how the same words can mean different things to different people. Bento's great friend, Escobar, has just proposed to his schoolmate an ingenious way of getting him out of a promise he had made to his very pious mother, a promise that, if kept, would make him a priest, which Bento did not wish to be. Escobar's plan itself rests on a certain finagling of the original intent of Bento's mother, but both Bento and the reader readily accept it as both clever and likely to gain the desired result—liberation from the seminary and from his promise. After Escobar has just declared that he wishes to leave the seminary with his friend (thus hinting at an incipient homoerotic attraction between the two boys) and go into business, where he would not need the Latin that he was required in the seminary to study, Bento laughingly declares, in reference to Escobar's plan, *In hoc signo vinces* (With this sign you will conquer; *DC*, 185, translation mine). It is for the alert and engaged reader to pick up on the ironic play of meaning involved. The quote, which, in its original usage (where the word *signo*, or "sign," serves as a clue to the reader), involves words written next to a cross and on the standard of the Roman emperor, Constantine, who established Christianity as the official religion of the empire. While the intended meaning of these same words was, for Constantine and the Roman Christians, a sacred statement of how faith will allow a believer to prevail against all of life's trials and tribulations, here a youthful and not very committed seminarian, Bento, willfully uses the same words (or signs) to mean something very different—that it is the business acumen of Escobar, and not his faith, that will allow him to prevail in life. Fully ten to fifteen years before Saussure would come up with his theory of how the linguistic sign is fluid in terms of its production of meaning, Machado has built this same idea into the heart of his novel. Skilled at Latin (another language/sign system), Bento knows full well that he is deliberately changing the meaning of the quote. What could seem to the unsuspecting reader a simple joke, actually functions (for the new reader Machado wants to create) as an illustration of the relative, uncertain nature of meaning, this issue being central to the novel's plot. While the chapter appears to be one thing, a mere change of strategy in the pursuit of a certain goal, it reveals itself, upon a careful and considered reading, to be about something else entirely—how the same words generate multiple and sometimes (as in this case) sharply askew meanings. Context and intent, Machado, "Dom Casmurro," the narrator, and the text show us, determine meaning, not something stable and inherent in the words themselves.

The problem of resemblances (and, one could argue, of meaning) continues on in chapter 99, titled (prophetically, as the text will soon demonstrate) "The Son Is the Image of His Father" (*DC*, 188). Once again, the concept is how things can, sometimes, seem to look, if not exactly alike, then at least similar, similar enough for Bento's mother to exclaim that her son is "the image of his father" and (a few lines later but in the same chapter) that he is "the picture of my dear departed" (*DC*, 188). Further, and in the process emphasizing the mutable nature of artistic interpretation (which recalls for us the discussion of verisimilitude offered in chapter 10), she also declares, of what she is now beholding (the flesh-and-blood reality of her son), "I always thought I saw a resemblance; now it is much greater," a point with which her religious counselor, José Dias, quickly concurs (*DC*, 188–89). With the question about whether we interpret art forms with objectivity or whether we respond to them in terms of our desires and experiences held in abeyance here, there is no doubt at all but that the narrative structure itself is centered, as it moves inexorably toward its conclusion, on the problem of appearances, on the way things can, by design (as in artistic imitation) or by accident, resemble each other and relate to each other. As we shall soon see, the entire plot structure of *Dom Casmurro* turns on exactly this question.

Chapter 106, "Ten Pounds Sterling," emphasizes, in disguised form, the same motif, and in the process subtly reminds the reader that everything in this novel is an exercise in self-referentiality. The chapter concerns an effort by Bento's wife, Capitú, to economize, to save some money for her family from their budget. She does this (to surprise him, the text tells us) without her husband's knowledge and, as she is no expert in financial matters, by availing herself of the advice of her husband's dear and very sharp friend, Escobar. Although in a certain sense Capitú and Escobar do conspire behind her husband's back (ostensibly to do something that will please him), Capitú's secretive actions here would, on the surface, easily be interpreted as being entirely laudable. Indeed, the nondiscriminating, nonengaged reader is led, by "Dom Casmurro's" presentation of the story and its facts, to feel that she is deserving of praise. But, as the same reader moves closer to the novel's tragic conclusion, she could, if reading the text as Machado wanted his "new reader" to do, see how the narrator's telling of what appears to be an innocent tale is actually a prefiguring of the novel's plot, which centers on the narrator's belief that he was betrayed by his wife and his best friend, Escobar. But in order to see this possibility, the reader must understand how the meaning ascribed to, or taken, initially, from, the events narrated in chapter 106 and the novel's basic conflict relate to each other in transforming ways, with the one (chapter 106) encapsulating and anticipating the other. Even more important, the same aware, engaged reader must grasp how her initial reading of chapter 106 becomes radically altered by reading through to the novel's end. It is only then that the reader can understand how her original reading of this same, key chapter is changed by its relationship to the larger, self-referential, and constantly offsetting narrative structure that Machado erects.

In terms of Machado's continuing development of a "new narrative," the reader's active, engaged role in it becomes more and more apparent. Chapter 109, "An Only Child," links the problem of appearances, or resemblances, with the closely related question of how we respond to the things of life, how we try to interpret the signs that surround and envelop us. Once again setting up a comparison, Machado devotes most of this short chapter to a brief discussion of how Bento and his wife, Capitú, responded to every cough and sneeze of their child, whose name, Ezekiel, evokes, of course, biblical allusions to his role as a prophet, a harbinger of things to come. As Machado does not fail to show us, however, the role of the parent with respect to a child has a parallel in what a careful reader does to a literary text; they both interpret signs. And so it is that the concluding line of this chapter involves words of advice for Machado's "new reader": "there are readers so obtuse that they understand nothing unless you tell them everything—and what's leftover. Let us go to what's left over" (*DC*, 206). Echoing chapter 17, in which worms, like critics, are chatting pointlessly as they devour texts they know nothing about and cannot understand, Machado here shows somewhat less asperity and, instead, gently chides the reader about what she needs to do—not to be so "obtuse" that she requires everything to be explained to her, as in the case of the old Realism.

More than this, chapter 110, preparing us for the grand finale, also echoes the very unrealistic discussion, in chapters 9 and 10, between God, responsible for the words in life, and the Devil, who was in charge of music, "the tune," as it is referred to here, goes beyond its relevance to the plot of *Dom Casmurro* by incorporating the core theoretical problems raised by this extraordinary novel, art, nature (more specifically, human life), imitation, verisimilitude, and interpretation. Ezekiel, we are told by our once again unreliable narrator (who may, we will think later, have some ulterior motive in linking a person he, at this point in the narrative, presents as his own son, with the Devil), puts some music "to good use" in the disproving of a "text," one not unlike, we may later surmise, the very one we are reading. The child and Bento then engage in a commentary of the nature of artistic creation, one here involving soldiers, music, and a kind of painting, a lithograph of a scene from a war. At issue is the question of verisimilitude; why, in the painting of a battle, a soldier does not "bring his sword down and have done with it?" to which his father responds that it was an issue not of reality but of artistic representation, of the choice the artist had made about how to best render this scene (*DC*, 208). Reality, once again, is one thing; its artistic representation is quite another, yet it is the issue of verisimilitude, as we learned in chapter 10, that we, as humans living in human society, must so often deal.

The role of Ezekiel, an Old Testament prophet, grows in chapter 112, "Ezekiel's Imitations." Connecting chapter 83 and foreshadowing chapter 136, this chapter turns entirely on the issues of artistic representation (or, the alert reader will counter, on another of the "strange resemblances" that we know exist in life; see chapter 83) and verisimilitude. Here, however, Bento and Capitú, presumably the father and mother of a child, Ezekiel, are discussing one of the boy's habits—his tendency to imitate others. It is, I suggest, not too much to suspect that this very fact is yet another form of mirroring employed by Machado. Read from this perspective, the child in question, Ezekiel (with the biblical implications of his name suddenly looming larger in our interpretation of his artistically presented actions), is imitating other people just as we, the readers, are interpreting another artistic imitation, that offered by the novel, *Dom Casmurro*. We are, in short, being asked to interpret the interpretations and imitations of a fictional character. Remembering that, at the point he writes these words (or gives us these signs, and in this particular order), it is the aged narrator, "Dom Casmurro," reinventing, via language, an earlier time in his life (when he was a young married man), he has Bento, the young innocent say, of his son (or, more precisely, of the child he thinks is his son, this being yet another form of interpretation), that he finds "only one little defect in him: he likes to imitate people" (*DC*, 211). Ezekiel, in other words, likes to imitate people for the same reason that Aristotle said all we humans do—because it gives us pleasure to do so (see *The Poetics*, 5–6).[9] Bento's wife, Capitú, then responds (via words that the narrator, "Dom Casmurro," has placed in her mouth) with a question: "Imitate? In what way?" (*DC*, 211). After her husband explains what he has seen, or thinks he has seen, Capitú then looks at him, "thoughtfully," and says that they "should correct him" (*DC*, 211). There ensues a short exchange between husband and wife in which we learn that, as a child, Bento, too, had imitated people and that Capitú did not want imitations in her family (*DC*, 212). No reason is given, though the reader who finishes the novel and concludes, with the narrator, that Capitú was guilty of adultery and that chapter 112, with its indication of Capitú's position on the matter of Ezekiel's imitations, is one of the first "sure" indications of it.

Crucially, Bento then asks his wife if, in those earlier days, she had loved him, and, according to "Dom Casmurro's" narration, "Capitú's answer was a sweet, mocking smile, one of those smiles that can never be described, and rarely painted" (*DC*, 212). Invoking yet another allusion to the various modes of imitation, the narrator also declares that the nature of Capitú's mysterious smile was such that he was sorry there was no sculptor around to capture the moment, and her "pose," in marble (*DC*, 212). "Only the artist," "Dom Casmurro" continues, emphasizing the role imitation and verisimilitude play in this novel, "would win glory by it, that is certain" (*DC*, 212). He then ends this critical chapter by pushing this point even further: "When a figure or group comes out well, no one is concerned about the model, but only about the work. It is the work that endures" (*DC*, 212). If the reader substitutes the word "reality" for "a figure or group," and the word "reality" for "model," then, as the sentence ends, and with "the work" seemingly meaning "art," then this same sentence, which seems, on the surface, to be little more than tangential to the issue at hand, turns out to be a statement about the ancient relationship between reality and its artistic re-presentation, its imitation. And, clearly, as per what the text itself actually says, it is the work of art, and not the reality imitated, "that endures" (*DC*, 212).

Why, I ask myself in making my argument here, would Machado take such pains to set up this scene, and to deliberately reference all these different modes of imitation, if he were not genuinely interested, as an artist himself (though one who works in language, not paint or stone), in exploring this relationship? Given what we learn in chapter 10 about the nature of verisimilitude and truth (that the latter is often a matter of the former, that is, of appearances and resemblances), I believe the novel, Machado's own artistic creation and a narrative he intends to be a contribution to this same question, is, first and foremost, an artistically rendered demonstration of how language imitates reality, what its real characteristics are, and how we, as readers, citizens, and human beings, must learn to deal with their fluidity and semantic mutability. This is the new Realism that Machado creates for us. And while it is intensely verisimilar in terms of its authenticity and in terms of its replication of the true nature of most human reality (that it is more a function of language than it is of scientifically verifiable fact), Machado's new Realism is also profoundly disturbing.

It is this issue, our intense and deeply rooted desire—our need—to know and to understand, that drives *Dom Casmurro* to its terrible conclusion. Chapter 118, "The Hand of Sancha," is a key part of this narrative movement. We learn two things in this chapter, both of which are, once again, related to the intertwined issues of (1) artistic imitation and verisimilitude and (2) interpretation. It is the second of these that turns up first in the chapter. We witness our narrator interpreting certain actions of Sancha, the wife of Escobar, Bento's business confidante and his closest personal friend. Bento believes that his eyes, and those of Sancha (which *seem* to him to be "sultry" and "imperious"),[10] meet and lock together, as if (in the telling of our narrator) to suggest her desire for some sort of elicit union. Immediately, he follows this thought to a physical act, to which he will impute the same meaning as he had taken from Sancha's eyes—that she is interested in having a tryst with him. "As we were leaving," he tells us, "my eyes spoke once more to the mistress of the house," that is, to Sancha (*DC*, 223). "Her hand pressed mine, and lingered there longer than usual," he then tells us (*DC*, 223). On the one hand, this handshake could be an innocent matter of friends saying good-bye; on the other, it could (as Bento, correctly or incorrectly, interprets it to be) be a sign of Sancha's desire to initiate an affair with him. But how can he know this? He cannot, of course. But, and more to the point I am making here, how can we know? We cannot know, either. We can only guess, or speculate. The reader, performing her own process of interpretation of these very same words, or linguistic signs, realizes that she cannot possibly know, in any certain terms, what is going on here or what it all means. All is interpretation, even in the mind of Bento, who, seemingly, is only too pleased to think that his best friend's wife wants to seduce him. Read this way, of course, the text rebuts, undercuts, or at the very least offsets the charge that Bento will eventually launch against his wife, Capitú—that she committed adultery with his best friend, Escobar. But here we witness Bento making his interpretational decision, and he seems to have no doubt about the correctness of it. This, I contend, is an example of how the mature Machado builds into his basic narrative structures the kind of language-based indeterminacy that characterize his later and greatest novels.

Having brought the question of interpretation front and center, chapter 118 then comes to its own conclusion (its own structuring within the larger structures that connect with it and that provide it with context and a variety of potential meanings), one that, once again, brings into the fray the issue of imitation by portraiture. Speaking of the "picture of Escobar" that our narrator kept alongside that of his mother, "Dom Casmurro," our narrator and the one person who controls every word that anyone says or thinks in this entire narrative (no one speaks for herself or himself; the entire text is a deliberate and calculated creation of our narrator), tells us, "I cast from me the image of my friend's wife, and called myself disloyal" (*DC*, 224). With this utterance, it *seems* that Bento is suddenly remorseful about the salacious thoughts he had imputed to Sancha and her actions. Again, we cannot know what Sancha wanted or intended. But offsetting this more generous reading of Bento's reaction to what he had been thinking (he had been "disloyal" to his friend), we then learn, suddenly, a bit of information that undermines what we had just surmised about Bento and his integrity: "Besides," the narrator tells us, "who could say there had been any intention of that sort in her goodbye gesture and in the previous ones? . . . Even if there had been some sexual intent, how could I be sure it was anything more than a swift flash of sensation, destined to die with night and sleep?" (*DC*, 224). The penultimate line of the narrative brings up once again the nature of painting, now contrasted with imitation by narrative, and the human desire to know, to understand: "The picture of Escobar seemed to speak to me" (*DC*, 224). While we are told not that in fact it did but that his picture *seemed* to speak to him, we, as readers, and as with people who gaze at paintings and sculptures, are stuck in interpretive limbo. We do not know what to think or what to believe. We are, in art (as with this novel) and in life, unable to decipher what these signs are telling us. Thus it is that both interpretation and our inability to know (for sure, at least, which is what we want) surface here, late in the novel (albeit in complex and interconnecting metaphoric form, as is the nature of linguistic imitation), to guide the story to its conclusion.

Although chapter 120 again invokes both the imitative and verisimilar presence of Escobar's portrait and its impact on our narrator (his reception of it and all it meant to him), it is only in chapter 123, "Eyes Like the Tide," that the closely and organically related question of interpretation surges forth to dominate this moment in the narrative's development. Unexpectedly, Escobar has drown while swimming and, in chapter 123, we are gathered around the casket, mourning. Our narrator, reconstructing (perhaps with an ulterior motive, perhaps not; as in real life, we cannot know) the events of that moment, when he was still the callow young man, Bento, tells us, ominously, "Many men wept; all the women. Only Capitú, supporting the widow, seemed able to control herself" (*DC*, 228). In the midst of the general consternation, we are further told, Capitú's response stood out as different. Being closely observed by her husband, our now white-haired narrator, we learn that she "gazed down for a few seconds at the corpse, gazed so fixedly, with such passionate fixedness, that it was no wonder if tears spring to her eyes, a few quiet tears " (*DC*, 228). But for "Dom Casmurro," who has, we are beginning to suspect, structured this entire narrative to prove the argument that, like a prosecutor in front of a jury (whose role is played by the reader), he wants to make—that his wife, Capitú, and his trusted friend, Escobar (for whom he may well have held a homoerotic attraction; see chapter 118), conspired behind his back to commit adultery, the act of interpretation leads to only one conclusion. In reference to the tears shed for whatever reason by Capitú, "Dom Casmurro" tells us that his "ceased at once. I stood looking at hers; she wiped them away in haste, glancing furtively around at the people in the room, . . . but the corpse seemed to hold her too" (*DC*, 228). For the reader, this reaction could be entirely normal, devoid of any suggestion of adultery on her part with the recently deceased. While Capitú may well have shed a couple of tears, and she may well have "wiped them away in haste," there is no way the narrator could be sure that she did so "furtively" or that the corpse "seemed to hold her too" (*DC*, 228). These interpretations, and conclusions, are entirely subjective, a function of the narrator's mind and narrative art and not of the hard facts of the situation. It is worth noting, yet once again, the omnipresent role the word "seemed" plays in this narrative, where nearly everything is a matter of how it seems in relation to something else, which, in a nutshell, is an apt description of the world-as-defined-by-language vision that drives the late Machado. As with everything else in this narrative, we cannot know for certain what all that goes on in the scene means. We can only speculate. But now the reader has to deal with the interpretational stance of the narrator/protagonist, whose reliability is, for the serious reader, the reader Machado wants to create, in question.

Chapter 126, "Musing," finds our narrator, who has, in the previous chapter, compared himself with Priam, bringing up another word, "illusion," that, like "seemed," occurs throughout the narrative of *Dom Casmurro,* as if to remind us that all art is an illusion.[11] This topic extends into chapter 127, "The Barber," where in contrast to the self-serving and coolly analytical chapter 126, we are treated to a rather humorous defense of art,[12] with the additional factors being the role of the artist (here, another barber), the mode of imitation (music), and yet another comparison of the various ways an imitation of nature may occur. In spite of its droll presentation, in fact, chapter 127 actually amounts to an exaltation of art; as an illusion, yes (and in this sense unrealistic), but, more importantly, as an illusion that, as Aristotle contended in his defense of art, was superior to the looseness and inconsistencies of life, and most especially of human life, which, in Machado's view, is rife with randomness, imbalance, and deception. Though he does not discuss it in terms of imitation by language, which is the mode of imitation practiced by Machado, this is an important point that Lucas has made.[13] Machado de Assis does, indeed, defend art and its superiority over nature.

But while all of this is true, I believe the most revolutionary aspect of Machado's writing, here and in his other post-1880 novels, lies in his modeling of narrative art, or imitation, after his new thinking about language, about how it simultaneously constructs meaning and then, sometimes in the same sentence, undercuts or decenters it. Of all of Machado's later novels, it is *Dom Casmurro* that most brilliantly demonstrates this new understanding of the, for Machado, necessary connection between linguistic theory and narrative structuring. Though the other novels come at this problem in different ways and from different perspectives, *Dom Casmurro* stands out for being, arguably, the most perfectly structured of all these superb later texts, with every line of interpretation offset by other, equally defensible and plausible but alternative arguments. It is a masterpiece not merely of ambiguity but of an ambiguity that is perfectly poised and that stems from the semantically fluid nature of language itself.

In my reading of *Dom Casmurro,* the denouement comes in chapters 131, "Anterior to the Anterior," and chapter 132, "The Sketch and the Color." And it is entirely an issue of imitation, verisimilitude, and interpretation that ties these two chapters together. A true turning point in the action, chapter 131 also features, once again, the problem of resemblances, in life and in art, and how we respond to them. In this structural sense, chapter 131 links up with chapter 10 (where the issue of verisimilitude is first broached in this novel) and in both chapter 83, "The Portrait," and chapter 112, "Ezekiel's Imitations," though no certainty as to the nature of the connections is given or alluded to. It is for the reader to make of them as she will. The chapter begins with Capitú bringing up to her husband, Bento Santiago (later to become transformed into the narrator, "Dom Casmurro"), the question of how much the boy, Ezekiel, resembles the now dead Escobar. Bento agrees, though we do not know if this is merely a continuation of his old habit of agreeing with whomever he is talking with (see chapter 83) or if he genuinely sees Escobar in the face, physiognomy, and habits of his former friend, Escobar. And, for the discerning reader, this very fact serves to offset the motivation behind the narrator's entire story—to convince the reader that Capitú and Escobar committed adultery. Why, the discerning reader asks herself, if Capitú knows she is guilty of having betrayed her husband and of giving birth to her lover's child, the very one in front of them, would she call Bento's attention to the child's resemblance to Escobar? While the aged and embittered man, "Dom Casmurro," tells his story, the text we know as *Dom Casmurro*, in order to convince the reader of his wife's alleged infidelity, the careful reader—the very reader Machado wants to create—begins to perceive how the narrative's own language undercuts itself and reveals other, quite different interpretational stances. Although chapter 131 is the epitome of this process, it appears throughout the text, so much so, and so deftly so, that it becomes impossible to believe that this was not by design on Machado's part. Indeed, it is no exaggeration, I believe, to argue that "Dom Casmurro" is the prototype of the text that "deconstructs" itself and that illustrates Machado's belief that this process reflects how language itself works.[14]

Yet the more Bento stares at Ezekiel, the more he becomes convinced, or the more he convinces himself (given the decision about Capitú's guilt that "Dom Casmurro" has already made when he begins to narrate his life story, the text that we are reading) that, yes, Ezekiel does resemble Escobar, so much so that he must, in fact, be Escobar's son and not his. At this moment, the nature of verisimilitude and our human response to it looms large in the plot, becoming essential to our response to the text's presentation of its subject matter, the reality it is reproducing. This devastating line of interpretation and the determination about guilt or innocence that springs from it are then couched, by Machado, in images relating to art and to various forms of imitation, including both painting and narrative. "Not only his eyes," our narrator exclaims, "but the remaining features also, face, body, the entire person, were acquiring definition with the passage of time. They were like a rough sketch that the artist elaborates little by little," until, finally, the entire, completed "picture" "hangs . . . on the wall" (*DC*, 238). Moving the reader dizzyingly back and forth between the worlds of reality, art, and interpretation, the narrator leads us either to accept his point of view or to wonder whether what we are being told via the meanings inherent in the writing of the novel itself (another art form) is true or the result of Bento's own (willful) interpretation of "facts" carefully, and perhaps strategically, selected and presented by him to give the "illusion," or appearance (see chapter 10), of truth? The text, having made this question entirely plausible, offers no explanation about it. The reader, confronted here, as in life, with multiple and conflicting interpretive possibilities, is on her own.

What is more certain, however, is that, in terms of the novel's overall structure, this chapter does give us a clear description of Bento's shocking transformation, one brought about by his conclusions about what he is seeing in the child, Ezekiel. In gazing at him, "Escobar emerged from the grave, from the seminary, from Flamengo; he sat at table with me, welcomed me on the stairs, kissed me each morning in my study or asked me for the customary blessing at night. All this repelled me . . . and I would vow to kill them both . . . so as to transfer into their dying, all the moments of my dulled, agonized life" (*DC*, 239). As powerful and as seductive as these words are, however, the reader Machado wants to create for his "new narrative" and his new Realism wonders if this is really true or is it his misguided interpretation, his own perverse creation of meaning from the "tatters of reality"? In short, is "Dom Casmurro" doing here essentially what the reader does to the text she is reading? Is art here imitating reality, though in a new and, I believe Machado would say, more realistic fashion, one in which various attempts at interpretation clash and uncertainty envelops everything?

This crucial moment in the narrative's development is then quickly followed by chapter 135, "Othello," in which, clearly, one work of art, the novel *Dom Casmurro*, which we are reading, is mirrored by another work of art, the tragedy *Othello*. Here, however, the goal of the chapter is to use one art form to prove the veracity, or verisimilitude, of the other. The narrator, "Dom Casmurro," wants his reader to believe that the story of his life, which he has been presenting to us, imitates, resembles, or otherwise parallels what transpires in the play. And that this makes his presentation of his life true. Specifically, he wants us to believe, via the comparison, that the players in the domestic drama he lays out in his narration have parallels in *Othello*, with the critical difference being, he takes pains to tell us, that while Desdemona was innocent, his Capitú was guilty, the latter being precisely the point that, in spite of all his arguments and protestations to the contrary, remains moot, a matter of, in this case, artistic imitation and verisimilitude (*DC*, 244).

What happens in the following chapter, "The Cup of Coffee," is prefigured by what almost happens in chapter 111, wherein Bento was on the verge of poisoning some dogs whose barking he believed was bothering his family. In chapter 136, however, the poison is intended for Bento himself; he is contemplating suicide. Interestingly, he grounds this plan in the process and nature of imitation and justifies it by referring to the parallels just established between the tragedy *Othello* and the narration being played out here. In a sense, we can say that Machado is here having "Dom Casmurro" / Bento use art to justify what, horrifically, he is about to do. Life, in an ironic switch, will here (in terms of the reality re-created in the novel) imitate art. The entire chapter, in fact, is built around interlocking images of and references to art (including drama), reality, and imitation. By referring, in a wryly ironic and disparaging way, I believe, to the narcotic power he seems to feel is possessed by the novels of traditional Realism, which, in his view, are so full of "moral cocaine" that they would do anyone in, Machado is able here to talk about his new, more realistic Realism and the "new narrative" that it has spawned: "Nevertheless," his narrator/artist/protagonist declares, "as I wished to avoid all suspicion of imitation" (*DC*, 245), that is, of copying these exemplars of the kind of Realism Machado now finds old-fashioned, simplistic, superficial, and unrealistic, he is offering us here, in the text that is *Dom Casmurro*, an example of his new theory of narrative Realism.

Moving quickly now to bring *Dom Casmurro* also, we are about to see, a tragedy (though with one less character than Shakespeare needed in *Othello*),[15] Machado has his narrator set up chapter 138 as the novel's great confrontation scene, the one in which the two antagonists, Bento, who thinks he is the cuckolded husband, and Capitú, whom he (spinning out the narrative) believes to be an adulteress, face off to settle the issue. In classic Machadoan fashion, however, the issue is never settled; at the end of this scene, with all its back and forth, there is no clear decision, no clear understanding. Capitú never categorically rejects Bento's charge against her, but neither does she ever categorically admit to any wrongdoing. Critically, however, for the argument I am making in this book, Capitú's final speech, and the one that brings this chapter to a close, has her saying this, I believe, key line: "I know the reason for this" (the charge Bento has brought against her); "it is the chance resemblance," the one between the child, Ezekiel, and Escobar (*DC*, 249). For the attentive reader, the reference here, in Capitú's final words to Bento (and to the reader), to the "strange resemblances" mentioned in chapter 83 undercuts Bento's damning interpretation here and in chapters 131 and 132. In life, there are indeed these "strange resemblances," and it is difficult to discern, or believe you discern, resemblances in art (which may or may not be there) that allow one to conclude that what is true of art must also be true of reality—unless the artist wishes to indulge the "moral cocaine" of falsity. And Machado does not.

Mentioning once again, in the very next chapter, the omnipresent problem of "illusion" in life and in art, and referencing in the process our struggle to find, or create, meaning in them, Machado reengages, in chapter 140, with the accompanying problem of "resemblances" (*DC*, 250, 251). The point must be important to Machado the narrative artist because he asks us, openly, to "reread," that is, reinterpret, chapter 83; "there *are* these inexplicable resemblances," and they can exist in both life, where they are common enough, and in art, where things can and do seem like other things (*DC*, 251). So the question of verisimilitude can trap us as well, just as reality can. While the questions of imitation and verisimilitude are certainly crucial to art, the role of interpretation may be especially so, and, if it is, then the role in plays in the interpretation of narrative art, that is, art made of language, emerges as being uniquely critical, a point alluded to in a number of earlier chapters, including chapters 62 and 73, among several others. The crucial difference, I believe Machado is proposing, is that while painting, stone, and even music, once placed into their forms of imitation, are basically static (they are as they are, for others to engage with on their own), language, as a mode of imitation, is different in that it is kinetic, it generates meaning and it does so endlessly. So imitation by language, and, in the case of Machado, imitation by narrative and the novel form, is of a different sort and must be approached from this perspective.

These questions carry on in chapter 144, "A Tardy Question," where, yet once again, the concept of artistic reproduction, which we can think of as imitation, comes openly into play along with the role played by interpretation, in art and in life. Rejecting the linear form of the old realistic novel, Machado here imparts a circular structure to his narrative, one that, like words in their structures, is self-referential. Thus it is that in this late chapter our narrator brings us back to the motivation that he spoke of in the novel's second chapter, his desire to build a new house in his old age that "reproduced" the house he had grown up in as a child. The parallels with art's attempt to reproduce reality that undergird this chapter are simply too powerful to miss, and so the chapter stands as both a summarizing of the novel's story line and, more importantly, I contend, a concluding statement about the complexities of artistic imitation, and most especially about the complexities of artistic imitation by means of language, as Machado is doing here.

As is so typical of the mature Machado, this same issue carries on in the following chapter, "The Return," in which Ezekiel (the boy whose eyes and manners seemed to so truthfully reproduce Escobar) returns from abroad. And, once again, the text itself actually calls our attention to the supposed similarities between the boy's appearance and a "sketch" of him that another character (Aunt Justina) had found and had wanted to use to verify the lad's identity (*DC*, 259). Ironically, art (the sketch) was to be used to verify reality. Its verisimilitude was that strong. And yet, as this text has shown us time after time, the semblance, or appearance, of truth (which is all that artistic imitation is) can lead us astray, for "sometimes, in life, there are these strange resemblances" (*DC*, chap. 83, 162).

All these issues carry on into chapter 146, where, merging, they link up with the symbolic role here of "the Prophet Ezekiel," with his "creation," or engendering, and with the diverse ways portraits, or "sketches," imitate him as opposed to the "texts" that do so, too, but via language (*DC*, 261). With the narrator's stunning revelation that, instead of the financial help he did give him, he would have rather given Ezekiel leprosy (which recalls chapter 90 and Bento's also callous treatment of poor Manduca), we see both the anger over a perceived injustice that has so devoured Bento and, more germane to my point here about language as a medium of imitation, the degree to which this same revelation reveals how twisted and unreliable Bento / "Dom Casmurro" has allowed language to make him.

As we learned in chapter 10, from the lips of an old Italian tenor as he imbibed another glass of chianti, "All is music, my friend," and, as we also learned in this same, early chapter, music, or desire, has, in the metaphor of life as an opera, been presented to us as the deforming domain of the Devil. In the reading of *Dom Casmurro* that I propose here, the "music" of the narrator's narration is not heavenly, as we commonly take music to be, but perverted. And the same applies to the words he uses to advance his agenda; they are not those of God (as suggested in chapter 10), but, as with his "music," also perverted. Although Verlaine has been invoked, the comparison is ironic. The music of Bento and of "Dom Casmurro" will not serve them well, and it will not redeem what they are showing us through their narrative imitation of a life, that is, the life that, by means of a crafty and manipulative use of language, reproduces the horrifying and repellent transformation of Bento into "Dom Casmurro." In the end, the good reader suspects, God and the Devil are both within Bento Santiago, and it is the Devil (who takes form in the text as "Dom Casmurro") who wins out in the struggle for control of "the opera" of life (again, chapter 10). "Dom Casmurro's" uncontrollable desire to believe, absolutely, that Capitú is the cause of his suffering and his ruined life becomes the ruinous "music" that destroys him. In his narrative, the reader watches him become his own Devil (just as he is his own Iago),[16] and so we watch him giving free rein to what amounts to his own linguistically rendered self-destruction. He destroys himself by means of the language, the "music," he uses to define himself, and the reader, responding to the tragic artistic imitation that his narrative is, witnesses the process of this demise in the verbal structure that is the novel *Dom Casmurro*.

Dom Casmurro's final chapter, "Well, and the Rest?," sums up the burning proposition that, though only gradually revealed by our narrator, has driven this narrative from the start—that Capitú was guilty of adultery. But, with the reader now playing the role of the juror in the box, the prosecutor, whose role is played by "Dom Casmurro," demands a verdict (a specific and single interpretation) of guilty from us. Setting himself up as the aggrieved victim (by referencing Jesus), and by paralleling the spousal deception referred to in a Bible verse with what he absolutely believes he was made to suffer, our narrator presents his summation to the reader and says, at the end of his self-serving peroration, "and you will agree with me" (*DC*, 262). From the perspective of the good reader, the kind of reader (and, I believe, citizen) that Machado wanted to have, a decision must now be made. But what will it be? Evidence has been compiled and organized to lead to one decision, the one desired by the narrator (Capitú is guilty). And for those readers who believe the argument put forth by the narrator, the decision is clear—guilty. The artistic verisimilitude of the text known as the novel *Dom Casmurro* is sufficiently strong and compelling that, as readers (and interpreters), we are convinced by it. But, as we have seen, the very same evidence (every word of which is a matter of carefully crafted language use, even those moments when imitation and verisimilitude achieved by language are compared with imitation and verisimilitude achieved by painting, sculpture, and music) undercuts itself and allows for other lines of interpretation. The very same words lead us in multiple directions, in art and in life, and the longer we ponder these same words, the more words will be generated and the more interpretational stances will come into being.

Moreover, the good reader begins to suspect, it is not so much a question of the older, more treacherous (according to "Dom Casmurro") Capitú being inside the younger, more innocent one, as "Dom Casmurro" insists ("What remains," he says in the final chapter, "is to discover whether the Capitú of Gloria was already within the Capitú of Matacavallos," like the fruit within its rind, "or if this one was changed into the other as the result of some chance incident") as it is a question of whether the Devil and his seductive "music" were present in the young Bento as much as were the words of God (*DC*, 262). Instead of what should have been the beautiful and harmonious music of his life, Bento, in allowing himself to become the monster "Dom Casmurro," turned his life into a discordant and cacophonous source of pain. In the novel's final scene, then, what seems to be an indictment of Capitú can also be interpreted as an indictment of the narrator himself. The real question raised in the novel's final lines must be directed, by the reader, not to Capitú (who, in the final pages of the text, gains a very positive characterization) but to how Bento Santiago became "Dom Casmurro."

5 • ESAU AND JACOB

Esau and Jacob (1904), Machado de Assis's penultimate novel, like the three before it, comes alive as an allegory of late nineteenth-century Brazil and as another exercise in debunking the modes, forms, and conventions of traditional Realism. In its pages, the reader "will find no red-blooded realism" or, indeed, any of the trappings of the old realistic novel.[1] Instead, it offers the reader the experience of a self-conscious text that, in the hands of yet another unreliable narrator, manages to discuss its own status as artifice even as it radiates meaning to a host of extratextual considerations directly related to the politics, conflicts, and social structures that foregrounded the establishment of the Brazilian Republic in 1889. Not only "a portrait of Brazil," the text of *Esau and Jacob* puts into practice a "method of narration" that, as I will once again argue, stems from the nature of language as a medium of imitation, and that, for this reason, "is so subtle, so strangely modern that it still fascinates and baffles."[2] Invoking a line from Dante, one of Machado's favorite writers, *Esau and Jacob* continues, as per my argument, to probe the questions of artistic imitation and verisimilitude. Taking as his epigraph a line from *The Inferno*, canto 5 ("Dico, che quando l'anima mal nata"), Machado puts into play the idea of predestination but, as if to offset that, the very real possibility that, in the world of human affairs, we do not always fulfill our expectations. Once again, though in a different way, we confront the fact that resemblances can be deceiving, in life and in art. Here, in the fourth of his five great novels, he focuses specifically on the issue of how even brothers do not necessarily "resemble each other" and how "children often do not resemble their parents."[3] The title itself, *Esau and Jacob*, "embraces the whole destiny of a people. By carrying forward the message of the epigraph, it explains how the Republic was born of" a "society to which it bore no resemblance—just as the youthful heroine, Flora, did not resemble *her* parents."[4] While the narrator's voice once again beguiles us, Flora is the key character, the one who must be most carefully watched. Because children do not always resemble their parents, generational change can take place. This is important both to Machado's view of human life and to his new thinking about how language actually works, how a word means whatever it means (whatever we decide it means) only because it is different from all other words in its system.[5] Flora, as we will see, is compared not so much to something in the real world as to Orpheus and his sweet song. And, in fact, Flora is largely defined in terms of music and flowers, these being fundamental to her imitation as a character. For her, music could provide the kind of harmony that was lacking in "Dom Casmurro's" view of his own life and, in her novel, it allows her to love the twin boys, Pedro, with his conservative bent, and Pedro, who favored a more liberal politics. In fact, Flora comes to symbolize Brazil as it stood, poised between its conservative past and its liberal future (as defined by the Republic); she "*was* the present, as the twins where the past," Pedro, "and the future" (Paulo). In stark contrast, however, to *Dom Casmurro*, which must be taken as a towering human tragedy, *Esau and Jacob* emerges as a comedy, albeit one that does not offer the reader the sop of the expected "happy ending." *Esau and Jacob* offers us a gentle satire of Brazil, and, by extension of the larger human experience, in which the language of politics leads to both rigid, death-dealing ideology (Conservatism) and to a flexible, life-affirming Realism, the one that, aware of its own very fluid semantic productivity, the mature artist Machado de Assis is now promoting and demonstrating.

More than in any of Machado's other novels, the identity of his narrator is both deliciously complicated and a matter of what we might call auto-intertextuality, in that he here identifies his narrator, Ayres, by referring to other fictional works that involve him, either as a character or as the author. This is all presented to the reader in the novel's "Preface," a dazzling bit of creative writing that, aside from weaving a narrative cloth that moves between both reality and fiction and between what we used to think of as fiction and nonfiction, also manages to clue the reader in to another text, one to be published later under the title *Counselor Ayres' Memorial* and that will stand as a separate narrative that is destined to become the fifth of Machado's last five novels. Thanks to what narrative art and imitation by means of language can do, we are suddenly dealing with things that have not happened, that may yet happen, and that are, perhaps, "fated to be!," and we are doing so simultaneously and on more than one level (*EJ*, chapter 1, "Things Fated to Be!").

In *Esau and Jacob*, Machado de Assis experiments with a form of narrative imitation in which the narrator, a man known as Ayres, writes about himself and another man, also named Ayres, who is a character in the narrative the first Ayres is telling and who seems to resemble the narrator. This sleight of narrative hand begins to show itself in chapter 11, "A Unique Case!," and chapter 12, "This Fellow Ayres," in which the omniscient author of the text we have in our hands (and a personage who is himself a fictional creation) introduces both himself, as narrator, and another character known, also, as Ayres: "This fellow Ayres, who appears here, still retains some of the virtues he had at that time, and almost none of the vices" (*EJ*, 37). To the reader, he then offers this bit of interpretational advice: "You are not to attribute this state to any plan of his, nor imagine this is homage to his moderation" (*EJ*, 37). Non-Doppelgängers, that is, the two Ayreses that we now have, with one commenting on the other, are here mirroring each other in ironic yet complementary ways, a situation that may be unique to imitation by narrative. A bit later, in chapter 12, "This Fellow Ayres," we get another example of how the two personages, both named Ayres, relate to each other: "Don't imagine," says narrator Ayres about the character Ayres, who has just (earlier in this same chapter and at the very end of chapter 11) entered the story that we, the readers, know as *Esau and Jacob*, "that he was not sincere; he was. . . . He used to keep a record of his discoveries, observations, reflections, criticisms, and anecdotes, using for this purpose a series of notebooks," the very ones, the reader notes, that are described in the novel's "Preface," "to which he gave the name of *Memorial*," a word that will be key to the title of Machado's next novel, *Counselor Ayres' Memorial*. But references to this same *Memorial* dot the narrative that is Esau and Jacob; the later narrative enjoys a constant presence in the earlier one. Clearly, intertextuality gets a thorough vetting in this 1904 novel. Bored by the insipidity of some of the people (characters he himself has created) around him, our narrator then tells us that, in the hopes that he can escape their boring clutches, he will try "to escape into" his "memory," which means that he will attempt, as "Dom Casmurro" did but for very different reasons, to use narrative, the art of storytelling, to sew together the "tatters" of his life and give them an order, a cohesiveness, and, above all, a unity (that is, art) that, as the mere components of a personally lived and perceived reality, they would not otherwise have. Again, we see, in Machado's handling of it, an exploration not only of how language creates order in life but of how, in terms of the human experience, realistic this is. What Machado's narrator does here, use language, and specifically narrative, to reconstruct the past so as to make sense of it, is largely what people do. But, as Machado warns us, for all of this, for all its seeming verisimilitude, even this new version of Realism is not without its own pitfalls, its own illusions. This has to be so, Machado would, I believe, say, because the same is true of language itself.

But, Machado's text seems to ask, can they really be the "same" person? What is the nature of the characterization of each and of their relationship? Can a narrator and a character (whom the narrator is describing) be the same entity? What happens (as it does in *Esau and Jacob*) if the narrator develops himself as a full-blown character as well? And, finally, how is the reader, who is drawn into the whole affair, to respond to it, to this type of linguistic imitation and the various levels and degrees of verisimilitude that it produces? Eventually, the real author, Machado de Assis, turns control of the narration over to the character, Ayres, and he, in turn, defers constantly to his reader, particularly in matters of interpretation.[6] Here, however, there is less of what seems to be an intentional manipulation of the reader (or a manipulation of the reader to elicit a particular response), as there was in *Dom Casmurro*, and more of a genial invitation to work with the narrator and with the text itself to discern meaning but also to contemplate new meanings that arise from the text. As in Machado's other late novels, the artistic narrative structure that is *Esau and Jacob* is full of "blank spaces" (more instances of "aporia") that the reader is invited "to fill in."[7] Machado and his narrator, the retired diplomat, Ayres, reminds of this in chapter 55, when, comparing the reader's role in the game of fiction to a bovine, he says, "the attentive, truly ruminative reader has four stomachs in his brain, and through these he passes and repasses the actions and events," of the novel being read, "until he deduces the truth which was, or seemed to be, hidden" (*EJ*, 142). Without the active, engaged assistance of the reader, the linguistic imitation of life that we are reading as the novel *Esau and Jacob* will never reach its full potential, its predetermined destiny (as the epigraph reminds us), if the reader does not do her interpretational duty. So, whereas in the previous novel, *Dom Casmurro*, the exploration of how narrative can imitate life focused overwhelmingly on the motivations and interpretations of the character telling the story ("Dom Casmurro"), here Machado is focusing on the role played by the reader, working in consort with, and not against, both the efforts of the narrator and the nature of language itself as a medium of imitation and meaning.

This point, the importance of the new reader to Machado's new narrative, opens chapter 13, "The Epigraph." Still concerned with showing us how unorthodox his novel is, and what it requires from the person, both male and female, who reads it, Machado and his narrator begin by partially explaining their seemingly peculiar narrative method. Three interconnecting points are then made, in rapid succession. Arguing that the epigraph, the line from Dante about people not fulfilling their destinies, rounds out literary characters and "their ideas," and thus serves as an aid to the attentive reader, they also claim, employing a wonderful metaphor, that the epigraph, echoing chapter 34 of *The Posthumous Memoirs of Brás Cubas*, is also "a pair of glasses with which the reader may penetrate whatever seems not quite clear or wholly obscure" (*EJ*, 41). Concerned here with the problems of perspective and understanding, Machado then goes on to stress the importance of the reader's active collaboration in the creation in the text's various meanings. Clearly, Machado and his Ayres, his narrator, are suggesting to the reader that the meaning of a text, and most especially a literary text, is never static and unchanging; it cannot be, given the nature of language, its medium of imitation.

This first point is pushed even further when the text offers a comparison between how language operates and how chess is played. On the critical point of creativity, the comparison favors language. Chess is a game with a finite number of possible moves by pieces whose movement is strictly prescribed and limited. This is why computers can be programmed to play chess very well. Language, however, is quite different, and to illustrate this difference the narrator sets up an analogy between playing chess and writing by suggesting that while "the chess-player" controls his pieces, which, of course, are limited in terms of how they can move, the writer only partially controls his words, which can and do move about and which change meaning, in the minds of their readers, as they do. A knight, we are told, cannot be a castle, nor a pawn a rook. In language, by way of contrast, there are no such limitations; its words, or signs, are infinite in the number of transformations they may take, the moves they can make, and the meanings they generate. Lest the reader miss the point of this droll little comparison, point three is made directly to the reader herself; "it may be that you have enough vision to reproduce the various situations," on the chessboard and in terms of how words generate new meanings by speaking to other words, "from memory. Yes, I think so" (*EJ*, 42). And to employ memory, of course, involves narrative. Then, and employing the subjunctive to suggest to the reader that we are, in fact, not really speaking here about a chess game but how words in a narrative produce a multitude of meanings, everything proceeds "as if" we "were actually witnessing a game between two players," two different words, "or," in a possible reference to chapter 10 of *Dom Casmurro*, "between God and the devil" (*EJ*, 42). Machado's new reader must, in other words, reproduce, through the same language system that gives rise to her initial thoughts about the text she is reading, more possible interpretations, more explanations about what seems to be happening in the novel and what it means. The chapter ends with this third point, which is shown, but not explained, to the reader.

In chapters 24 through 27, which must be taken as another of Machado's interconnecting units, another comparison is made, this time, however, between words and a group of portraits and prints, all with some historical or sociopolitical significance attached to them. This entire series of chapters centers, however, on one issue: the tension (or line of interpretation) that results when, from the same art shop, Paulo, the liberal twin, buys a portrait of Robespierre while Pedro, his conservative brother, buys a portrait of Louis XVI. But, wonders the sentient reader, is the conflict really over what the two paintings represent, or is it also (and more meaningfully) over how, in life, the same signs signify various things, in various ways, to various people? Moreover, in the haggling over value and the prices of the various paintings, it is not difficult to see how a similar, or parallel, haggling over meaning plays into our reading of these chapters. What the reader sees is that both pricing and meaning are negotiable, that is, relative to other things and meanings within the systems (one economic, the other semiotic) that are in play. Prices go up and down, and meanings vary, through time and within specific situations.

This same narrative technique, that of linking several seemingly separate chapters together into the probing of a single issue, occurs again in chapters 33 through 44. Here, the focus is once again on the problems of artistic imitation, resemblance (a word that, as in *Dom Casmurro*, recurs often in *Esau and Jacob*; see *EJ*, 87 and 102, and passim), verisimilitude, and interpretation. In preparing the reader to respond to the thematic unit that is formed from this writing strategy, chapter 31, "Flora," the problem of imitation, how an artist reproduces life, comes to the fore, and in a specifically linguistic fashion. In a discussion with Dona Claudia over the meaning of the word "mysterious" (*inexplicável*, or inexplicable, in the original), Ayres says flat out that "everything depends . . . on how we define the word" and then asks his host if meaning is not merely a function of "point of view" (*EJ*, 79). Fluidity of meaning in language serves as its defining characteristic, one that connects this scene to the block of chapters to come.

Chapter 34 opens the divagation with another contrasting of painting and language and their capacities for reproducing reality in art. Flora finds the discussion "obscure," but, we learn, Ayres, our narrator (and the artist who, ostensibly speaking, provides us with the imitation of life that we are reading), does not add "another word" of explanation (*EJ*, 86). His recommendation, moreover, to Flora is that she think and learn more, that, more specifically, she learn to draw, to paint, to practice her music, and to learn more languages, notably English and French. Flora's name, which translates as "flower," implies that she has the potential to bloom into something beautiful and fragrant, just as Brazil itself does as a newly born Republic. In her close identification with music, moreover, Flora also comes to represent the kind of harmony in life that we all desire, and that language, which is constantly constructing and deconstructing itself, is hard-pressed to reproduce. As a kind of life force in the text, Flora and her love of music also remind the reader of the German philosopher Arthur Schopenhauer, who is often mentioned in the same context as Machado de Assis and for whom music was, itself, a form of Eros, an affirmation of life and an escape from its brutalities. As her studies progress, the discerning reader notes, Ayres, the artist, then advises her to concentrate only on music and language, and "nothing more," he adds, making what we might think of a rather pointed point that, in fact, ends this paragraph (*EJ*, 86).

In chapter 37, "Disaccord in Accord," a title that, in and of itself speaks to one of language's most singular qualities, agreement in disagreement, and vice versa, we are presented, indirectly, of course, as is consistent with the mature Machado's working techniques, with the key question: What do words, understood as arbitrary linguistic signs, mean? In this chapter, the words in question are two in number, abolition and emancipation, both being terms that, in the novel and in real life, had, and still have, a very specific social, political, and historical significance but words that, for the argument I am making here, also demonstrate the fluid, arbitrary, nature of meaning in language. For the brothers, who were also struggling to deal with these immensely important words, the "only difference in their opinion was in respect to the significance," or meaning, "of the reform, which for Pedro," the conservative, "was an act of justice and for Paulo was the beginning of" a much broader and more profound "revolution," one destined to change the nature of Brazil as a modern nation and of the Brazilian people (*EJ*, 91). Significantly, however, it is the liberal twin, Paulo, who gets the job of delivering the key line: "Abolition," he declares, "is the dawn of liberty, we await the sun; the black emancipated, it remains to emancipate the white" (*EJ*, 91). Machado's brilliance as a writer is that he does not allow these two functions of language, the social or political and the aesthetic or linguistic, to separate into two warring camps; to the contrary, he insists that since language is the same system that produces literature and, in this case, political discourse, these two forms of language use, which (wrongly, Machado would, I think, say) *seem* so different, really face the same problems, and they (these two uses of language) must be understood in this context. There is, Machado is saying, I believe, in his late novels, no basic difference between what is commonly called "fiction" and what is commonly called "nonfiction."[8] Machado and Ayres raise the question of emancipation in the context of 1888 and Brazil's move to free first its slaves and then its women (a point seen more clearly in Machado's next novel, *Counselor Ayres' Memorial*), and they speak only of "the significance," or meaning, "of the reform" (*EJ*, 91). But while the text itself presents the question in the context of the emancipation of the slaves and of the white people who are still shackled to their racism, violence, and the easy acceptance of buying and selling people, the reader sees that Machado is also speaking of the need to emancipate fiction from the shackles of the old Realism. Subtly made, the parallel is there for the engaged reader to contemplate.

In chapter 38, the characters bring up, in a discussion of the natures of Natividade's twin boys, Pedro and Paulo, the linguistic problem of semantic slipperiness and change. Ayres, the narrator, says, to Natividade (a woman he loves, despite her being married and to a man, a banker named Santos, whom he cannot abide), she always demands "definite answers" in life, and Ayres avers that nothing, in life or in conversation (that is, language use), is ever "definite" (*EJ*, 94). Natividade here expresses the very human desire we all have to know with absolute certainty and to get definitive answers to our questions. But, as Ayres points out, gently but insightfully, there is precious little in this world that is "definite," and, the alert reader by now thinks, meaning in language must surely rank as among the least definite issues that we can think of. But how, the same reader will ask, do with deal with uncertainty in literary texts like this one, and in life generally?

This, I believe, is the key question and the one Machado wants us to think about. As if to lay to rest this now broached but not pursued ontological and epistemological quandary, Ayres kindly allows that while "conversation," the exchange of ideas and points of view, is pleasurable and core to the process of human communication, it is never final; there are always "houses" full of other opinions to be considered (*EJ*, 94). Mutability, in life and in the meanings of words and opinions, is a basic fact of life, and we fool ourselves in thinking that it is not. At issue is how, in art, in social discourse, and in politics, we deal with this basic truth. The chapter then closes with a celebration of harmony (the kind of harmony, we think, that art alone can deliver), even when it is a matter of seeking harmony through language, "in words," as Ayres declares, to the woman he adores, and even when misunderstanding is a living part of the process. Even then, the reader is reminded, harmony still stands as a desirable goal, one to be worked toward by all parties involved.

The opening lines of chapter 46, which speak of the reader's need to piece together and then decipher the meaning of the narrative that is emerging from Ayres's effort to understand the twins, recall *Quincas Borba* and its admonition about how she, if she wishes to be truly and authentically realistic, must content herself with trying to piece together the "tatters," or shreds, of reality. Calling to mind the argument made in chapter 94 as well, chapter 66 then moves to a discussion of art, reality, illusion, and resemblances. With the text we are reading performing the comparison, Machado's narrator returns to a discussion of how well, relatively speaking, the scenery of stage props, painting, and fiction imitate reality. At the heart of this particular discussion is the question of illusion, a problem that, as subtly laid out in the rest of this chapter, affects not merely the world of art but the world of politics and social interaction as well. The keen reader begins here to realize how much the words, illusions and resemblances, are proliferating in the narrative and creating one of its principal, if less than obvious, conceits—the world as illusion, a linguistic construct that imitates life with verisimilitude less than it creates a vision of life that someone, an artist or an ideologue, for example, wishes to construct (see, for example, chapters 25, 35, 44, 79, 80, 90, and 118, and passim). Though different in terms of their intentions, Machado suggests to us, both life and art are, in their own ways, illusions, and this becomes a basic motif of *Esau and Jacob*. The chapter ends with Machado's narrator summing up for us this troubling concept: in art and in life, "reality takes the place of fiction" (*EJ*, 111). Then, as if with a colluding wink to the reader/collaborator, the narrator declares, of his own artistic efforts, "I am speaking here in metaphors: you know that everything here is the pure truth and without tears" (*EJ*, 111). And he says this even though his own narrative is full of gaps, omissions, and, as in chapter 48, even openly admitted mistakes of interpretation. Though different in his own ways, Ayres, Machado's narrator here, is as unreliable as his others have been, and what we learn from this is that, as a function of language, unreliability takes many different forms and manifests itself in many different ways.

Following hard on the heels of chapter 46, chapter 49, "The Old Signboard," which deals, appropriately enough, with how the wording on a sign can be altered so that it means a multitude of possible things, nakedly mentions "writing," as involving "a Philosophy of Signs" (*EJ*, 124). For the modern reader, this line jumps out of the text for linking Machado's "new narrative," as well as his new theory of narrative and narrative imitation, to a field known today as semiotics, the science of signs, in all their myriad forms, and how we interpret them. It is precisely this issue, a concern with how much of human life is based on language (and, more specifically, on language understood as a stable referential mode of expression but as a fluid and highly unstable semiotic system), that drives the next several chapters (see, for example, chapter 55, which offers the reader the comic metaphor alluded to earlier in which "the truly ruminative reader has four stomachs in his brain, and through these he passes and repasses the actions and events, until he deduces the truth which was, or seemed to be, hidden"; *EJ*, 142).

In chapter 57, "Shopping," however, this discussion comes to a head. Here, Machado and his narrator open the narration by saying this: "I would not write this chapter if it was really about shopping, but," no surprise to the reader who is doing the job Machado has wanted her to do, "it is not" (*EJ*, 144). This line is immediately followed by another, even more telling one, one that, packed with the kind of linguistic and intellectual prescience Machado had in great abundance, seems to epitomize the semiotic view of life as a system of interlocking systems: "Everything is an instrument in the hands of Life" (*EJ*, 144). With "Life" being capitalized and with the reader interpreting "instrument" as either symbol, sign, or even word, it is very easy to read this chapter as proof that Machado's later texts being about much more than they seem, on the surface, to be about. Having already talked about "writing" as "a Philosophy of Signs," chapter 57 goes so far as to openly advise the reader further as to that critical point; chapter 57, though titled "Shopping," is not about "shopping." What it *is* about, I maintain, is language, and the reader must come to understand this and deal with it.

This exploration of what we know today as semiotics carries on into chapters 62 and 63, and also chapter 92. Clearly, it is central to Machado's new thinking about narrative theory and its relationship to both narrative art and human life. In chapter 62, "Stop on the D," even the title calls our attention to the ways words, and the various combinations of letters they make use of, create and change meaning. Couched once again in comic language and in an ironic sociopolitical context (how a shopkeeper will have to change the name of his store to accommodate a change in government, change once again being the catalytic agent, in life and in language), chapter 62 shows us how, as with the words, or signs, "cat," "hat," and "bat," a change as small as that of a single letter can, and regularly does, change meaning. Although for the reader of *Esau and Jacob* it is amusing to follow the shopkeeper as he frets about what will happen to his business if he cannot rename his store sign successfully, this same reading also suggests to Machado's new reader something much more serious, something fundamental to our ability to deal with both life and literature. It is difference, as Ferdinand de Saussure would later contend, that makes all the difference, as far as meaning is concerned, and these chapters plumb this point.

As Saussure has taught us, a sign means something because it differs from another sign. With the terms "substitution," "change," and "opinion" (used in the context of interpretation) strategically employed, chapter 62 flows into chapter 63, "New Sign," where Ayres, keenly aware that a "name," that is, a word, was not "definitive" in terms of what it meant, proposes to the anxious shopkeeper "a middle term," one that, in his mind, "will serve as well for one political system as another" (*EJ*, 160, 161). Actually, and in full parodic mode, Machado and Ayres suggest to Custodio no fewer than six different names, none of which meet with his approval. The silliness of Custodio's anxieties about his sign, and his inability to accept any of Ayres's very sensible ideas, amounts to a parody of Brazilian politics at the time the novel describes. Just as Custodio cannot agree to any of Ayres's suggestions, neither can Brazil's Liberals and Conservatives agree on any reasonable and workable ideas, a point illustrated by the clash between the two twins, Pedro the conservative and Paulo the liberal. For Machado's new, more semiotically sensitive reader, chapter 63 is provocatively titled "New Sign," a subtle but unmistakable suggestion about the mutability of signs and meaning. The reader gets two clues about what is really being discussed in chapters 62 and 63. The first one comes toward the end of chapter 62, when Custodio says to his painter, "But what will you lose by replacing the last word with another one? The first word can stay, and even the *d*. . . . Didn't you read my note?" (*EJ*, 159). The second, and more telling one, comes toward the end of chapter 63, when Ayres, offering Custodio his final suggestion, says, to the distraught shop owner, that he "would spend something on the changing of one word for another, *Custodio* in place of *Imperio*," but, then, he drolly adds, "revolutions always entail expense" (*EJ*, 164).[9] At this point, the engaged reader realizes that the real substance in chapters 62 and 63 has to do with signification, with how language produces meaning. Chapters 62 and 63 are thus splendid examples of Machado's skill at employing his poetically based metaphoric method, a kind of writing that shows the reader rather than tells the reader and that opens the text up to a much wider range of interpretations. Much to the reader's delight, these chapters demonstrate how language is a living, changing thing, a web of letters (as we see in chapter 62, "Stop on the D," a reference to where Custodio wants the painter to stop his repainting of the sign), words, their fluid relationships with reality, and their unstable, protean status as semiotically productive parts of a larger signifying systems, systems in which the reader participates in her interpretations of the text she is responding to.

Later in this same semantically energetic chapter, Custodio, the confectionary shop owner, is reflecting on how different the different signs that he could choose to identify his business would affect his business. His existing sign, the *Confeitaria do Imperio*, has proudly identified his very popular shop for more than thirty years, but now, with the advent of the Republic, he is worried, reasonably enough, that it will drive away customers or provoke violence. But, like Flora, he cannot make up his mind and so ends up stewing in a state of "despair" (*EJ*, 164). Of his musings, the narrator notes that "one could read neither *yes* nor *no* in him," a comment appropriate enough given its context in the chapter but a comment that, for the attentive reader, suggests not only the fluidity of meaning and interpretation but the danger of relying on simplistic binary thinking, the kind of passive, unchallenged thinking that the readers of the old Realism had been weaned on and that Machado wants to do away with (*EJ*, 162). Showing how much human reality depends on words speaking to other words, Ayres then stresses what we all need to do as readers and citizens; we need, always, "to calculate the bad results of an ambiguous word," which, I believe, shows Machado urging us all to carefully consider the impact of the words we hear, read, write, and speak and not to simply assume that their various meanings, or interpretations, are stable and definitive, for they are not. The implications for this bit of advice are tremendous, both for our understanding and appreciation of literature and for a variety of social, political, legal, religious, and civic questions. Machado then ends this chapter with another suggestion to the reader/citizen, that she not fall prey to conventional meanings and that she not make the common mistake of thinking that what is inherently arbitrary and subject to change is, instead, permanent, stable, and unchanging. "Yes, I'll think about it," says the shopkeeper to Ayres's suggestion, adding that "perhaps it will be best to wait a day or two, to see where the fad," the conventional but often erroneous thinking, "will end" (*EJ*, 164).

Chapter 69, "At the Piano," returns us to the realm of music and its own, unique ability to produce harmony. The chapter is then built around Flora's love of music (a form of imitation closely associated with her) and the harmony it produces, as opposed to imitation by language and the semantic fluctuations that are inherent in it. Larding the text of this chapter with words like "imagination," "definition," "music," and "mutability," or "flux," Machado presents change, in life and in literature (that is, meaning), as a constant and destabilizing force in human affairs. Flora, we learn, "did not share her parents' agitation" over the social and political changes that were sweeping Brazil (emancipation, for example, or the establishment of the Republic), these being functions of language use, so she chose music as her refuge from the world of political discourse (*EJ*, 176). By making this choice, of music over language as a way of dealing with the world, Flora frees herself from "the present" and, instead, enters into the harmonies of music, into an artistically rendered world that was "outside time and space, pure idea" (*EJ*, 176). Finding in music, we learn, a very special "kind of harmony," one that offsets the discord of "the present hour," that is, the era in which she is living, Flora finds that her sonata "gave her the feeling of an absolute lack of government, the anarchy of primitive innocence in that nook of Paradise that man lost through disobedience and will one day win again when perfection brings eternal and unmatched order" (*EJ*, 176). Music, for Machado, is unsurpassed in its ability to attain harmony, but, in contrast to language, which, like our human response to rhythm and harmonic sounds, is deeply linked to the human mind, it cannot realistically capture the often contradictory ebb and flow of human desire and sociopolitical interaction and organization.[10] The harmonic perfection that so attracts Flora comes to her through the melodic sounds she produces in her music, which speaks to her "without words" (*EJ*, 177). But as the reader who finishes *Esau and Jacob* realizes, while the musical harmony prized by Flora, who becomes to symbolize the forces girding the creation of the Brazilian Republic in 1889, suggests a perfect state of being, the Republic itself will not be achieved by means of music, harmonic or otherwise, and will, by contrast, be achieved, imperfectly, by means of the semantic slip and slide of language. Although music, Machado seems to be telling us, is a lovely diversion from the frustrations of life (and a good way to show a character in search of wholeness), language, in all its instability and imprecision, is how we create our human world. Language may not have the pure harmonies of music, but, in its imitative capacities, it comes closer to capturing the fleeting, often fragmentary realities of the human experience, the "tatters" of life that a novelist like Machado de Assis will seek to stitch together in a narrative form that, every step of the way, undercuts itself. How we deal with this is, for Machado the "new novelist," the reality of human existence.[11]

This thought carries on into chapter 83, "The Great Night," which reaches its own conclusion with a fairly lengthy demonstration of how the reader must respond to the challenges presented by Machado's "new narrative." "Believe me, my dear sir, and you, madam, who are no less dear to me," Machado and Ayres say to us as he prepares to launch into a carefully disguised discussion about the unusual kind of novel he is writing (*EJ*, 208–9). Telling us that he could, as other novelists of the realistic tradition have done, drench us in concrete detail and lengthy commentaries on what is going on and what it means, "it would be boring, but readers," those used to the old Realism, "would understand" because that is what they expect (*EJ*, 209). Likening this old, worn-out Realism to "the sputterings of the night lamp," the one "whose flame was dying," Machado proceeds to offer his new Realism as an alternative (*EJ*, 209). "Yes," Ayres and Machado declare, "the lamp's flame was dying," but it could still shed a bit of light (*EJ*, 209). Rapidly, though, this same old lamp, which the reader takes to be the old Realism, arrives "at its last gasp," and at that point it must be replaced with something better, a kind of narrative that, I believe Machado would say, is more language conscious and therefore more realistic (*EJ*, 209). Working an extended metaphor (the dying light of an old lamp) into the displacement the displacement of the old Realism by his new Realism and his "new narrative," Machado reminds his reader what it is that art does; fusing "shapes, so that where there had been two there was now only one," which we can think of as the art object itself, artistic imitation involves "a great deal of merging and dissolving, of forming and transforming" (*EJ*, 209). When the flame in Flora's lamp dies, she goes to relight it but sees that it is lacking the necessary harmony of elements to make it again produce light. Specifically, it has no wick. As a result, the "whole phantasmagoria" that art produces, its illusions, unities, and harmonies, is rendered inert and lifeless (*EJ*, 210). Doing to the lamp, then, in essence what the artist does to reality, that is, give it wholeness and cohesion, Flora (who replaces the old wick) brings light back into her room. "The lamp," Ayres and Machado tell us, in parallel form, "now with a new wick, lighted up her bedroom: imagination had created the whole thing" (*EJ*, 210).

The key word here, "imagination," is what the artist uses to "see" and to create. It is also a word that recurs constantly throughout this novel, as if to remind the reader of its importance not merely to the interpretive process but to the creative process as well (see, for example, chapters 79, 80, 102, 108, and 109).[12] The rich ambiguity that marks Machado's late work is highlighted in chapters 103 and 104, when a wealthy businessman decides he is enamored of Flora and determines to woo her. When his letter of interest arrives at Flora's residence, she bursts into laughter at the prospect and declares, "I do not want to marry" (*EJ*, 253). Her friend, Dona Rita, tries to cajole Flora into thinking it over "for a few days" what the older woman feels is a good match, but Flora, resolute, replies, "I've thought it over" (*EJ*, 253). In the first line of the following chapter, Flora goes further and informs Dona Rita what she is to tell her suitor, a man named Nóbrega: "Say I do not intend to marry" (*EJ*, 253). On the surface, this seems clear enough. But for the careful reader, who has paid attention to the complex and evolving relationship between Flora and the twin boys, Pedro and Paulo, other possible interpretations begin now to emerge from the text. Flora does not wish to marry Nóbrega and all marriage with him would represent, but how does she feel about marrying one of the twins, both of whom are attracted to her (she is the fresh and attractive new Brazil, after all), and she to them? Or is it that, attracted to them or not, Flora, symbolizing Brazil and its future as a free and independent Republic, the young woman does not wish to marry, period? Is it the state of marriage itself that she rejects? Do she and modern Brazil seek some other status, some other type of being? All of these possibilities are now in play—as are new ones about how the earlier metaphors involving the old lamp and its sputtering flame (now read as quite possibly referring to the old Brazil) might be leading the leader to consider Flora being the new wick that the old lamp needs to give off a new and brighter light. And in addition to generating all these new and potentially transforming lines of interpretation for the reader, Machado's deft rejection of the old Realism, which, in yet another reading, he can be seen as presenting, metaphorically, as the "dying lamp," combined with his understated celebration of his own "new narrative," the old lamp (narrative), is (like the old Brazil) now blessed by a new wick, a new vitality and a new understand of human reality, and it lights up the room (Brazil's vast potential as a modern democratic nation) better than ever. Few scenes in Machado's later narratives surpass this one, which gets its semantic richness and humanity from what the inquiring reader takes to be the many possible meanings of the words Flora says and the things she does, in terms of demonstrating what it means to "write and read" deconstructively.[13]

Far from being a depressing experience in nihilism, a charge often brought against deconstruction as a reading strategy (and one that hearkens back to Nietzsche), Machado shows us how profitable and invigorating it is to watch as writing and reading open themselves up to a perhaps infinite number of interpretational possibilities. With his new theory of how language signifies, and how it relates to real, human reality, Machado and his new narrative show his reader (who is expected to participate in the process) the unique ability of language to generate a perhaps endless number of ways to respond to the texts she is experiencing. Just as the appearance of *The Posthumous Memoirs of Brás Cubas* in 1880 was startling, so, too, is the effect of Machado's new theory of narrative startling, and, I contend, for the same reason; even as an author seeks to "construct" a tightly woven but deliberately open text and the reader responds to it in an engaged and thoughtful fashion, that text comes alive, at the moment of its reading, by "deconstructing" itself, by demonstrating to its reader that, because it is a function of language, its meanings can never be closed, pinned down to a single one, or limited in any way. Even when a single meaning seems to be promoted by the author, it can never really be the only one that emerges from a good reading of the text. The reader, responding to the language of the text with the language of reading, is the catalyst in the game of literature, and this, I believe, is why Machado takes such pains in his later narratives to write the way he does and to insist that his reader become actively involved in the production of meanings that results from it.

In the very next chapter, 84, Machado and Ayres add to this an explanation about how Santos, ironically enough (given that he is not one of Ayres's favorite characters), actually ends up improving "on the truth" of the visit Natividade had made to "the cabloca of the Castello" early in the novel (*EJ*, 212). In retelling the story, Santos inadvertently does what Aristotle, in his defense of poetry over the objections Plato brings against it in *The Republic*, said art does for nature—improve it by completing what it does not do naturally or demonstrate clearly. Discussing, then, what is "true," in life and art, and how we can know, Ayres's text ends on a reminder of how change (in this case, political change) brought about a plethora of new meanings for old words and about the necessity of careful, considered interpretation, by readers of novels and by citizens.

This same discussion of what art, and especially narrative art, can do continues on in chapter 94, titled, appropriately enough (given the argument I am making here), "Contradictory Gestures." The chapter opens with a seemingly innocuous sentence about how "a single roof" can "cover such diverse thoughts," about life, art, imitation, and verisimilitude, that we have been cogitating in the past several chapters. But art's ability to imitate the immense diversity of human and natural life is surely the starting point for this discussion; I believe that, with the reference to the "single roof," Machado is suggesting that, of all the imitative modes, it is language, and specifically the art of narrative, that is most successful in reproducing the full, ever metamorphosing nature of reality. Painting, sculpture, music, and the others all have their strengths, but it is language, Machado and Ayres here seem to be declaring, that is best able to provide the single, imitative "roof" for the endless vagaries of human existence. As critic Elizabeth A. Drew observes, "All literary art is . . . 'impure' compared with the arts like painting or music; the latter are more removed from the actualities of human experience since they do not have to use speech as their sense medium—the medium in which we carry on our everyday living. But first among all the impure arts, the novel is the most impure. . . . The novel" concerns itself "directly" with the ever fluctuating "the emotional and moral standards," the confusion, and the turmoil that inform our lives and that "beset us every day."[14] That it possesses a semantic productivity capable of doing this constitutes the great strength of language as an imitative mode.

Forging ahead with his musings, Ayes, the narrator, then, again seeming to refer to the power of art to capture the diversity of the human experience, avers that "it is the same with the sky, whether it is clear or clouded—a vast roof that covers a multitude of them," "a vast roof" being an image that we may think of as our potentially infinite slate of "interpretations," "with the same zeal" (*EJ*, 233). "And then," he adds, as if we had missed his point, "do not forget the human skull either, which," as is notably true of language as an imitative medium, "also houses thoughts, not only diverse ones, but even contradictory ones" (*EJ*, 233). How all of this sometimes formless and chaotic language use fits together our narrator says he does not know, adding, a few lines later, all these "words" always seem to lead to different "alternatives" and different reactions, which is precisely what language use does (*EJ*, 234).

This same line of thought, how art can make life seem manageable, more attractive, and more comprehensible, chapter 109, which puts us in the cemetery, close to Flora's fresh dug grave, sees the narrator telling us, "The cemetery had an air almost of gaiety, with its wreaths of flowers, bas reliefs, busts, and the whiteness of the marble and lime. Compared with the fresh grave, *it seemed a rebirth of life* that had been forgotten here in a corner of the city" (*EJ*, 264, emphasis mine). Art, the reader is led to feel, can achieve vitality and the re-creation of life itself. After saying some "special words," the narration here has converted itself into a life-affirming art form, one brought to life through the imitative force of language, which, for all its instability and uncertainty, can, under certain circumstances, achieve the kind of elevated verisimilitude that Aristotle expected from art. From the reader's perspective, this remarkable scene truly does seem "*a rebirth of life*," and it is the art of narrative imitation that carries it forward.

6 • COUNSELOR AYRES' MEMORIAL

Published in 1908, a few months before the author's death, *Counselor Ayres' Memorial* was striking out on a new track with regard to Machado de Assis's exploration of imitation by way of language and narrative. Several factors distinguish this final novel from the four that preceded it. First and foremost, there is his use of the diary form. As a subgenre within the Western narrative tradition (which Machado knew well), the diary imparts a strong sense of realism, or reality, to this particular text. But the reader must remember that it is not at any point a "real" diary; rather, it is a complete fiction, an illusion, as it were, one, however, that makes use of the conventions of the "real" diary to further its examination of narrative's ability to imitate human existence. Machado clues his reader in to this technical ploy on his part in the entry for September 30, 1888. As a consciously deployed literary device, which is how Machado makes use of it here, the diary thus offers a particular illusion of reality, one in which seemingly confidential or private ruminations are being constantly accessed by the reader, who can feel she is now privy to a special kind of verisimilitude. In this final text, then, we see once again how important the question of genre—and the expectations, on both writer and reader, that come with it—becomes a major part of Machado's experimentation here. Second, there is the complex relationship that exists between this text and its predecessor, *Esau and Jacob*. Machado brings this up in his prefaces to both *Esau and Jacob* and *Counselor Ayres' Memorial*, and while the earlier of these is longer and more opaque, the second is short and much more canny, suggesting that in this last novel Machado knows exactly what tact he wants to take in his exploration of narrative and its imitative capabilities. And while many commentators have concluded, not without reason, that when Machado speaks here of the "single theme" that "ties together" the pages of this physically slight but intellectually rich text, he is speaking of the restorative power of love, I believe he is simultaneously speaking about something else as well—how language helps us both envision and erect our human institutions and our human relationships and how it shows these to be an illusion, an illusion that guides our lives and that orders them but an illusion nevertheless (*CA*, 5).[1] And third, there is in it a sense of "optimism," "an aura of happy success" and of "wholeness," or unity achieved.[2]

This "wholeness," "oneness," or sense of unity, I believe, shows Machado coming full circle with his new thinking about language, narrative, and imitation. Whereas in 1880 and *The Posthumous Memoirs of Brás Cubas* the reader is confronted with a brilliant if fragmented narrative structure, *Counselor Ayres' Memorial* presents us with a demonstration of how the same theoretical divagations that guided the writing of *The Posthumous Memoirs* can, in fact, also produce unity. And while the text makes it painfully clear to us that this same unity, or sense of wholeness, may well be as fleeting as the language that expresses it, for a time, at least, it can create if not permanent, lasting unity, then at least the appearance of such. To put this another way, *Counselor Ayres' Memorial* shows us how the fluidity of language, the basis of so much of our human institutions and relationships, can achieve for us a hint of what we want in life. In this sense, the 1908 novel, Machado's last, provides the answer to the painful dilemma set up by *Quincas Borba*, the text that, also concerned with imitation by means of language, refused to give the reader the sense of artistic unity that she wanted. *Counselor Ayres' Memorial*, then, is a different take on this same theoretical problem, the one that I believe animates Machado's last five novels. In addition to demonstrating (and, through Ayres, commenting on) his "new narrative" and its essentially antirealistic techniques, this 1908 novel (and, the reader must remember, it *is* a novel) also discusses a host of such related topics as the nature of art and representation, style, verisimilitude, interpretation, self-conscious narrators, metafiction, the nature of metaphors, control (over a text's meanings), time (which had played such a profound role in *Esau and Jacob*), structure, meaning, and the deeply interactive roles of both the narrator and the reader. It is, in short, a commentary on narrative art, a point touched upon in the entry for January 25, 1888. Here, Ayres, discussing how the ravages of time have not dimmed the beauty or charm of Dona Carmo, notes that her white hair, arranged with both *arte* (art; *CA*, 23) and *gosto* (taste, in the sense of good taste; *CA*, 23), marries, in its demonstration of proportion, harmony, and unity, all of the qualities of imitation that we take pleasure in viewing. And, the reader understands, it is language that allows her to know this, to feel it, and to begin to understand all that it means and that, under different circumstances, it might mean. In short, I believe this early reference to a single physical aspect of Dona Carmo's being speaks to the reader both as a concrete and verisimilar detail that creates her as a fictional character and as a ringing statement of why art is important and of what it can achieve. In terms of enunciating his new theory of narrative art, *Counselor Ayres' Memorial* can be thought of as Machado's richest and most complex novel.

The challenge to the reader to recognize and accept the revolutionary newness of what she is reading here appears in the entry for February 4, 1888, when, as if speaking directly to the reader, Ayres, the ostensible author of the diary we are reading, allows that one of his characters, Aguiar, had had, in his life, to "learn new ways," a point with which Machado's reader, aware, by now, of the new role she would have to play in Machado's "new narrative," would readily agree (*CA*, 25). As for Aristotle, change through time is, for Machado de Assis, a decisive aspect of human reality; as a writer, the question, for Machado, is: How can this fact, this most critical decentering and destabilizing fact about life, imitation, and reality, be most truthfully depicted in art?

A few days later, on April 7, 1888, Ayres continues this discussion, though coming at it from a different perspective, that of the artist who, keenly aware of the difference between reality and its imitation, seeks not falsity but truth. To do this, he employs, in the original Portuguese, the phrase "a mesma aparência de realidade" (the same appearance of reality; *CA*, 38), which clearly calls attention to the most venerable question about art that we have—how well, or how poorly, does it produce the "appearance of reality"? The phrase has its place in the context of what is going on in the diary/novel at this point, but it can also be taken (and, indeed, in this particular text and at this point in Machado's career, it all but demands to be so taken) as another statement on the nature of narrative art and its particular potency as an imitative mode. Musing over how he might best put into words a thought he has about some incident that has taken place concerning his characters, Ayres is acutely aware of not wanting to lose "the appearance of reality" in his narration (*CA*, 40). This concern then leads him directly into an amusing and self-conscious but decidedly nonrealistic dialogue with the paper he is writing on, one that speaks simultaneously both to the problems inherent in imitation by language and to the reader's responses to the language used. "Paper, dear foolscap," he writes, "do not gather up everything this idle pen writes," going on, then, to expand the metaphor into a short but pithy commentary on the strengths and pitfalls of practicing imitation by narrative (*CA*, 40). Though this is its first appearance in the novel, this narrative ploy, where Ayres, the narrator, his pen, and his paper all engage in a discussion of what they are doing and how the reader might respond to it, will later recur several times, becoming, in the process, a key motif of the text.

The short entry for June 15, 1888, which expands upon an issue, the problem of "improbability," that pops up toward the end of the previous day's entry, echoes the very same issue as taken up by Aristotle in *The Poetics*.[3] In reading what Ayres feels he needs to say about the veracity of the narrative he himself is writing, the reader can easily think, in fact, that Aristotle's own discussion of this issue was here exerting a direct influence on the words of Ayres (which, of course, are the words Machado, the real author, directs him to pronounce). Ayres begins his entry by writing something that reminds the reader of *Dom Casmurro* and the question of unexpected similarities: "There are in life unexpected symmetries" (*CA*, 59). Then, and all but inviting the reader to compare what he is doing to a well-known point made by Aristotle in *The Poetics*, he writes, "If this were a novel," which, of course, it is, albeit one draped in the diary form, "some critic would tax this agreement of occurrences with improbability; but long ago the poet said that truth at times can be improbable" (*CA*, 59).[4] These words come close to imitating those of Aristotle himself, who wrote, of how a writer must decide between "probable impossibilities versus unconvincing possibilities," that "poets should choose impossibilities which are probable rather than possibilities which are unconvincing."[5] For Machado de Assis, as for Aristotle's poet, "a convincing impossibility is preferable to an unconvincing possibility."[6] Machado and Ayres then end this embedded exercise in theoretical speculation about the nature of narrative imitation in the entry for June 16, 1888, and a return to the similarly theoretical discussion involving the narrator, his pen, his paper, and, of course, the reader. Centering now on the question of "artistic order," and how that of the music Fidelia plays so delightfully compares with that the reader receives from her reception of this narrative, Ayres opines, "Let this be confided to thee alone, dear paper, to whom I tell all that I think and all that I do not think" (*CA*, 60).

This important but, in classic late Machado fashion, slightly opaque statement is then followed, in short order, by the entry for June 30, 1888, which stands as the text's most distilled statement of Machado's sense of his own "new narrative," of its own imitative characteristics, and of the reader's role in it. Different here, however, is that this same entry also reveals the late Machado's new theory of narrative art. As laid out in the entry for June 30, this new theory, however, links up with and then expands on a comment made at the very end of the previous diary entry, that of June 27. There, and under the guise of discussing how individual priests give Mass, Ayres writes "each priest says Mass in his own regular style," a comment that parallels what each writer does in terms of how the story gets told and what the reader does with respect to how she interprets what she is reading (*CA*, 67). Moving on to a summary of the content and style of a letter "the widow Noronha" wrote to Dona Carmo, Ayres tells us that he had "proposed to find it interesting even before" he "read it" (*CA*, 67). Then, and as if he were describing the very text that he himself was writing and that we are reading, he proceeds to laud the style of the letter and the degree to which it was faithful to its subject and an authentic, or verisimilar, portrait of Dona Carmo's "soul," her core, or "real," identity (*CA*, 67). The letter, like the text we are reading, constitutes "a genuine page of her soul," one that, in its accuracy and truthfulness, awakens long-buried "memories" of how her life had been (*CA*, 67). Like Aristotle, defending poetry (and all art, including, we can deduce, that produced by creative writing as well) against Plato's charge that the poet is nothing more than "a mere imitator of appearances," Machado clearly understands the poet, or creative writer, to be a much more active and creative agent, one who, in truth, is both an "imitator *and* a creator."[7] And it is language, Machado seems to feel, that, as the medium of imitation, can best achieve the level of creativity *and creative engagement with the reader* that is required. "Nature's last boast is over and done with," Ayres writes here of the corrosive effects of time on physical beauty and its "appearances," adding, crucially, that now, as he is writing his diary/novel, "there are left only" his "aesthetic tendencies," "the power of conception and analysis," and the acumen and perceptivity of the reader (*CA*, 68). As this entry moves to its poignant conclusion, the power of art, and especially narrative art, to, as Aristotle would say, complete or perfect reality becomes more and more manifest.

This focus on what happens when narrative art imitates nature continues on in the entry for July 13, 1888, a year of momentous importance for Brazilians. Morphing into a discussion more focused on how, in the process of imitating something else, art becomes a form of reality itself, one replete with its own standards and criteria, this diary entry shows how one singular strength of narrative art is that it is not the passive and superficial imitator of the appearances of reality that Plato alleged that it was. Ayres and Machado show us here how and why it is that imitation by language, and specifically by narrative, more than painting, sculpture, and even music, can capture the ebb and flow through time of its subject while, at the same time, providing insight into the same subject's inner world of motivation and desire. A new imitative mode is also here introduced, the photograph, though Machado and Ayres view it as functioning within the older tradition of imitation by painting. A photograph of the Aguiars' grandson is framed and placed on display, and while, a function of its own technology, the photograph offers a newly verisimilar likeness of its subject, it is still seen, by the imaginative reader, to be superficial, that is, limited to its subject's exterior appearances, as these are, moreover, locked in time and place. Standing in sharp contrast to this new imitative technology (photography), imitation by narrative, which the text we are reading provides us a nuanced example of, which can go further and, given the nature of language, which works in more creative, semantically productively fashion, gets a sturdy defense in this entry.

The entry for July 28 ties all of this to questions of how time, memory, and desire affect imitation and meaning. Pondering the meaning of an event that had taken place when he was a boy, Ayres reminds his reader of how relative, how ephemeral meaning really is. "What significance," he writes, "do such incidents have now in this year of 1888?" (*CA*, 74). The reader well schooled in modern literary theory, might well see in this entry a justification of what is usually meant by the term "logocentrism," and if she did, she would not be incorrect. *Logos*, the Greek word for "word," "speech," or "discourse," and the spirit of rational ordering that accompanies these terms, has particular resonance for Machado de Assis, an artist who uses language as his preferred imitative medium precisely to demonstrate that such language structures as meanings, systems of belief, and efforts at communication are never as stable and as clear as we want them to be. They are constantly subject to change, and (important for my argument here about the nature of Machado's late novels) they are, in terms of their meanings, always functions not of some reality beyond them but of themselves as self-referential units.

The point Ayres is making here, however, about how meaning changes through time is true for everyone, but, in this particular case, with the year 1888 being referenced, his point is uniquely apt for his Brazilian readers, who would have known that 1888, the year abolition was achieved, was when everything changed in Brazil. Indeed, the very meaning of Brazil itself changed. The long-running stability of Brazil as a slave-based monarchy run by a small but powerful clutch of wealthy white male oligarchs was fast coming to an end. A new age was, in 1888, about to set in in Brazil, and the text that we read as *Counselor Ayres' Memorial* deals with the vast and profound changes that are already taking place. Two of these, as I have tried to show elsewhere, involve the emergence and emancipation of the new Brazilian woman and her growth as a productive citizen while the other relates to Machado's prescient view that white Brazilians had to be emancipated, too—from their old, conservative ideas about the legitimacy of enslaving both the black slaves and the women of Brazil.[8] Machado knew perfectly well that no modern society built on such reactionary ideas could long endure, and if Brazil was to progress successfully into becoming a democratic Republic, which it does in 1889, slavery in all its forms and manifestations would have to be done away with. A discussion of this very point pervades not only *Counselor Ayres' Memorial* (where the role of Fidelia, the main female character, greatly increases in terms of its symbolic importance), but its predecessor, *Esau and Jacob*, as well. And in both of them, the need to reform the nation and its culture finds its literary analog in the triumph of Machado's "new narrative." As if to reinforce not merely the importance of this momentous date to Brazilians but the certainty of change for everyone, Ayres concludes this section by writing, "Customs and institutions, like all else, pass away" (*CA*, 74). Time, the great catalyst of change, is an inherent strength of narrative and its ability to imitate it, a point we see continuously made in this generally optimistic but occasionally elegiac novel.

The issue of the photograph as a particularly verisimilar imitative form returns in the entry for August 21, 1888. Here, Ayres writes that Fidelia had recently had a photograph of her father, the implacable Baron of the Santa Pia plantation, and her beloved husband "placed in one frame and hung in the living room" (*CA*, 86). Though the two had been at odds in life, death—and art—would now unite them. And, in the photograph, no one would see the enmity that had kept them apart when they were alive, though it would be there in the language used by people, including Fidelia, who knew them. The two photographs are cropped and brought together into a new work of art, the representation of the two of them now together. Art has harmonized reality; balance and proportion have been achieved. The text, if it does not explicate this for us, does lead us to this conclusion; as Ayres looks at the newly produced picture of the two deceased men, whose long-running conflict he knew well, he sees both Fidelia's "delicacy" and "her present determination" to achieve in her art (and, we recall, Fidelia is a gifted musician) "the same spiritual harmony of her nature" (*CA*, 86). It is our human quest for precisely this kind of "harmony" that, while so often lacking in our lives, we find attainable in art, constitutes the core of this last of Machado's novels. And yet, when perceived through the medium of a different form of imitation, it is an illusion, since this newly established "harmony" could not have been seen in its tangled entirely in the photograph but only in the narrative that brings to life the hidden conflicts that lay behind the now apparent harmony. What we see, Machado is telling us, is not always all that is there. Thus it is that what happens in the entry for this date (a harmony is established through art) mirrors what happens in the novel as a whole, where time, language, and interpretation continue to change even what appears to be stable and harmonized. This, Machado would tell us, is the reality of life, and it is the basis of his new language-based Realism.

Calling our attention, metafictively, to "this diary of facts, impressions, and ideas," Ayres then informs us, in the following entry (August 24), that, invigorated now by engaging with language, he "cannot leave off writing the *Memorial*!" (*CA*, 87, emphasis original). Just as the playing of music will "resurrect" Fidelia and bring her back of the realm of the emotionally dead (her grieving for her deceased husband), so, too, does writing return Ayres to the land of the living. "Here I am," he tells us, "again with the pen in my hand. Truly, it gives a certain pleasure to pour out on paper things that want to come out of the head by way of memory and reflection" (*CA*, 87). By here reiterating the main reason Aristotle believed we humans like to imitate (because it gives us pleasure to do so),[9] Ayres gives us, in this final novel, an insight into Machado's new theory of narrative: while it seems to be true that "all is fleeting in this world," and that (like his "new narrative") a new "*Ecclesiastes* a la moderne" would show us this, it is nevertheless also true that narrative, as an imitative medium, can change;[10] and Machado has done this—he has given us a new kind of narrative, one that reflects the truths about language and one that therefore shows us that "everything is thus contradictory and unstable also" (*CA*, 88). It is, I contend, unlikely that a writer as meticulous as Machado de Assis would compose a text this way if he did not want his readers to consider how and why he writes as he does. In addition to underscoring the vicissitudes of life, and by referencing *Ecclesiastes* (along with the idea of "the modern"), Machado is also showing us once again his "new narrative" and how, in its constant demonstration of semantic instability, it contrasts with the old Realism. And by constantly reminding us of the importance of writing, Machado also reminds us that nothing is more fluid and changing than language, an awareness of which is the driving force behind his new theory of narrative.

Ayres follows up this short if profound discussion of the Machadoan "new narrative" by contrasting what it can do, as far as imitating nature and women and men in action with music, the force that will return life to Fidelia and an art form that keenly interested Machado de Assis and that appears regularly in his late novels. "How I still love music!," Ayres tells us in the entry for August 27 (*CA*, 89). Indeed, this entry basically amounts to a loving paean to music and all it represents (its ability to produce harmony, for example), to Machado, to his characters, and to Ayres, our narrator. It is Ayres himself who lets us know that "music was always one of my loves, and, if it were not for my dread of the poetic," which I take to be another of Machado's irony-drenched comparisons of music and literature as imitative forms (I say ironic because Machado had no "dread of the poetic"; far from it), he might well have been a musician, a point he himself ponders (*CA*, 89, 90–91). But this entry is less about Ayres than it is about Fidelia, who, we learn, begins to play Schumann and, in the process, resurrects not only herself but her entire household. Art, of the musical kind, reanimates her, and though the reader can only imagine what this is like, she can, and does, read about it in the text that is *Counselor Ayres' Memorial* (*CA*, 89–91). Little by little, the reader now begins to suspect, Machado is suggesting that, as different as they are (and most conspicuously so on the issue of harmony), music and literature are, perhaps, the two most evocative imitative forms.

The entry for September 12, 1888, puts music aside for a moment to show how we must not allow what is today called "binary thinking" to dominate our interpretive processes. Reality, and especially the realities of art, are not this simplistic, and to believe that they are is to result in misinterpretation and misunderstanding. The key to avoiding the pitfall of binary thinking, Ayres suggests to us, is reflection, and not quick judgment, and especially not the common kind of quick judgment that is based on superficial appearances. This recurring theme of how and why our thinking about a text (like the one we are reading) changes through time and through the lenses of the different interpretational stances that we may apply to it, emerges as a new feature of *Counselor Ayres' Memorial*. "Neither the one nor the other," Ayres tells us as he himself has led us to consider one of two ways to interpret a point he has just made (*CA*, 103). The truth is not this simple, and only the reader's careful and open-minded consideration will discern it. Offering us more angles on the issue he is writing about, Ayres then closes by saying, "Everything is possible under the sun—and above it for that matter," which implies that things are always more complex and tangled than they look, even in art, where, as with Fidelia's father and husband, conflicting forces can be harmonized (*CA*, 103). In this diary entry, the reader is led to feel that this is precisely what art does; it makes us think, and no imitative medium does so more successfully than language does. While painting, photography, and sculpture can all imitate at least the superficial forms of life, language can go further. Narrative art in particular can make us think even more than the reality can; while we tend too often to respond to what we think of as reality in ways that reflect our standing attitudes, ideological systems, and prejudices, the more perfect, more completed, and more selective nature of narrative imitation makes us think, and see, in new ways, ways that challenge our conventional ways of thinking, about life, art, existence, and meaning. And this is precisely what Machado's "new narrative" makes us do.

This current, this concern with the aesthetics of art, imitation, and the reproductive capabilities of painting, photography, music, and literature, reaches its climax in the entry for September 30, 1888. Ayres himself brings the issue to a head when he opens this section by asking us, albeit indirectly, to consider what we are reading and thinking about as we do. "If I were writing a novel, I would strike the pages of the September 12 and 22. A work of fiction would not permit such an equivalence of events," as, of course, being "improbable," and therefore unbelievable, in the sense that Aristotle speaks of this question.[11] "I would delete the two chapters," Ayres goes on to tell us, "or make them quite different from each other. In either case I would lessen the exact truth, which seems to me more useful for my present purpose," the writing of his diary, "than it would be in a work of imagination," that is, fiction (*CA*, 110–11). Machado and the reader know full well that Ayres *is* writing a novel, and, according to the argument I am making here, they also know (Machado more clearly than the reader, perhaps) that they are probing the limits of narrative's ability to tell the truth, to present a more verisimilar imitation of life than conventional Realism could. After he refers to the entries for these two days as "chapters," and after he asks his reader to consider the narrative without them, Machado is rather clearly asking his reader to think critically about the "new narrative" she is reading, about her role in it, and in the new aesthetics of semantic instability that inform it (*CA*, 111).

Ayres does not let go of this issue. Instead, he expands it, first by referring, self-consciously and metafictively, to something he had written earlier. "A number of pages back," he tells us, calling our attention to the very text, the very fictional text, we are reading and the nature of its own, peculiar verisimilitude,

> I spoke of the symmetries one finds in life. I cited the example of Osorio and Fidelia, both with sick fathers away from here, and both leaving here to go to them, each to his own. All this is repugnant to imaginary compositions, which demand variety, and even contradictions, in behavior. Life, on the other hand, is like that, a repetition of acts and gestures, as in receptions, meals, visits, and other amusements; in the matter of work it is the same thing. Events, no matter how much chance may weave and develop them, often occur at the same time and under the same circumstances; so it is with history and the rest. (*CA*, 111; see also *CA*, 88)

When Ayres then says, slyly and with a wink, I think, that he makes "these excuses" to himself so that he can more easily include a reference to his aching knee, which, in "another parallel of situations," is "exactly like Dona Carmo's," he is really inviting his reader to do what he is here doing: critiquing the difference between so-called "fiction" and the so-called "nonfiction" diary form and, along with "history and the rest," their abilities to represent the many and sundry "symmetries of life," which, along with their constant contradictions, Ayres and Machado contend, the old Realism could not abide. The reality of Machado's "new narrative" is that it can and it does, and so, being more realistic than its predecessor, it achieves a higher level of verisimilitude.

In the diary entry for February 2, 1889, the year the Brazilian Republic is formed, Ayres notes that while it may be "an illusion" on his part, he now perceives Fidelia differently (*CA*, 159). "Change," a word Ayres uses to describe what is going on, is again in the air, and in the telling—and receiving—of this tale (*CA*, 159). "I do not know how to put it," he says, self-consciously, of his ability to reproduce what he feels are his new perceptions and insights (*CA*, 159). Considering what he has previously written about this subject, he then says, "Back there, three weeks ago, on the 9th of the month, I wrote something, which in a certain fashion, explains and ties together the two states" (*CA*, 159; see also *CA*, 154 for another reference to the same issue, how narrative art imitates a changing reality by emphasizing its semantic mutability).

Stressing now, as his narration moves to its conclusion, this very point, Ayes begins, very subtly but in a way that clearly reflects how, in language use, words gain and lose meaning by referring to other words in the same structure, to show the essentially circular structure of his narrative. His tale, we can see, refers more and more to itself; it is its own point of reference. Then, by changing the focus to the role of the reader and her skill at interpreting what she is responding to, Ayres writes, "Let her read it," as another character, Mana Rita, may one day do, in reference to "this page," "and let her read also this confession that I make of her qualities as a lady and relative" (*CA*, 161). Albeit brief, this metaphor about the potency of reading shows what we have seen is a crucial aspect of Machado's "new narrative," its demonstration of how it is the act of reading, when applied to the product (a text, understood, once again, as *texte*, that is, in the sense that Barthes uses the term) that comes from the act of writing, that brings a text to life, and that imbues it with new and hitherto unconsidered meanings. The certainty that comes from the old Realism and its exemplary "works" has been supplanted, by Machado and his narrators, by uncertainty, undecidability, and ambiguity.[12]

By March 21, 1889, with change and problems of interpretation occurring on all fronts, Ayes tells us, frankly, "I will explain yesterday's text," which, it turns out (in what I take to be a clue to the reader), comes to involve a reference to the imitative force of narrative art (*CA*, 174). Ayes tells us, making reference to one of his characters, Dona Cesaria, that she was able to bring her potentially conflicted but nevertheless semantically rich words together "with such art that at times one thing appeared to be the other, and both the two combined," the latter serving as yet another example of the theme of unity, or harmony, that runs through the narrative (*CA*, 174; see also *CA*, 5 and Machado's "Foreword"). Only in language can this happen. Ayres follows this same thought by declaring, in the entry for March 25, that, in life as in this narrative, "Everything fits together and accommodates itself" albeit in "diversified" ways (*CA*, 175). In rapid fashion (his entry for

March 26), he follows up this revelation with another one of the same sort: "Now," changed by the passage of time and events, "many a thing slips away from me, many things get confused with one another, many are altered. . . . I am not sure whether I explain myself clearly, but it is enough that I understand" (*CA*, 176, 177).

And what is it that Ayres claims here that he understands? I believe it is this: that language, even as it can more or less accurately describe, in a verisimilar way, both the inner and outer aspects of human reality, cannot and will not pretend, as an imitative mode, to tell us the absolute truth. Indeed, it leads us to wonder whether, in the nonscience world (which is largely the human world of linguistically based institutions and systems of thought and belief), there is anything, any kind of external, objective truth, beyond language.

Linked, in the main, to the characters whose story Ayres is commenting on, the epistemological problem, how we claim to know things, deviates from this focus, as the text draws to its final entry, to make a close to naked commentary on Machado's "new narrative." The line that yanks the reader in this direction is couched in the context of her efforts to understand the meaning of Dona Fidelia's decision not to sell the plantation she inherited from her father. In the midst of a tangled but (for the careful reader) easily discernible process of interpretation involving Tristão, Fidelia, Dona Carmo, Ayres, and the reader, Ayres, our narrator, suddenly blurts out what he thinks is a witty "exclamation": "And critics fight over romanticism and naturalism!" a jarring declaration that has little or nothing to do with the discussion at hand (the giving of the plantation to the ex-slaves) but that most certainly could be taken as one of Machado's own, final statements of frustration with how he, his "new narrative," and his "new novel" have been received (that is, misunderstood) by the Brazilian literary establishment, which we know was engrossed in debates concerning this very question, the remnants of Romanticism and the new, fractious force of Naturalism in Brazilian letters (*CA*, 180).

Surprisingly, since the reader has been led to think something else was going to happen with the land, the buildings, and the former slaves (now free men and women) who still lived there, the first line of the entry for April 15, 1889, is this: "Santa-Pia is no longer up for sale, not for lack of buyers—on the contrary" (*CA*, 179). Once again, the reader, seeking to make order of things, is forced to deal with the surprising, unexpected, and unforeseen nature of life—and of Machado's "new narrative." Fidelia, the new Brazilian woman, is "not going to sell it," even though she could make a great deal of money by doing so (*CA*, 179). Instead, and much to the astonishment of everyone in the text (and perhaps to the reader herself), Fidelia, showing her newfound power and independence as well as her freedom from a thirst for money and from the constraints of patriarchal society, is going to give the plantation to the former slaves. Those who wish to will "work it for themselves" (*CA*, 180). This surprising decision leads Ayres to attempt to understand the meaning of Fidelia's action, and it is his effort to do this, to interpret (a word that stands out in this entry) what Fidelia has done, that dominates the end of the entry for April 15. Interpreting Fidelia's interpretation of Tristão contribution to her original plan (simply to give the plantation to the now free men and women to operate as their own), Ayres, who is told this by Dona Carmo, is now aware (as the reader may not be) that Tristão, a budding politician, is quite capable of "concealment" and of dissembling (*CA*, 180). On the other hand, Ayres muses, doing to Dona Carmo's interpretation exactly what the reader is doing to *his* words, it was also quite possible to interpret Tristão's advice to Fidelia as a sign that he did not want anyone to think that he, as husband, stood to enjoy financial gain from what might have been his wife's sale of the Santa Pia *fazenda* (a Brazilian plantation), either to buyers or to the bank. For the reader who either sees them or imagines them as possibilities, other possible readings emerge from this section of the text as well.

The point, as far as my argument is concerned, is that Machado is here, and elsewhere, deliberately writing a text that emphasizes its own openness and polysemy, its own sematic multiplicity. In a few brilliantly done pages, Machado sets up a multifaceted scene in which different characters are interpreting each other, while a narrator interprets them in the process of interpreting others and the reader, processing all of this in the text she is responding to and according to her own beliefs, attitudes, and experiences, generates her own possible interpretations, all of which, based on what the text tells her and what she can surmise about it and the mores of the time and place in which the novel's action is happening, are reasonable. Readings here mirror other readings, but each of them, functions of language and its natural state of "plurisignation," endlessly generates still other meanings.[13] Machado's text does not merely reflect the way language works, it embodies it, it exemplifies it. While all language use produces this effect, some texts do it more systematically than others, and it is this quality of language that, I contend, Machado so cannily exploits in his later novels.

But this open concern with interpretation, with how we read not merely words, as in this text or in the things people say, but in their actions as well, continues on in the entry for April 19, and the one for April 28. In this latter, very short, and cryptic entry, Ayres vents his doubts (which may well have echoed Machado's own doubts) about the efficacy of Fidelia's generous and humane but also not yet fully understood decision. The careful, involved reader, the kind of new reader that Machado spent so much time and trouble trying to create, gets a whiff of this additional uncertainty early in the entry for April 19, when Fidelia's husband, Tristão, lets it be known to Ayres that hitherto "secret motives" are involved (*CA*, 180). In literature as in life, things are never as they appear to be, nor even as we think they are. More is afoot here, though exactly what it is will remain a mystery. But of what can be seen and known leads Ayres, still struggling to decipher it all, to this conclusion, one itself dripping with uncertainty: "There goes Santa-Pia to the freedmen," he writes, ostensibly to himself, on April 28, 1889, "who will probably receive it with dances and with tears; but it also may be that this new, or first, responsibility. . . ." (*CA*, 181). The ellipsis, ever a technique Machado employs to engage his reader, is his. Or Ayres. Even that is in doubt.

This most basic of human desires, our desire to know and to understand, continues on as the novel/diary comes to its close. It is, in fact, the dominant motif of the final pages, and of the reader's response to them. In the entry for August 30, 1889, for example, Ayres is trying to explain a point he was making to Judge Campos, who, we are told, simply does not grasp what Aires is telling him, "neither at once nor completely" (*CA*, 195). While the paragraph in which this statement occurs starts out referring pretty clearly to the judge, by its end it seems to be speaking directly to the reader. Ayres, whom we can think of as Machado writing his "new narrative," tries once more, by adding more words, to explain. As if he were speaking of his reader, and not Campos, Ayres concludes, "He did not agree, which shows that he still did not understand me completely," an utterance that could easily be construed as Machado, a bit frustrated, lamenting, even in 1908, the still puzzled reaction of his readership, still addicted to the certainties of the old Realism, to his new theory of narrative. He does not succeed; more words do not explain the ambiguity already caused by other words.

But Ayres and Machado are not the only ones who must understand this; his reader, too, must also understand, though, responding to this and Machado's other late texts, she must also perceive and accept that literature, like life, is never static, eternal, and unchanging in its meaning. Yet we humans seek the unity of meaning in both life and in art, and while this is more elusive in real life, we can find it in art. And, indeed, it is art that has the final word in this, Machado's final novel. The old couple, Dona Carmo and Aguiar, are devastated by the departure of their two beloved young friends, Fidelia and Tristão, for Portugal, where the young man seems destined for a life in politics. Whether they are read as abandoning Brazil or not, their leaving plunges the two old people into near despair. They feel a keen sense of loss. Deciding, kindly, to go visit them and to try to cheer them up, Ayres enters their house and, seeing them sitting together on the back patio, stops. Then he quietly retreats and, undone by what he sees, leaves. This final scene, possibly the most poignant Machado ever wrote, is built around the twin problems of interpretation and knowing. The old couple were just sitting there, "gazing at each other" (*CA*, 196). "As I went through the gate into the street," writes Ayres, trying to understand what he had just seen, "I saw on their faces and in their attitude an expression for which I find no clear, exact name; but this is what I think it was. They wanted to laugh and be merry but they could do no more than console themselves—console themselves with the sweetly melancholy remembrance of their own love" (*CA*, 196). Ayres, the narrator and the supposed master of the words that make up this narrative, can do nothing more with it in terms of understanding the predicament of the old couple than the reader can by reading the same words. In life as in literature, interpretation, words trying to divine other words, is all.

On the basis of this particular conclusion for this particular narrative, I believe Machado would say, it is narrative art that allows us both to see this problem of instability and relativity and to assemble out of its "tatters" some semblance of meaning and coherence. Life, to put this another way, is very much like this narrative, but while life is typically messy and aleatory, and lacking in coherence, the self-conscious narrative that is *Counselor Ayres' Memorial* is ruled more by the "aesthetic truths" of art, and particularly those of narrative art, than it is by the "historical truths" that he also recognized and that were so very important to him. And these seemingly different realms are, in fact, connected by their dependence on language. Making this point repeatedly in *Counselor Ayres' Memorial*, and from its beginning to its end, Machado shows his reader that just as love makes life whole and harmonious, so, too, but in its own way, does narrative make an art form that is similarly, and simultaneously, whole, fluid, and harmonious, a harmony in which, as per the nature of language, disharmony also occurs but a kind of harmony nevertheless. The harmony of linguistic imitation, one might say, is the harmony of disharmony, a kind of endless settling and unsettling; or (as Machado might say if he had lived during the 1980s), a kind of endless construction and deconstruction. As a function of language, Ayres suggests to his reader, meaning *is* always relative, but this does not have to lead one to be despairing or nihilistic. It is simply a fact of life that we must recognize and come to terms with. We can, of course, and we do, but we must learn to do it much better. And with greater honesty. It is precisely this essentially positive point that drives Machado's "new narrative" and its essentially antirealistic modernity.

CONCLUSION

In the previous pages of this study, I have tried to show three things: one, that Machado de Assis, concerned with the venerable issues of imitation, verisimilitude, and literary art, invents Latin America's, the New World's, and the Western tradition's first "new narrative"; two, that, in its conceptual basis, this "new narrative" anticipates the linguistic breakthroughs achieved by Ferdinand de Saussure in the early years of the twentieth century; and, three, that Machado deserves to be regarded as a major theoretician of the modern novel form, in the Americas and globally. His sense of what a new, more language-based Realism would be like deserves a much greater audience than it has so far been given.[1] In making these arguments, I have sought to demonstrate that, for the Brazilian master, language is not, as it was for the traditional Realists, the frosting on the cake; it is, so to speak, the cake itself. It is what the modern literary artist needs to understand in order to properly interpret and imitate reality.

The reader who has paid close attention to the revolutionary critical thinking that begins with *The Posthumous Memoirs of Brás Cubas,* that spills immediately into *The Psychiatrist* and *Quincas Borba,* and that connects *Dom Casmurro, Esau and Jacob,* and *Counselor Ayres' Memorial,* by now realizes that multiple readings must be given these texts in order to fully grasp the enormity of their theoretical implications about the nature of narrative art, imitation, and reality. Indeed, about the nature of human life itself, in all its myriad contexts. As David T. Haberly (making reference to *Quincas Borba*) aptly puts it, in words that apply to all of Machado's late novels, even "those readings may fail to capture" what appears to be "an ultimately unknowable reality."[2] Machado, grasping the core dilemma of modernity (our sense of displacement) and linking it to how we use language to attempt to deal with this sobering situation, seems now to clearly understand that "our human vision of our own lives, of the lives of others, of the world in which we live, is vague, fragmentary, and formless—just a bit more complex, perhaps, than 'the ideas of a dog, a jumble of ideas' (Chapter XXVII)."[3] For the post-1878 Machado, "language is a profoundly mysterious technology so constitutive of the human mind that we can only get glimpses, from inside the fishbowl of consciousness, of how it works."[4] Inscribed in a new kind of thinking about language and given form in both a "new narrative" and a "new novel," this is the radically new kind of Realism that Machado de Assis offers us.

If one can accept the possibility that my thesis here might be an accurate assessment of what I argue is Machado's new theory about the nature of language and of its functioning as a system of signification and of imitation, then logical follow-up questions would be: Where did he get these new ideas? Did they simply appear, spontaneously, in his mind? Were they the product of years of thinking about language, writing, reading, and the novel form? Or could they have been the result of his lifetime of reading and by his catholic interests? Could his ideas, once beginning to gel in his mind, have been influenced by other authors, texts, or theoretical issues? All these possibilities are plausible. Like Jorge Luis Borges, Machado was a voracious reader, one who consumed not only an astonishing number of different authors and texts but an astonishing variety of them. He appears to have read everyone, other fiction writers, artists, historians, philosophers, religious scholars, and assorted thinkers, both classical and modern and both Western and non-Western. And it also appears that Machado, again like Borges (but many years in advance of the great Argentine writer), used all of his vast and varied reading as grist for his own creative mill. He absorbed what he read and then refashioned it, along with his own ideas, into a kind of narrative that was, at once, an amalgam of world literature and his own, unique prose, a kind of literary *texte* that was uniquely and unmistakably his. So, if what I take to be Machado's radically new theorizing about language, the novel form, and imitation is correct, it could have come from virtually anywhere, including his own restless, endlessly creative imagination. Issues of influence and reception, as they pertain to a writer of Machado's rank, are fascinating but notoriously difficult to pin down.

Nevertheless, there is one explanation of how the Brazilian master might have come to the focus on language that I contend controls his post-1878 narratives that deserves special consideration. Could Machado have come to his new thinking about language and its special relationship to reality because of his reading of, first, French symbolist poetry (and particularly that of Stéphane Mallarmé) and, second, the more socially conscious Brazilian symbolists, prominent among whom is João da Cruz e Sousa? The importance of Baudelaire, Rimbaud, Verlaine, and Mallarmé to Machado is obvious and goes without saying. But what about the influence of *Symbolisme* itself? Could the intellectual arguments and defining tenets that underlie Symbolism, in both France and Brazil, where, as in the case of Cruz e Sousa, it takes on a more socially conscious aspect but without compromising its more aesthetically defining qualities, have influenced Machado and his thinking about how his own theoretical divagations about language might manifest themselves and, consequently, what his "new narrative" would be like? I believe the answer is yes.

But what does this have to do with Symbolism? A great deal, I suggest. First of all, the fact that *Helena* openly experiments with the use of symbols in an otherwise realistic narrative suggests fairly strongly that Machado was, as a writer and an artist, keenly interested in the nature and function of symbolist verse. For the French symbolists, art, and specifically the art of poetry, was a way of reacting against the crudity and materialism of life. Their goal was to capture, via a certain kind of language use, a world beyond physical reality, an evanescent realm of music, color, artistic perfection, and harmony in which the inexpressible was evoked. But all of this was to be achieved by and through a new vision of poetry. As Mallarmé famously expressed it, the purpose, the raison d'être, of this new type of poetry was not to inform or to teach; it was, rather, to evoke and suggest, in the mind of the reader, new realms of existence and new ways of thinking and feeling. In symbolist poetry, it is the atmosphere created by language, and not the world of specific things, that is important. For the symbolists, language was no longer a mechanism by which the world could be specified, explained, or even imitated; it was a magic key that could open up new and hitherto unseen worlds and hitherto unexperienced thoughts and emotions. Language was able to transform what was thought of as everyday reality and, in its best moments, even create new, higher realities based on artistic unity and new demonstrations of linguistic self-sustenance, of the myriad ways words lead to more words.

This vital connection between Symbolism and language is all important, and Machado would have understood it immediately. In the world of symbolist poetry, language shows itself to be the link between what can be said and what, seemingly, cannot be said. It becomes, in the best symbolist poetry, the real subject of inquiry, and Machado, already interested in the power of the symbol and in the nature of narrative, would not have failed to see this. But, as I believe Machado clearly realized as he contemplated it, symbolist poetry also reveals how language really functions, how, as a self-contained and self-referential semantic system, it generates, in the mind of its reader, an infinite number of possible meanings. Aside from its efforts to touch the ineffable, symbolist poetry demonstrates how language itself is a living, breathing semiotic system. It is a system of symbols. This, I believe, is the more radical, and revolutionary, lesson that symbolist poetry revealed to Machado. And it is this that forms the basis for his "new narrative" and, more specifically, his "new novel." While we expect this in poetry, we do not, in 1880, expect it in narrative, which, as a genre, has, at this same time, long been associated more with the "real" world. For the symbolist poets, however, words were signs that pointed less to this same "real world" than to higher, more perfect forms of existence. From this, is it not unimaginable to speculate that Machado, armed now with a better understanding of the mysterious power of poetry and able to apply it to narrative, could have extended this interest to the realm of language itself and to its function as an imitative mode? And from this, he could have moved to a contemplation of how this new understanding of language would affect his sense of how his "new novel" would have to be written. Indeed, it is all but unimaginable that he would not have done so. The theoretical importance between symbolist poetry and Machado's creation of his "new narrative" cannot, I believe, be overestimated.

We know that Machado loved and admired poetry and that he wrote it his entire life. Indeed, his best poems appear in his final years, as do his best narratives, novels as well as short stories. And we know that much of his best, semantically richest fiction is driven by the conceits and techniques of poetry. His marvelous use of the metaphorical method is an example of this, as is the fact that, on page after page, his late narratives suggest much more than they say. They make their reader think about and reflect on a multitude of possible meanings very much as the best poetry does. In Machado's late novels and stories, a single word and its location relative to other words matters as it does in poetry. A poet himself, Machado knew full well what poetic language could do, the evocative power it has. His interest in symbolist poetry would have clinched the deal for him. It is not, therefore, impossible to imagine that, perhaps after he had completed *Helena*, a novel that, more than Machado had done before, aggressively cultivates the use of symbols, and after *Iaiá Garcia*, the last of his so-called early novels and the one that gives us at least a glimpse of the brilliant originality to come, Machado was beginning to formulate how he might successfully integrate the allusive power of poetry with the descriptive, storytelling power of narrative. The result, I believe Machado may well have envisioned, would be the creation of a new, hybrid genre, the "new narrative," a self-consciously figurative and poetically driven kind of fiction that, in 1880 and *The Posthumous Memoirs of Brás Cubas*, would blossom into his first "new novel." Although Verlaine's immensely influential *Art Poétique* did not appear until 1884, Machado, who knew and admired French literature, would surely have read it. Moreover, Machado would have been following the poetry of the French symbolist masters, all of whom produced much of their best work earlier, in the 1870s. And *Helena*, we remember, was published in 1876. Machado would not have needed Verlaine to explain to him what this new poetry was about or what the symbolist movement was seeking to achieve with its understanding of language usage. And he would not have needed Verlaine, or Mallarmé, to explain to him how the themes and techniques of symbolist poetry could be applied to narrative art.

In taking what I contend is this distinctly theoretical step (from the use of symbols in poetry to thinking about their function in narrative, his chosen mode of artistic representation), Machado almost certainly came to understand that language was not the clear, stable mechanism for representing the world that the realists had taken it to be. Language was something else, and it is this "something else" that Machado's later novels explore, albeit in ways that constantly remind the reader that for however much they and their novelistic structures are symbols communicating with other symbols, words also have very definite social and political functions as well. It is this latter quality that moves Machado's late prose fiction from the rather ethereal realm of the best symbolist poetry to the real world of men and women in action and that retains for it a powerful and knowable social context. The one quality (language's status as a figurative and symbolic system) does not, in Machado's world, cancel out the other quality (language's status as a communicative system that we human beings use to try to deal with our real human experience, in all its uncertainty and confusion); indeed, language exists for human beings in precisely this dual fashion.

We see this point being made as early as 1881–82 and *The Psychiatrist*, where the supposed certainty of science, or our perhaps unfounded confidence in it as a panacea for our problems, is contrasted to the semantically productive fluidity of language and interpretation. The trouble with the old Realism, I think the post-1879 Machado would say, is that it made us believe that language was something it was not (a perfect, perfectly transparent, and neutral medium of expression and communication), and that it could do something it could not, in fact, do (give us perfect knowledge and understanding). For the post-1878 Machado, when he declares, in effect, that while human reality is endlessly fascinating, Realism, that is, the old Realism, is an illusion, a misnomer, since, on the most basic ontological and epistemological levels of human existence, it is not realistic at all. Machado, I posit, intends his "new narrative" to remind us of how language really is, how it relates to the human condition, and how we, as readers and as citizens operating within the social, political, and economic systems that we ourselves create, must learn to understand its true nature.

In Machado's revolutionary view, language is never a neutral or transparent artistic medium; and it does not imitate nature in the ways that painting, sculpture, and music do. In contrast to these other modes of imitation, Machado I believe feels, language has a very special and unique relationship with the human mind, one that is deeply tangled in issues of human identity and that relates directly to the great and timeless questions about human existence: Who are we? Why are we here? How and why do we claim to know things, and to understand them? Why are we so easily mislead and deceived? Why do we so easily choose to mislead and deceive others? Why are we so prone to self-delusion? What are our motivations, and how do we deal with them? Why are we so prone to saying one thing and then doing another? Why do we love ourselves so ardently when it is clear that we need to love and care for others? In reading Machado de Assis, it is not difficult to understand why he is so widely hailed as a writer who is deeply philosophic in his concerns as well as one who is innovative in questions of technique and style but also cares deeply about the social and political lives of people, his characters, male and female, but also the people who read his poems, comedies, crônicas, stories, and novels. A brilliant innovator and iconoclast, Machado is no ivory tower dweller; he is very much a writer grounded in the politics of his time and place as well as an incisive commentator on the larger human condition. He is a writer for all times and all places.

For Machado, it is language that determines who and what we think we are; it determines how we seek to understand (and manipulate) the world around us, and how we seek to make sense of it all. And, because of its endless, and often offsetting, semantic productivity as regards the eternally changing questions of meaning and motivation, language is, inescapably, the source of the famous ambiguity that permeates his best work. Inevitably, there is "slippage" whenever we use language to deal with reality. Words, Machado had come to realize, are symbols, but reality (or, more specifically, physical reality) is not. But the sundry "realities" we use to define and order our human experience, "realities" such as the concepts (or, as Saussure would term them, the "signifieds") of truth, identity, honesty, clarity, and understanding, are all functions of language, of words/symbols speaking to other words/symbols. To have realized this about language has tremendous and far-reaching implications for all manner of human endeavor, from law and religion to politics and human relationships. Such an understanding about language even affects (and, one might venture to say, effects) our individual senses of identity. Indeed, few, if any, writers have ever revealed the core anxiety of modernity as tellingly as Machado de Assis. But, crucially for the argument I have made in the preceding pages, just as there is "slippage" in meaning between words, so, too, is there "slippage" between words and reality. This is the ground that Machado tills in his "new narrative," and it is the conceptual basis for what I argue is his new Realism as well.

This is also why the roles of both writing and reading are so consistently stressed in Machado's final six novels. For Machado, as for J. Hillis Miller and others, both writing and reading are "deconstructive" activities, and they need to be considered together, as the two sides of the same language coin.[5] This realization that language is not merely self-referential but self-interrogating is the core of Machado's new narrative theory, his "new narrative," and his "new novel," and all of these require a "new reader" to bring them to life. What we need to appreciate more in these texts is that "instead of seeking a resolution to the stresses," conflicts, and uncertainties that "are present within" them, they use "those stresses to explore the play of differences engendered."[6] Machado's post-1880 novels lead the reader, as they do the citizen, to get beyond our human desire for "resolution and to an awareness of the enigmatic openness of the text and of the reality to which it alludes."[7] His late, great novels "reject . . . (or transcend) the" conventional realistic "attitude that makes cohesiveness of structure and meaning a value in itself."[8] As in the case of Saussure's linguistics, in Machado's mature period there are only differences without positive value. Sobering though this may be, it is not nihilistic, for we humans do muddle along, in spite of the many problems our worlds of language cause us. The message Machado sends us is that we need to understand the nature of our situation and stop expecting it to give us something—perfect communication—that it cannot give us. His new, language-based Realism begins with this proposition.

Though it might at first seem more appropriate for a note or side bar, the question of deconstruction and its relevancy to Machado's late narratives and to the argument about them that I am making here is actually more logical than one might at first think. The issues inherent in the still divisive term "deconstruction" riled departments of English in the 1980s and 1990s much more than they did departments of foreign languages. And within departments of English, the same fractious "ism" tended to split professors of literature and professors of composition, or rhetoric.[9] Why this happened is a question that deserves more attention, and the answer is germane to the argument I am advancing in the current study. Perhaps it was partly because students and scholars who work in foreign language departments, like those who concentrate on composition and rhetoric, tend to study language very closely and as a system of thought, expression, and signification, one, moreover, whose idiosyncrasies have to be carefully studied and understood. Each and every word must be scrutinized and considered in and of itself and as a part of the larger structure in which it appears. And while in U.S. departments of English, at least, there occurred something of a schism between the literature people and the composition people, in language departments such rifts rarely rear their ugly heads. Perhaps this is because to study a language different from one's native tongue is to constantly remind oneself that language is an elusive, constantly evolving system of meaning, and this is true for both professors of foreign language literature and for professors of language; indeed, both work with the same materials, and both confront the very same problems. In foreign language departments, while there are legitimate concerns about such issues as salary difference and scheduling, rancorous splits between those who teach "language" and those who teach "literature" are far from common. For scholars who work with languages other than their own, these tasks are one in the same, and everyone recognizes this. Indeed, those who presume to teach "literature" are fully aware that they are, at the very same time, teaching "language" as well. And the reverse is also true. Professors of "literature" teach composition as a normal, routine part of their teaching duties. As far as the advent of deconstruction to foreign language departments is concerned, the typical response was, "Of course! Why would anyone be surprised by this? It's how language works."

In the case of departments of Spanish and Portuguese, which have historically been geared to French literature and French intellectual thought, discussions about deconstruction (which I believe is more usefully understood as poststructuralism) caused hardly a ripple. In his 1969 article on the special importance of language to the new novel of Brazil and Spanish America, Emir Rodríguez Monegal makes this point when he discusses the instantly warm and enthusiastic reception of Cuban author Severo Sarduy, who uses a "language which critically turns on itself, as happens with the French writers of the *Tel Quel* group," one with which Sarduy was himself very involved.[10]

But in contrast to departments of Spanish and Portuguese, where, after decades of such language-conscious writers as Machado de Assis, Mário de Andrade, Oswald de Andrade, Clarice Lispector, Guimarães Rosa, Borges, Cortázar, Lezama

Lima, and Sarduy, the concepts behind deconstruction and poststructuralism were easily received, the reception of deconstruction by U.S. English departments and their teachers of composition and rhetoric and their teachers of literature was, to say the least, conflicted. In many places it was quite fractious, and the discipline of English was itself seriously rent. The 1980s produced a spate of studies, by Barbara Johnson, Edward M. White, Mariolina Salvatori, and Nancy R. Comley and Robert Scholes, among many others, that sought to study the problem and, by finding common ground, reestablish a sense of comity and peace. One study, a 1985 collection of essays titled *Writing and Reading Differently*, edited by G. Douglas Atkins and Michael L. Johnson, was particularly successful at achieving this goal. As the editors write, the goal behind their efforts in putting this book together was "to bring together composition and literature, writing and reading, and the teaching of them, thereby 'bridging the gap' between them and displacing the either/or thinking that has too long dominated the pedagogy, especially of English, in secondary and postsecondary education."[11]

What struck me when I first read this book many years ago is this: The denying of "either/or" thinking, on the part of the reader, who is instead urged to take a more imaginative and participatory position about the multiple meanings inherent in what she is reading, is precisely what the later narratives of Machado de Assis do. And they do it, I maintain, by design, by intention. His writing, his "new narrative," demonstrates this page after page and novel after novel. For Machado, and for the other, later Latin American new novelists, it is "the reality of language," the "creative and even revolutionary role of language," that emerges as preeminent in their texts.[12] For modern Latin American novelists, led, first, by Machado de Assis and later by Borges, "the *form* of the book becomes what used to be called its *content*."[13] Although Machado de Assis was, apparently, not known by the scholars who wrote their fine essays for *Writing and Reading Differently*, he was, in 1880 Rio de Janeiro, not only writing the kind of texts they were concerned with but creating a reader who could appreciate it. Machado himself was reading and writing differently, and he wanted his reader to do the same. Indeed, he all but insists on it. When, decades later, Miller writes that reading and writing are close to being the same thing and involve the same issues, the deciphering and production of signs that are themselves part of still larger structures of similarly interlocking signs, these other, semantically ever expanding totalities are not separate sets "of nonlinguistic objects" but fields "of signs to be read," thought about, and written about, "which means to have more signs added to them," Machado would have been nodding his head in approval.[14] Like his U.S. colleague, Machado would have known, and already demonstrated, that "reading and writing are . . . intimately connected," as both actions require the interpretation of an endless supply of signs and symbols.[15] And Machado, who couched it all in serious political overtones, was making what, if we wished to do so, we could call his prototypically deconstructive narratives all seem perfectly normal and even funny, a surprisingly realistic view of human reality.

Hence the other thing that struck me when, back in 1985, I first read this excellent book: Had the contributors been better versed in the literature being produced "south of the border," in Spanish America and Brazil, they would have found numerous examples of the kind of writing and reading they were advocating. This is, after all, some twenty years after the Boom period. Only the essay of Andrew P. Debicki, a celebrated professor of Spanish, reminded the readers of *Writing and Reading Differently* that there was, on their geographical and cultural doorstep, a rich plethora of texts that had, and for a very long time, been engaging with the issues they link to deconstruction. Borges in the 1930s, yes, of course; but also Miguel Ángel Asturias and Clarice Lispector in the 1940s, Juan Rulfo and Guimarães Rosa in the 1950s, and, again, Clarice Lispector, Julio Cortázar, Carlos Fuentes, José Donoso, and José Lezama Lima in the 1960s. But preceding all of them was Brazil's Machado de Assis, whom Roberto González Echevarría, Enrique Pupo-Walker, and Haberly hail as "the first world-class" writer to come out of Latin America, with the great Sor Juana Inés de la Cruz being his "only worthy predecessor."[16] Indeed, Rodríguez Monegal's 1969 essay, titled "The New Latin American Novelists," discusses at length precisely the issues with which the contributors to Atkins and Johnson's book are concerned. "At the core" of Machado's new narrative and of these other new Latin American novels "stands the lucid conviction of the 'fictional'"[17]—Barbara Johnson and others would use the term "figurative"—"quality of all narration. They are, first and foremost, formidable verbal constructions."[18] Understanding this was the key to understanding the new Latin American novel. But it was Machado de Assis who, in Latin America, in the Americas generally, and perhaps in the Western tradition, was the first writer to explore a form of narrative that was "an attempt to interpret as exactly as possibly" (I would say as realistically as possible) "the oscillations in meaning produced by the irreducibly figurative nature of language."[19]

Why, the reader might well ask, am I bringing this up now? The answer is that the subject of my current study, Machado de Assis, still ranks as foremost among these new Latin American novelists. And readers outside the ken of Latin American literature need to know much more about the writers from Brazil and Spanish America, a point that González Echevarría argues in an important but not widely enough read 1990 essay titled "Latin American and Comparative Literatures."[20] The students and scholars of Spanish and Portuguese tend to be very well grounded in the authors of other Western literatures and in the latest theoretical fads and debates, but the opposite is still not true; students and scholars in other literature and language departments tend, even now, in 2017, not to be knowledgeable about writers working in Spanish and Portuguese. This needs to change.

Part of bringing that needed change about returns us to the question that opens this section. To wit, I am not interested in dredging up once again the pros and cons of deconstruction. Far from it. Enduring its rancorous but (from the perspective of foreign language departments) sometimes risible debate once was quite sufficient. I am, however, very much interested in arguing that, taken together, the late novels of Machado de Assis constitute a corpus of narratives that undertake what I believe is Western culture's first systematic exploration of what it would mean, as Atkins and Johnson put it, "to write and read differently."[21] And to do it in ways that, for both the writing and the reading, are eerily prescient, early harbingers of the reading and writing strategy known, decades later, as deconstruction. Whether one considers Machado to be a deconstructionist or not is, in my view, irrelevant; what matters is that we recognize the extraordinary originality of his post-1879 narratives and what he is seeking to accomplish with his new theories about narrative, art, and imitation.

But how does this discussion of deconstruction relate to the work of a late nineteenth- and early twentieth-century iconoclast from Brazil, a writer who, I contend, was very far in advance of his time in terms of his critical theory, his narrative techniques, and his demands on the reader? To answer this question, we do well to begin with the very distinctive nature of Machado's late narratives and the surprising extent to which, already in 1880, they epitomize certain key aspects of twentieth-century literary theory. In his essay "Machado and Modernism," Brazilian scholar Raúl Antelo sums up the nature of Machado's deliberately decentering new narrative: In this hitherto unseen kind of writing (and in the hitherto unseen kind of reading it would require), Machado's post-1880 texts show how "the enigma of the state (the aporia of reading) generates other enigmas that point out the verbal decomposition of truth, the perpetual ambivalence of texts, and even the secret of literature as a social institution."[22] In his distinction between "lisable" (or closed) texts and those that are "scriptable" (or open), those that engage themselves and the reader in the play of language and meaning, Roland Barthes provides us with an interpretative lens that allows us to better appreciate the radical newness of what Machado is doing between 1880 and 1908. My choice of the term "text" over the term "work" thus reflects my belief that Machado's last six novels epitomize Barthes's notion of the "scriptable," or semantically open narrative. What Machado was seeking, in 1878, when he rejected traditional Realism, had no name, no term, to describe it, but he clearly knew he wanted something different, something new. And while he might not have known what to call it (as Barthes would, some eighty years later), his vision of a new kind of narrative, one based on his new thinking about how language worked, how it signified, would create a new theory of narrative and a new novel to demonstrate it. In my view, and as I have tried to show, Machado's final novels are, in fact, not "works" at all but "texts," and in the sense that Barthes uses the term. By writing this new kind of narrative, Machado must have felt he was starting to capture the reality that was so fascinating to him and for which he, as a writer, elected to part company with traditional *Realismo*.

To paraphrase something Denis Donoghue once wrote about the difference between literary "works" and literary "texts," Machado's last six novels are "lavish" in their featuring of semantic plurality and ambiguity, as opposed to the ways the old Realism that Machado categorically rejects after 1878 is "parsimonious" in doing so, "because they are *ourselves writing*," reading, and thinking, "engaged in the play" of language and "the world."[23] Or, to put this another way, Machado's post-1878 novels exemplify, in my view, the basic distinction "between 'work,'" understood as "a static repository of set meanings," and "'text,'" understood as describing a "system of signs, the value of which can be open to question."[24] This is the turf that Machado works, and it is the main reason we regard him as such an eerily modern writer. He lays bare the modern malaise as well as anyone ever has. With the Machado de Assis of the late 1870s and early 1880s, narrative Realism is freed from being little more than a "frozen form," one that congeals into "stereotype" and the most unrealistic kind of supposedly realistic "literature," and allowed to come alive for the reader in the "licentious play of signifiers."[25] And, quite clearly, I think, Machado also insists that his reader learn to be cognizant of this process, as destabilizing and as decentering as it necessarily is.

Nearly all scholars who study Machado's work come to wonder about how to explain the extraordinary leap, in thinking and technique, that separates the pre-1880 novels from the post-1880 ones. While the seeds of the later ones are clearly there in the earlier ones, the leap from *Iaiá Garcia* (1878) and *The Posthumous Memoirs of Brás Cubas* (1880–81) is still difficult to explain. It remains, as Alfred J. Mac Adam and Flora H. Schiminovich write, "one of the mysteries of literary history."[26] I have sought, in the previous pages, to provide an answer to this long-standing question. My argument has been that, beginning in 1878, Machado the narrative theoretician determines to quit the old Realism and create, instead, not merely a "new narrative" but a "new novel" as well, one that is built around the nature of language. Between 1878 and 1906, he explores the various ways he might do this and the consequences, both aesthetic and political, that would stem from doing so. As I have sought to argue, Machado's decision to write "a radically different kind of prose fiction," one that flies "in the face of realism," is not merely a matter of style;[27] it deals with something much more ontologically and epistemologically important—the opaque and changing nature of human existence and our attempts to understand it. Machado's post-1878 novels do not so much deal, thematically, with this problem, they embody it. His texts, we might say, *are* the ambiguities they present. They exemplify them. Form and content have become one. And this, he seems to tell us, is the nature of life; we yearn, through language, to know, and to be sure of things, but we cannot.

And so, as Machado shows us, our lives are exercises in seeking to deal with this situation. In fusing the semantically fluid and productive nature of language with the ephemeral and inscrutable nature of human existence, Machado engages his reader with the modern condition, one that would later be further explored by such greats as Proust, Woolf, Kafka, and Borges. But it begins with the great Brazilian master and his iconoclastic thinking about language, meaning, and artistic reproduction. This is not, of course, a uniquely Brazilian problem; it is a human one, and a major part of Machado's enduring greatness is his ability to use Brazil, in all its tangled complexity and hope, as a metaphor for the human condition. It is not for nothing that Zephyr L. Frank describes Machado, who "apprenticed in the hothouse of the literary world of Rio de Janeiro" and who produced, beginning in 1880, several "unquestionable masterpiece novels," as "one of the marvels of world literature."[28]

As the harbinger of both our modern *malaise* and our ability (by means of our language use) to deal with it, Machado de Assis deserves greater respect, both within the European modernist tradition and globally. Machado's later novels and stories, as Franco Moretti writes, "train us without our being aware of it for the unending task of mediation and conciliation."[29] Machado and his "new narrative" do this, I would add, by means of their constant insistence on the need for careful, thoughtful interpretation and on the reader's active participation in the creation of the text's meaning. Neither the reader nor the modern woman or man can afford to be passive and disengaged any longer; ideas have to be evaluated and decisions, about literary texts and about the nature of the cultures in which we live, have to be made. By thinking about Machado's post-1878 narrative art and theory in this fashion, we can see more clearly that his "techniques and grasp of the social world are more attuned to those of contemporary literature than any of the nineteenth-century writers mentioned before. Not only does he usher in the twentieth-century, but in many ways he anticipates and even exhausts it. . . . Had he been born French or English," or, one might add, German, Russian, or Italian, "there is little doubt that his works would be prominently featured in the Western canon."[30] He should, now and henceforth, be so featured.

Machado's new theory of verisimilitude (that the truthful appearance of reality must derive from the truth about the nature of language as a self-aware and self-referential semiotic system and not from illusions about the stability and reproducibility of reality), thus forms, I believe, the basis of his new theory of narrative art and of the novel form in particular. His post-1878 writing cultivates, in the opinion of Gilberto Pinheiro Passos, the radically new concept of fiction being "overlaid by fiction," and producing, finally, a narrative art consciously built around interlocking structures of symbol, metaphor, irony, self-consciously, and illusion.[31] *Quincas Borba*, following hard on the heels of *The Psychiatrist*, is a powerful demonstration of this belief on Machado's part. To the extent that life is what we say it is, life becomes a "fiction," a structure of words, an illusion, a "sublime masquerade" (*QB*, 119). As such scholars as Araripe Júnior, Haberly, John Gledson, and others have maintained, Machado's evisceration of Brazil's desire to see itself as a modern and progressive Empire that would transform itself into a modern and progressive Republic stands as a case in point. Yet it is also true, as I believe Machado understood, if Brazil (or any nation) is ever to achieve such lofty goals, it will have to be through language use. Law, like literature, is a function of language, as is the world of politics and political persuasion. Because, as I argue, Machado came to realize between 1878 and 1881, language is a semantically fluid and constantly self-interrogating system of signification, so, too, must literature, a self-enclosed artistic form made up of language, in its status as art, also be. But, as I have indicated, the same is true of a nation's legal code and its sense of identity, whether political, social, or personal.

In Machado's view, what is true of language must, if one wishes to present life realistically, also be true of literature, as it must also be of social commentary. Even history requires interpretation, a point hurried over by Plato. Otherwise, the whole notion of Realism in narrative would be an illusion (as, I contend, the post-1878 Machado took the old Realism to be), an essentially false and misleading representation of reality, and the Machado de Assis of his last six novels is loath to do this, whether in terms of narrative theory and art or political analysis. Indeed, for the Machado of 1878 and afterward, and his famous rejection of traditional Realism in favor of the complexity of reality and the role language use plays in our perception of it, the old view of language as a "straightforward" and "referential" system was a *mirage*, an illusion that fosters self-delusion and that is foisted on readers and citizens by outmoded thinking about language, being, and meaning.[32] Every word that goes into the construction of a line of meaning sows the seeds of its denial or blunting by another word, and this, I believe, is the principle by which Machado's post-1880 novels are structured. Every line of interpretation that a reader might undertake is countered by another.

For Machado, I contend, this realization about language—that it is constantly destabilizing itself—constitutes the basis of his new theory of narrative. But it is also the theoretical basis for his also new theory of narrative art and its applicability not merely to the world of novels but to the real world of human beings. In life and in art, as I have argued, determinations have to be made. When George Steiner speaks of the "vital ambiguities of chimeric potentiality and undecidability" as the hallmarks of "natural language," he could be talking about the driving force behind Machado's new theory of narrative.[33] The "instability" of meaning "is perhaps the most telling of the evolutionary adaptations, of the reaching outward, that determine our humanity," and this is, in essence, the insight that Machado has during the late 1870s.[34] Whether we read him as a breathtakingly original literary artist or as an acute observer of our civic life and political systems, Machado's writing is best understood not as something static and absolute but as *écriture*, a kind of language use that stresses its own fluidity, self-referentiality, reader involvement, and semantic play; his deeply humane writing is thus not "separate from 'reality' but constitutive of it."[35]

Having arrived, by 1878 at this conclusion, Machado realized, I believe, that the only questions facing him as an artist who worked with words, as opposed to paint, marble, or sound, would be these: How can I create the new narrative that reflects these basic truths about language, imitation, and verisimilitude? What will it look like? How will it take shape? How will it work? And how can I create a new reader who, fully engaged in its process, can respond appropriately, that is, thoughtfully, to it? Beginning, in 1880, with *The Posthumous Memoirs of Brás Cubas,* his answers to these questions are to be found in the famous texts of his late, mature period. This is the argument I have made in this book. While it might be argued that in making my argument, and in seeking to allow the texts themselves to demonstrate it, I parse Machado's sentences too much, I would counter that this technique is the heart and soul of close reading, which is, indeed, the way I approach literary criticism. I prefer to let the texts speak for themselves. Machado's do, and they have a lot to tell us.

In defending my position (which some will find controversial), I find that I cannot resist taking the stance taken by Machado's first great narrator/protagonist, Brás Cubas (who, we remember, is, perhaps like me, fundamentally unreliable), as he addresses his potential readership in his novel's prologue: "The work itself is everything; if it pleases you, dear reader, I shall be well paid for the task; if it doesn't please you, I'll pay you with a snap of the fingers and goodbye."

ACKNOWLEDGMENTS

The author wishes to thank the many fine scholars, in Brazil, here in the States, and around the world, who have labored to bring the genius of their beloved author, Machado de Assis, to the attention of others. To the extent that this book helps secure Machado's rightful place in the canon of great world literature, it is due to your efforts.

NOTES

INTRODUCTION

1. I speak of his final six, and not final five, novels because I include in this classification a text, *The Psychiatrist* (1881–82), that some regard as a long story, while others see it as more of a novella. For my purposes, I consider it a short novel. Hence its inclusion here. For references in the text, see Machado de Assis, *The Psychiatrist and Other Stories,* trans. William L. Grossman and Helen Caldwell (Berkeley: University of California Press, 1963) (hereafter cited in text as *Psy*).

2. I use the term "text" quite deliberately in this study, and in the tradition established by Roland Barthes, who, by the late 1960s and early 1970s, had established a distinction between the concept of a "work," understood as a closed piece of writing that illustrates the nature of traditional literature (where the reader's job is to absorb and accept the information given her by the author), and "text," understood as an open, semantically productive piece of writing that demands the reader's active participation in the creation of meaning. Importantly, however, I argue that Machado's final six novels seek to give the illusion of being "works" even as, and quite subversively, they explore the new and hitherto unseen aesthetic, ontological, and epistemological realities that come from their being "texts." Machado's new and quite revolutionary thinking about language and its ability to reproduce human reality has consequences that are profoundly social, political, and aesthetic in nature. Machado's revolutionary theorizing, I maintain, about the role language plays in both narrative art and human discourse changes how we think about language and life, and for this he deserves much more recognition than he has so far received.

3. Roberto González Echevarría, ed., *The Oxford Book of Latin American Short Stories* (Oxford: Oxford University Press, 1997), 16, 95; see also Michael Wood, "Master among the Ruins," in *The Author as Plagiarist—The Case of Machado de Assis,* guest ed. João Cézar de Castro Rocha, Portuguese Literary & Cultural Studies 13/14 (Dartmouth, MA: Center for Portuguese Studies and Culture, the University of Massachusetts Dartmouth, 2005), 294; and Paul B. Dixon, ed., "Preliminary Note," Special Issue: "Machado de Assis: The Nation and the World," *Santa Barbara Portuguese Studies* 8 (2004): 10.

4. Alfred J. Mac Adam, *Textual Confrontations: Comparative Readings in Latin American Literature* (Chicago: University of Chicago Press, 1987), 22.

5. K. David Jackson, *Machado de Assis: A Literary Life* (New Haven, CT: Yale University Press, 2015).

6. While *Cratylus* considers the relationship between words and the things in the world, including ideas, it is in *Phaedrus* that Plato takes up the issue of how rhetoric impacts both writing and reading, two functions of language use that are crucial to the development of Machado's new theory of narrative art, imitation, and the reader's role in responding to them.

7. Aristotle, *The Poetics,* trans. Preston H. Epps (Chapel Hill: University of North Carolina Press, 1942), 3–4.

8. While Laurence Sterne's *Tristram Shandy* (1760–67) was undoubtedly an influence on Machado, the latter's understanding of self-reflexivity in language went much further, I believe, than that of the Irishman. Sterne served Machado less as a model to be emulated than as a springboard for more radical experimentations. For Machado, linguistic self-reflexivity went to the core of human consciousness and being, which, for him, made it a very different issue,

one that linked language to human existence. Hence, what I regard as the very distinctive nature of Machado's use of language and his constant serio-comic haranguing of the reader about how to respond to the plurality of meanings in his texts (this in contrast, for example, to Sterne's stated desire for "an uncritical reader"; see Elizabeth A. Drew, *The Novel: A Modern Guide to Fifteen English Masterpieces* [New York: Dell, 1963], 79). While *Tristram Shandy* is often judged, because of what for many is its stream-of-consciousness style, to be a precursor of such modernists as Woolf and Joyce, I maintain here that, because of his understanding of language, its semantic productivity, and its imitative capabilities, Machado and his later novels should be considered even more so. More than Sterne, for whom comic effect was a primary goal, "Machado de Assis wrote for profoundly literary reasons" (Jackson, *Machado de Assis*, 110; see also Drew, *Novel*, 75, 84, 88, 91, 94).

9. Fredric Jameson, *The Prison-House of Language: A Critical Account of Structuralism and Russian Formalism*, 2nd ed. (Princeton, NJ: Princeton University Press, 1972), 3.

10. Carlos Faraco, "Machado de Assis: Um Mundo Que Se Mostra Por Dentro E Se Esconde Por Fora," in *Memórias Póstumas de Brás Cubas*, 18th ed., by Machado de Assis (São Paulo: Série Bom Livro/Editôra Ática, 1992), 29, translation mine.

11. Chris Power, "A Brief Survey of the Short Story, Part 47: Machado de Assis," *Guardian*, March 1, 2013, 2, https://www.theguardian.com/books/booksblog/2013/mar/01/survey-short-story-machado.

12. Power, "Brief Survey," 2.

13. Such as the nature of literary verisimilitude; see Machado de Assis, "A Nova Geração" [The New Generation], in *Obra Completa*, ed. Afrânio Coutinho (Rio de Janeiro: Editôra José Aguilar, 1962), 3:825 (hereafter cited *OC*, by volume and page).

14. For more on Aristotle's views on the *dénouement*, see Aristotle, *Poetics*, 30.

15. Aristotle, *Poetics*, 11; see also 26–28; 30.

16. Earl E. Fitz, "The *Memórias Póstumas de Brás Cubas* as (Proto) Type of the Modernist Novel: A Problem in Literary History and Interpretation," *Latin American Literary Review* 18, no. 36 (July–December 1990): 7–25.

17. Helen Caldwell, *The Brazilian Othello of Machado de Assis: A Study of Dom Casmurro* (Berkeley: University of California Press, 1960), 165.

18. Brian Wilkie and James Hurt, eds., *Literature of the Western World* (New York: Macmillan, 1984), 2:2078.

19. Power, "Brief Survey," 3–4.

20. Assis, "O Punhal de Martinha"/"Martinha's Dagger," discussed in Roberto Schwarz, "Former Colonies: Local or Universal?," *Novel: A Forum on Fiction* 43, no. 1 (2010): 100–106. Although Nancy Armstrong and Warren Montag refer to the Machado text as a short story ("The Figure in the Carpet," *PMLA* 132, no. 3 [2017]: 613–19), it is not, although, as is often the case with Machado, it is very story-like; published August 5, 1894, it is one of his many *crônicas*, one that dates, I hasten to point out, from his later, or mature, period, which is the focus of the argument I am making in this book. The crônica is a nonfiction form, typically appearing in a newspaper and immensely popular in Brazil, even today, that deals with a wide range of topics, from art to politics. Armstrong and Montag, "Figure in the Carpet," 618; see also Zephyr L. Frank, *Reading Rio de Janeiro: Literature and Society in the Nineteenth Century* (Stanford, CA: Stanford University Press, 2016), 89–90.

21. Armstrong and Montag, "Figure in the Carpet," 618; see also Frank, *Reading Rio de Janeiro*, 183.

22. Wilkie and Hurt, *Literature of the Western World*, 2:2078.

23. Armstrong and Montag, "Figure in the Carpet," 618; Frank, *Reading Rio de Janeiro*, 85–86.

24. David Damrosch, *What Is World Literature?* (Princeton, NJ: Princeton University Press, 2003), 27; Héctor Hoyos, *Beyond Bolaño: The Global Latin American Novel* (New York: Columbia University Press, 2015), 88–89; Wilkie and Hurt, *Literature of the Western World,* 2:2078.

25. Wood, "Master among the Ruins," 297.

26. Pascale Casanova, *The World Republic of Literature,* trans. M. B. DeBevoise (Cambridge, MA: Harvard University Press, 2004).

27. Damrosch, *What Is World Literature?,* 5–6; Hoyos, *Beyond Bolaño,* 1–32; also Frank, *Reading Rio de Janeiro,* 1–19.

28. K. David Jackson, "Madness in a Tropical Manner," *New York Times Literary Supplement,* February 22, 1998, 15.

29. Emir Rodríguez Monegal, "Preface," in *The Borzoi Anthology of Latin American Literature,* ed. Emir Rodríguez Monegal and Thomas Colchie (New York: Knopf, 1984), 2:xiv; Mac Adam, *Textual Confrontations,* 20. See also Assis, "O Punhal de Martinha"/"Martinha's Dagger," discussed in Schwarz, "Former Colonies"; Roberto Schwarz, *A Master on the Periphery of Capitalism: Machado de Assis,* trans. John Gledson (Durham, NC: Duke University Press, 2001), 149–64; Roberto Schwarz, *Misplaced Ideas: Essays on Brazilian Culture,* ed. John Gledson (London: Verso Books, 1992), 1–32.

30. Roberto González Echevarría, "Latin American and Comparative Literatures," in *Comparative Cultural Studies and Latin America,* ed. Sophia A. McClennen and Earl E. Fitz (West Lafayette, IN: Purdue University Press, 2004), 89–104; Bill Ashcroft, Gareth Griffiths, and Helen Tiffin, *The Empire Writes Back: Theory and Practice in Post-colonial Literatures* (London: Routledge, 1989), 153–54; and Schwarz, "Former Colonies," 100–106.

31. Noting that "to love this book is to become a little less provincial about literature," Susan Sontag, recognizing "the relative neglect of Machado" as illustrating the marginalizing problem of "Eurocentric notions of world literature," also writes the she is "astonished that a writer of such greatness does not yet occupy the place he deserves" in the thinking of global literary scholars ("Afterlives: The Case of Machado de Assis," *New Yorker,* May 7, 1990, 108, 107, 107, https://www.newyorker.com/magazine/1990/05/07/afterlives-the-case-of-machado-de-assis; see also Sontag, "Foreword," in Assis, *Epitaph of a Small Winner,* trans. William L. Grossman [New York: Noonday Press, 1990], xi–xx).

32. Franco Moretti, *Distant Reading* (London: Verso Press, 2013); see also Assis, "O Punhal de Martinha"/"Martinha's Dagger," discussed in Schwarz, "Former Colonies"; Caldwell, *Brazilian Othello of Machado de Assis,* 165; and Jackson, *Machado de Assis,* 104–22.

33. Power, "Brief Survey," 1.

34. Sarah Lawall, ed., *Reading World Literature: Theory, History, Practice* (Austin: University of Texas Press, 1994); Damrosch, *What Is World Literature?*; Casanova, *World Republic of Literature*; Moretti, *Distant Reading*; and Hoyos, *Beyond Bolaño.*

35. Schwarz, *Master on the Periphery of Capitalism.*

36. Carlos Fuentes, *Machado de la Mancha* (México: Fondo de Cultura Económica, 2001).

37. Jorge de Sena, "Machado de Assis and His *Carioca* Quintet," trans. Isabel de Sena, *Latin American Literary Review* 14, no. 27 (January–June 1986): 9–18.

38. J. Hillis Miller, "The Two Rhetorics: George Eliot's *Bestiary,*" in *Writing and Reading Differently: The Deconstruction and the Teaching of Composition and Literature,* ed. G. Douglas Atkins and Michael L. Johnson (Lawrence: University Press of Kansas, 1985), 113.

39. Wood, "Master among the Ruins," 294–95; see also Hélio de Seixas Guimarães, "Fictionalization of the Reader in Machado de Assis' Novels," in Castro Rocha, *Author as Plagiarist,* 205–17.

40. Earl E. Fitz, "Machado de Assis' Reception and the Transformation of the Modern European Novel," in Castro Rocha, *Author as Plagiarist,* 43–57.

41. The need for this—for world literature studies to engage the historical, economic, and political contexts that inform the texts they seek to study—is a basic argument made by Casanova (*World Republic of Literature*, xiii).

42. Wood, "Master among the Ruins," 295.

43. Aristotle, *Poetics*, 2, 15.

44. Change, in fact, is omnipresent in Machado's last six novels. It plays a fundamental and multiform role in all of them, ranging from issues of time and the effects wrought by its passage to those of semantic instability and its impact on our ability to determine who and what we are, to create satisfying and rewarding relationships, and to build the many institutions of our social, political, and economic world. Machado's revolutionary thinking about linguistic change, and especially changes in meaning, anticipates that of Saussure, for whom the difference between the diachronic approach to language study and the synchronic is essential. In concentrating on *how language actually works*, in terms of the production of meaning, rather than concentrating only on how it evolves historically, Machado alters our view of how the modern novel would be written and read. For some very concrete examples of how important the concept of change is to Machado, see Machado de Assis, *The Posthumous Memoirs of Brás Cubas*, trans. Gregory Rabassa (Oxford: Oxford University Press, 1997), chap. 7 (hereafter cited as *BC*); Assis, *Dom Casmurro*, trans. Helen Caldwell, foreword by Elizabeth Hardwick (New York: Farrar, Straus and Giroux, 1991), chaps. 145 and 148 (hereafter cited *DC*); a novel in which time itself plays a fundamental role, Assis, *Esau and Jacob*, trans. Helen Caldwell (Berkeley: University of California Press, 1966), chap. 38 (hereafter cited as *EJ*); and Assis's final novel, *Counselor Ayres' Memorial*, trans. Helen Caldwell (Berkeley: University of California Press, 1972) (hereafter cited *CA*), in which a specific literary genre, the diary, is used to mark the flow of time and to explore the many consequences for narrative imitation that form produces.

45. Casanova, *World Republic of Literature*, xiii; see also Moretti, *Distant Reading*.

46. Aristotle *Poetics*, 39–48.

47. Hazard Adams, "Aristotle," in *Critical Theory since Plato*, rev. ed., ed. Adams (New York: Harcourt Brace Jovanovich, 1992), 49.

48. Erich Auerbach, *Mimesis: The Representation of Reality in Western Literature*, trans. Willard Trask (Garden City, NY: Doubleday, 1957), 489.

49. Auerbach, *Mimesis*, 487–88, 489–92.

50. Auerbach, *Mimesis*, 487.

51. Jackson, *Machado de Assis*, x; see also Raúl Antelo, "Machado and Modernism," in Castro Rocha, *Author as Plagiarist*, 143–60.

52. Auerbach, *Mimesis*, 488.

53. Auerbach, *Mimesis*, 489.

54. Mark Schorer, "Technique as Discovery," in *The Theory of the Novel*, ed. Philip Stevick (New York: Free Press, 1967), 66.

55. Jackson, *Machado de Assis*, 298.

56. Jackson, *Machado de Assis*, 6.

57. Raman Selden, *A Reader's Guide to Contemporary Literary Theory*, 2nd ed. (Lexington: University Press of Kentucky, 1989), 80, emphasis original.

58. Emir Rodríguez Monegal, "The New Latin American Novelists," in *The TriQuarterly Anthology of Contemporary Latin American Literature*, ed. José Donoso and William Henkin (New York: E. P. Dutton, 1969), 13.

59. Rodríguez Monegal, "New Latin American Novelists," 28.

60. Emir Rodríguez Monegal, *El Boom de la novela latinoamericana* (Caracas: Tiempo Nuevo, 1972).

61. Rodríguez Monegal, "New Latin American Novelists," 9.

62. Rodríguez Monegal, "New Latin American Novelists," 9.

63. Rodríguez Monegal, "New Latin American Novelists," 22.

64. Mariolina Salvatori, quoted by G. Douglas Atkins and Michael L. Johnson, "Introduction," in Atkins and Johnson, *Writing and Reading Differently*, 4.

65. Salvarori, quoted by Atkins and Johnson, "Introduction," 4.

66. Salvarori, quoted by Atkins and Johnson, "Introduction," 4.

67. Gregory Rabassa, "Osman Lins and Avalovara: The Shape and Shaping of the Novel," *World Literature Today* 53, no. 1 (Winter 1979): 35.

68. Echevarría, *Oxford Book of Latin American Short Stories*, 95; see also Wood, "Master among the Ruins," 295, 294–98.

69. Miller, "Two Rhetorics," 101.

70. Jackson, *Machado de Assis*, 3–58, 281–99; see also *Oxford Book*, ed. González Echevarría and Pupo-Walker, 95.

71. See also Guimarães, "Fictionalization of the Reader"; and Marisa Lajolo and Regina Zilberman, "Machado and the Cost of Reading," in Castro Rocha, *Author as Plagiarist*, 249–62.

72. Earl F. Fitz, *Machado de Assis* (Boston: Twayne/G. K. Hall, 1989), 2, 100–112; see also Jackson, *Machado de Assis*, x, xiv, xv, and 56–57.

73. J. G. Merquior, "The Brazilian and the Spanish American Literary Traditions: A Contrastive View," in *Cambridge History of Latin American Literature*, ed. Roberto González Echevarría and Enrique Pupo-Walker (Oxford: Cambridge University Press, 1996), 3:369.

74. Schorer, "Technique as Discovery," 67.

75. Schorer, "Technique as Discovery," 67.

76. Paul Northam, "Heuristics and Beyond: Deconstruction/Inspiration and the Teaching of Writing Invention," in Atkins and Johnson, *Writing and Reading Differently*, 118.

77. Robert Scholes and Robert L. Kellogg, *The Nature of Narrative* (New York: Oxford University Press, 1966), 84, emphasis original; see also Celso Favaretto, "The Misadventures of Unity: An Afterword," trans. David T. Haberly, in *Quincas Borba*, trans. Gregory Rabassa (Oxford: Oxford University Press, 1998), 280.

78. Auerbach, *Mimesis*, 486.

79. Helen Caldwell, *Machado de Assis: The Brazilian Master and His Novels* (Berkeley: University of California Press, 1970), 62.

80. Scholes and Kellogg, *Nature of Narrative*, 88.

81. For example, see the essays in Dixon, ed., Special Issue: "Machado de Assis: The Nation and the World," *Santa Barbara Portuguese Studies* 8 (2004): 9–11, esp. Regina Zilberman, "*Memórias Póstumas de Brás Cubas*: A Procura da História." See also Castro Rocha, *Author as Plagiarist*; and the essays of Maria Aparecida Ferreira de Andrade Salgueiro, "Machado de Assis: A Keen Look at Nineteenth-Century Brazilian Identity"; Christiane Costa, "Machado de Assis, the Apprentice Journalist"; and José Luís Jobim, "Machado de Assis and Nationalism: The *Americanas* Case."

82. Maria Luisa Nunes, *The Craft of an Absolute Winner: Characterization and Narratology in the Novels of Machado de Assis* (Westport, CT: Greenwood, 1983), x.

83. Afrânio Coutinho, *An Introduction to Literature in Brazil*, trans. Gregory Rabassa (New York: Columbia University Press, 1969), 245.

84. Ramón Xirau, *Octavio Paz: El sentido de la palabra* (México: J. Mortiz, 1970), 41, 52.

85. Gregory Rabassa, "A Comparative Look at the Literatures of Spanish America and Brazil: The Dangers of Deception," in *Ibero-American Letters in a Comparative Perspective*, ed. Wolodymyr T. Zyla and Wendell M. Aycock (Lubbock: Texas Tech University Press, 1978), 126; see also Mac Adam, *Textual Confrontations*, 17–18.

86. René Wellek, "The Concept of Realism in Literary Scholarship," in *Concepts of Criticism*, ed. Stephen G. Nichols Jr. (New Haven, CT: Yale University Press, 1963), 253.
87. M. H. Abrams, *A Glossary of Literary Terms*, 3rd ed. (New York: Holt, Rinehart and Winston, 1971), 141.
88. Wellek, "Concept of Realism," 223.
89. Wellek, "Concept of Realism," 254.
90. Wellek, "Concept of Realism," 255.
91. José Luiz Passos, "Realism and Moral Reasoning: An Analysis of Machado De Assis' Criticism of Eça de Queiroz," *Estudos Portugueses e Africanos* (Campinas) 36 (July–December 2000): 8, 11.
92. Passos, "Realism and Moral Reasoning," 11, 12.
93. Passos, "Realism and Moral Reasoning," 15.
94. Passos, "Realism and Moral Reasoning," 16.
95. Wellek, "Concept of Realism," 255.
96. Alexander Coleman, *Eça de Queirós and European Realism* (New York: New York University Press, 1980), 127.
97. Favaretto, "Misadventures of Unity," 275.
98. George Steiner, *After Babel: Aspects of Language and Translation* (Oxford: Oxford University Press, 1977), 233.
99. See also Caldwell, *Machado de Assis*, 106.
100. Ralph Freedman, *The Lyrical Novel* (Princeton, NJ: Princeton University Press, 1963). While Machado's "lyrical novel" exhibits nearly all of the defining characteristics of this genre that Freedman discusses in focusing on Woolf, Gide, and Mann, what is different in the Brazilian's case is his offsetting use of humor, the ways he couches serious themes in a comic mode. The result is that his later novels do not always seem, at first glance, as profound as they really are.
101. Louis Menand, "The Defense of Poetry," *New Yorker*, July 31, 2017, 69, https://www.newyorker.com/magazine/2017/07/31/can-poetry-change-your-life.
102. Menand, "Defense of Poetry," 69.
103. J. Hillis Miller, "Composition and Decomposition: Deconstruction and the Teaching of Writing," in *Composition and Literature: Bridging the Gap*, ed. Winifred Bryan Horner (Chicago: University of Chicago Press, 1983), 40.
104. Miller, "Composition and Decomposition," 43.
105. Mac Adam, *Textual Confrontations*, 12–13.
106. John Gledson, "Introduction," in Schwarz, *Misplaced Ideas*, xiv, xv.
107. Roberto Schwarz, cited by Gledson, "Introduction," xv.
108. Gledson, "Introduction," xv.
109. Mac Adam, *Textual Confrontations*, 21, see also 13.
110. With this distinction, Ferdinand de Saussure cautions us that while in language there are, indeed, only differences, linguists before him had taken it for granted that this concept of difference, as between different words within the larger Indo-European language system, was thought of in "positive terms," by which "the difference is set up" (*Course in General Linguistics*, trans. Wade Baskin [New York: McGraw-Hill, 1959], 120). What is revolutionary about Saussure's claim (still accepted by professional linguists today) that "in language there are only differences *without positive terms*" is that he understood that "whether we take the signified or the signifier, language," understood as *langue*, the system in which individual words (*parole*) appear "has neither ideas nor sounds that existed before the linguistic system, but only conceptual and phonic differences that have issued from the system" (120).

111. Adams, *Critical Theory since Plato*, 717; quotations from Dan Latimer, ed., *Contemporary Critical Theory* (New York: Harcourt Brace Jovanovich, 1989), 2; the *without positive terms* reference is from Saussure, *Course in General Linguistics*, 120.

112. Saussure, *Course in General Linguistics*, 2.

113. Earl E. Fitz, *Machado de Assis and Female Characterization: The Novels* (Lewisburg, PA: Bucknell University Press, 2015).

114. Selden, *Reader's Guide to Contemporary Literary Theory*, 102.

115. Adams, *Critical Theory since Plato*, 671.

116. Adams, *Critical Theory since Plato*, 671.

117. Adams, *Critical Theory since Plato*, 671.

118. Adams, *Critical Theory since Plato*, 671.

119. Favaretto, "Misadventures of Unity," 278.

120. Scholes and Kellogg, *Nature of Narrative*, 5.

121. Scholes and Kellogg, *Nature of Narrative*, 5.

122. Power, "Brief Survey," 3.

123. Wilkie and Hurt, *Literature of the Western World*, 2:1812.

124. Machado de Assis, *Quincas Borba*, trans. Gregory Rabassa (Oxford: Oxford University Press, 1998) (hereafter cited *QB*).

125. The problem of nullity can be traced to Saussure's famous assertion that, in language, there are only differences but *without positive terms*. Without positive terms to guide us, we are in danger of becoming lost, of not knowing what to think or what to do. As Machado's final novel shows, however, this absence of absolute, immutable meaning in words can be overcome by human beings who determine to make their own useful and productive meaning, to live their lives in ways that prove such positive meanings could, in fact, come from words. Machado's most memorable characters tend either to illustrate this or to show what happens if one simply gives in to the nihilistic impulse.

126. It is unclear whether Nietzsche himself ever used exactly this phrase. While he commonly makes use of the word *Gefängnis* in his writings, a search done by Vanderbilt University research librarian Ramona Romero turned up no instance where he links it with *Sprache*. Further investigation reveals that the term's first usage, in English at least, may be that of Fredric Jameson in his book *Prison-House of Language*. This influential study cites one of Nietzsche's epigrams where he seems to express the essence of what is now the famous term so often attributed to him, "the prison house of language." The epigram referred to by Jameson appears, in its English version, to be a somewhat imaginative translation of a line from *Der Wille zur Macht*. The line in question is as follows: "Wir hören auf zu denken, wenn wir es nicht in dem Sprach lichen Zwange thun wollen, wir langen gerade noch bei dem Zweifel an, hier eine Grenze als Grenze zu sehn" (Nietzsche, *Gesammelte Werke* [Munich: Musarion-Ausgabe, 1926–29], 19:34). The translation of this passage, presumably by Jameson (though this is not clearly indicated), reads, "We have to cease to think if we refuse to do it in the prison-house of language; for we cannot reach further than the doubt which asks whether the limit we see is really a limit" (*Prison-House of Language*, frontispiece).

127. Jameson, *Prison-House of Language*, 3, 101–216.

128. Adams, *Critical Theory since Plato*, 628; Vincent B. Leitch, *American Literary Criticism from the Thirties to the Eighties* (New York: Columbia University Press, 1988), 274.

129. Adams, *Critical Theory since Plato*, 638.

130. Fitz, *Machado de Assis and Female Characterization*.

131. Nietzsche, "Truth and Falsity in an Ultramoral Sense," quoted in Adams, *Critical Theory since Plato*, 638, emphasis original.

132. Steiner, *After Babel*, 176, 211.

133. Leitch, *American Literary Criticism*, 274, emphasis original.
134. See also Fitz, *Machado de Assis and Female Characterization*, 35n87.
135. Leitch, *American Literary Criticism*, 274.
136. González Echevarría, "Latin American and Comparative Literatures," 47–58.
137. While it is undoubtedly even now startling for some to think that a Brazilian writer, Machado de Assis, might have begun to explore this line of thinking before the German sage, or even as he was coming to it himself, there is no reason to think that it could not have happened. Indeed, as his post-1878 novels demonstrate, there is every reason, I contend, to think that it did happen, that his new theorizing about language, artistic imitation, and self-referentiality is precisely what distinguishes Machado's later novels.
138. Machado did enjoy some recognition in France, where his novel *Dom Casmurro* had been published by Garnier. One year after Machado's death, Anatole France saluted him in a speech the French critic presented on April 3, 1909, at the Sorbonne.
139. Translated into English as "mutable," the word in Portuguese is *modificável* (Assis, *OC*, 1:627).
140. Schopenhauer, who influenced Nietzsche, believed that the will, or desire, could never be satisfied, and so the human creature lived in a perpetual state of frustration and unhappiness. While Schopenhauer has long been linked to Machado as a possible source of the Brazilian's alleged "pessimism" (see Eugênio Gomes, "O Testamento Estético de Machado de Assis," in *OC*, 3:1097–120), I believe it is also possible to think that his best characters, and especially his best female characters, reject this position and, while not necessarily exemplifying Nietzsche's "will to power," do seek to live lives of meaning, personal integrity, and social, political, and economic justice. To succeed, as Alfred I. Bagby Jr. has argued, Machado's characters have to be strong and willing to fight for what they want in life (Bagby, "Introduction," in *Iaiá Garcia*, by Machado de Assis, trans. Albert I Bagby Jr. [Lexington: University Press of Kentucky, 1977], xx, see also n8).
141. Jameson, *Prison-House of Language*.
142. Jackson, *Machado de Assis*, 52–58.
143. Scholes and Kellogg, *Nature of Narrative*, 103.
144. Robert Con Davis and Ronald Schleifer, *Criticism and Culture: The Role of Critique in Modern Literary Theory* (Essex, UK: Longman, 1991), 127; Saussure, *Course in General Linguistics*, 16.
145. Davis and Schleifer, *Criticism and Culture*, 127.
146. Harry Levin, "Realism in Perspective," in *Approaches to the Novel: Materials for a Poetics*, rev. ed., ed. Robert Scholes (Scranton, PA: Chandler, 1966), 113.

CHAPTER 1. THE POSTHUMOUS MEMOIRS OF BRÁS CUBAS

1. Susan Sontag, "Foreword," in *Epitaph of a Small Winner*, by Machado de Assis, trans. William L. Grossman (New York: Noonday Press, 1990), xx.
2. K. David Jackson, *Machado de Assis: A Literary Life* (New Haven, CT: Yale University Press, 2015), ix-xv, 1–58.
3. For the reader interested in studying all of them, Machado's references to the "new narrative" he is beginning, with *The Posthumous Memoirs of Brás Cubas*, to write can be found in the following *BC* chaps.: 9, 14, 24, 27, 31, 34, 42, 55, 71, 72, 73, 86, 98, 124, 130, 136, 138, and 160. Some of these are more obvious than others, but, when taken as a whole, the reader can easily see a pattern developing, one in which Machado systematically seeks to educate his reader to the "new narrative" and "new novel" he is creating. If Machado were not seriously concerned with alerting his reader to what is new and different about the novel he is writing, he would not, I believe, have bothered to make so many references to it.

4. In suggesting that a discussion of his new theory of narrative art would be "interesting" but not necessary to its understanding or to its attractiveness, Brás Cubas anticipates what the great detective, Lönnrot, would later say about reality and artistic representation in the Borges "ficción," "Death and the Compass," namely, that while reality does not need to be interesting, our hypothesizing about it and what it means, does. So, too, Machado and Brás would say, does our artistic representation of reality have to be.

5. In Machado's original text, the line reads "eu não sou pròpriamente um autor defunto, mas um defunto autor" (*OC*, 1:511).

6. Jackson, *Machado de Assis*, 211; J. Hillis Miller, "Composition and Decomposition: Deconstruction and the Teaching of Writing," in *Composition and Literature: Bridging the Gap*, ed. Winifred Bryan Horner (Chicago: University of Chicago Press, 1983), 38–56.

7. There is an interesting translation issue that must be noted here. The original line in Portuguese reads, "o leitor, entretanto, não se refugia no livro, senão para escaper à vida" (*OC*, 1:619). The Grossman translation, which runs these two sentences together into a single sentence, goes like this: "To hop from a character study to an epitaph may be realistic and even commonplace, but the reader probably would not have taken refuge in this book if he had not wished to escape the realistic and commonplace" (*BC*, 180). Clearly, the Rabassa rendering hews closer to the original. See Machado de Assis, *Epitaph of a Small Winner*, trans. William L. Grossman (1952; New York: Noonday Press, 1990), 194.

8. René Wellek, "The Concept of Realism in Literary Scholarship," in *Concepts of Criticism*, ed. Stephen G. Nichols Jr. (New Haven, CT: Yale University Press, 1963), 255.

9. Celso Favaretto, "The Misadventures of Unity: An Afterword," trans. David T. Haberly, in *Quincas Borba*, trans. Gregory Rabassa (Oxford: Oxford University Press, 1998), 279.

10. In making this point, which a certain kind of reader will take to be couched in ironic humor, Quincas Borba contrasts what he argues is the changing nature of religious exaltation (a function of language) to the permanence of hunger, which (as a function of the human body) he views as "eternal, like life and like death" (*BC*, 186). The reader, of course, realizes that even hunger, and even hunger understood in this entirely corporeal sense, must also be interpreted and imbued with the kinds of meaning—its sociopolitical, religious, legal, and ethical import, for example—that only its consideration in language can deliver.

11. The reference to Pascal is not, of course, an idle one; nothing in the fictional world of Machado de Assis is. The French scientist and philosopher is remembered chiefly for having been concerned with the problem of knowledge and truth, and how these were, or were not, attainable through both science and religion. Pascal's conclusion was that truth was better recognized via religious revelation (and therefore by the particular form of language use this entails) than by science. Given that Quincas has already alluded to the mutability of religious "exaltation," and thereby undercut Pascal's position, it is easy to see why Machado, Brás, and Quincas all invoke the Frenchman to make their underlying point about the endlessly protean nature of meaning in language.

12. The term "birtherism" refers to a nonsensical, basically racist, and demonstrably untrue belief promulgated by President Donald J. Trump and some 70 to 80 percent of conservative Republican voters in the United States during the first two decades of the twenty-first century that former president Barack Obama was not born in the United States—when, in point of fact, he was born in Hawaii, as his official birth certificate clearly indicates.

13. Brás informs us that while he had once believed that the things and events of his life would mean one thing, he now sees that they really meant something else, something quite different from what he had earlier thought and expected. This misinterpretation is not lost on Machado's "new reader," who has been trained, thanks to Brás's constant hectoring, to be attuned to precisely this possibility.

14. George Steiner, *After Babel: Aspects of Language and Translation* (Oxford: Oxford University Press, 1977), 58.
15. Earl E. Fitz, *Machado de Assis and Female Characterization: The Novels* (Lewisburg, PA: Bucknell University Press, 2015), 15–17.
16. Gilberto Pinheiro Passos, "Afterword," translated by Barbara Jamison, in *The Posthumous Memoirs of Brás Cubas*, trans. Gregory Rabassa (Oxford: Oxford University Press, 1997), 212.

CHAPTER 2. THE PSYCHIATRIST

1. Hayden White, *Tropics of Discourse: Essays in Cultural Criticism* (Baltimore: Johns Hopkins University Press, 1978); and Jill Lepore, "Just the Facts, Ma'am: Fake Memoirs, Factual Fictions, and the History of History," *New Yorker*, March 24, 2008, 79–83, https://www.newyorker.com/magazine/2008/03/24/just-the-facts-maam.
2. J. Hillis Miller, "The Two Rhetorics: George Eliot's *Bestiary*," in *Writing and Reading Differently: The Deconstruction and the Teaching of Composition and Literature*, ed. G. Douglas Atkins and Michael L. Johnson (Lawrence: University Press of Kansas, 1985), 104.
3. Barbara Johnson, "Translator's Introduction," in *Dissemination*, by Jacques Derrida, trans. Barbara Johnson (Chicago: University of Chicago Press, 1981), xiii.
4. G. Douglas Atkins and Michael L. Johnson, "Introduction," in Atkins and Johnson, *Writing and Reading Differently*, 3.
5. A translation problem emerges here. While the original text uses the word *verossímil*, meaning "verisimilar," Grossman's English version omits it entirely, thus losing the impact of the term and its referencing of the act of imitation by language.
6. K. David Jackson, *Machado de Assis: A Literary Life* (New Haven, CT: Yale University Press, 2015), 213.
7. Atkins and Johnson, "Introduction," 3.
8. This is not as far-fetched as one might think. In January 2017, conservative Republicans and their spokespersons in the Trump White House are touting the use of what they praise as "alternative facts" in the production of their official policies and positions.
9. It is important to note here that, in the original Portuguese, it is *ilusão*, or illusion, and not "untrue." The Portuguese version of this text thus emphasizes more than the translation does the illusory aspect of language and its relationship to reality. It is also worth pointing out that Machado is here warning his readers about something that we, here in the United States of the twenty-first century, are experiencing nearly every day now: the proliferation of "false news" and false "alternative facts." While this is not much of a problem in the game of writing and reading fiction (indeed, there it makes for delicious fun), in the public arena where elections and political decisions matter, lying, deception, and the deliberate, systematic distortion of the facts are a much more serious matter, this being a point I believe would not have been lost on Machado de Assis.
10. The French anthropologist derived his thinking about human social structures directly from Saussure's structural linguistics. He believed, consequently, that things do not mean something in and of themselves but only through their myriad relationships with other things in the same society, or social structure. The conclusion reached in 1881 by Porfirio the barber, in a fictional narrative written by Machado de Assis, would seem to prefigure both Saussure and Lévi-Strauss.

CHAPTER 3. QUINCAS BORBA

1. This is, I believe it is fair to say, mostly because it makes use of a third-person point of view more than the novel that came before it, *The Posthumous Memoirs of Brás Cubas*, and the novel that comes after it, *Dom Casmurro*, both of which are built around articulate but deceptive first-person narrator/protagonists. Now, however, readers and critics of *Quincas Borba* agree that its narrator is at least as brilliantly and innovatively developed as are the narrators of these other novels.

2. Celso Favaretto, "The Misadventures of Unity: An Afterword," trans. David T. Haberly, in *Quincas Borba*, trans. Gregory Rabassa (Oxford: Oxford University Press, 1998), 275.

3. John Gledson, *Machado de Assis: Ficção e História* (Rio de Janeiro: Paz e Terra, 1968), 113; see also Maria Luisa Nunes, *The Craft of an Absolute Winner: Characterization and Narratology in the Novels of Machado de Assis* (Westport, CT: Greenwood, 1983), 14–16, 117–36.

4. It is on this point that Celso Favaretto cites John Gledson.

5. Favaretto, "Misadventures of Unity," 278.

6. David T. Haberly, "Introduction," in *Quincas Borba*, trans. Gregory Rabassa (Oxford: Oxford University Press, 1998), xxv.

7. Haberly, "Introduction," xxv.

8. Haberly, "Introduction," xxv.

9. Haberly, "Introduction," xxv.

10. Haberly, "Introduction," xxv.

11. Aristotle. *The Poetics*, trans. Preston H. Epps (Chapel Hill: University of North Carolina Press, 1942), 1–8, 15–18, 30.

12. Although I am loath to use academic jargon in trying to write about literary texts, I must say that, in this case, I do believe that what Machado is plumbing here comes very close to epitomizing the kind of text that Derrida has in mind when he coined the neologism *différance*, which is itself based on Derrida's thinking of Saussurean linguistics, where meaning reveals itself to be a matter of differences between signs but without positive terms. I also hasten to point out something that is nearly always forgotten when discussions of "deconstruction" take place: if Derrida is correct (and I have yet to see his theory refuted; objected to, yes, but not refuted), readers do not "deconstruct" texts; texts deconstruct themselves, and the reader merely takes note of this process and participates in it. The reader, then, responds to the text, a function of language, deconstructing itself. It is essentially for this reason that I consider Machado de Assis to be a poststructuralist without portfolio, that is, a writer whose best work exemplifies the basic tenets of poststructural thought but long before the term came into existence.

13. See Haberly's view in "Introduction," xix-xiv.

14. Favaretto, "Misadventures of Unity," 275.

15. Favaretto, "Misadventures of Unity," 276.

16. John C. Kinnear, "Machado de Assis: To Believe or Not to Believe," *Modern Language Review* 71, no. 1 (1976): 54–65.

17. This standing in sharp contrast to what Machado's narrator is doing in his narrative.

18. The reference to "method" reminds us of its similar usage in the "To the Reader" section of *The Posthumous Memoirs of Brás Cubas* as well as in chapter 1 and in the several other chapters of that book that were devoted to demonstrating how Machado's "new narrative" and "new novel" were taking form. My point in mentioning this is to underscore this most salient fact: for Machado the "new novelist," technique, "method," was everything.

19. I use the hyphenated term to emphasize how the process by which language constructs meaning is precisely the same one that, at the same instant, is giving birth to other forms of language use that undercut, undermine, or otherwise displace the efforts to construct meaning.

20. There is, of course, scientific truth, which is not, in 2016, highly regarded by conservative Republicans, but there is also the notion of truth in discourse and in human affairs, this being the terrain of the humanists. Machado, I feel, would have understood the difference—as well as the difficulty women and men of integrity and good will have in converting scientific truth into systems of understanding and belief that improve the human condition. This is where I believe it is useful to think of Machado's "new reader" as a kind of "new citizen" as well.
21. Earl E. Fitz, *Machado de Assis and Female Characterization: The Novels* (Lewisburg, PA: Bucknell University Press, 2015), 131–41.
22. Haberly, "Introduction," xiv–xvii.
23. As K. David Jackson notes, Machado was very interested in the idea of "human perfection" and whether it was possible to achieve or not, a point he elaborates in a crônica from *A Semana* dated February 26, 1893 (*Machado de Assis: A Literary Life* [New Haven, CT: Yale University Press, 2015], 215). Perfection in art was, of course, another, though not entirely unrelated, question, and one Machado wrestles with constantly after 1878.
24. In this sense, it is easy, for the comparatist who is also a Latin Americanist, to read *Quincas Borba*, and not Julio Cortázar's *Hopscotch* (1963), the English translation by Gregory Rabassa (New York: Random House, 1966), as Latin American literature's first "anti-novel."
25. Favaretto, "Misadventures of Unity," 285.
26. Favaretto, "Misadventures of Unity," 285; see, for example, chaps. 105 through 107.
27. Favaretto, "Misadventures of Unity," 285.

CHAPTER 4. DOM CASMURRO

1. Other than the ones I will discuss in the upcoming pages, here is a partial list of other chapters in *DC* in which the issues of imitation, resemblance, and verisimilitude appear: chaps. 2, 6, 17 (which also alludes, comically, to the act of interpretation and how Machado believes his critics had understood his "new narrative" to this point), 22, 25, 30, 31, 32, 34, 40, 45, 56, 62, 70, 71, 90, 92, 99, 116, 136, and 147.
2. Fábio Lucas, "Uma ambigüidade insolúvel," in *Dom Casmurro*, 39th ed. (São Paulo: Editôra Ática, 1971), 6.
3. In chapter 3, the reader is deftly lured into an active deciphering of the deluge of verbal signs, or words, that she has been assaulted with in chapter 2 by means of a series of sentences that end not with a period, or full stop, but by several ellipses, each of which functions as an invitation to the reader to think further and more carefully about the different, but related, topics that are here brought up. One of these open-ended sentences in particular seems clearly to reach out to the reader when one of the characters asks, making a question that the reader herself might well wish to ask here, "And am I to believe . . . ?" (*DC*, 8). The response to this very plausible question is similarly suggestive of the reader's response to this scene and, as we shall see, this entire text: "Brother Cosme, what do *you* think?" (*DC*, 8, emphasis original).
4. Aristotle, *The Poetics*, trans. Preston H. Epps (Chapel Hill: University of North Carolina Press, 1942), 5–6.
5. In accepting an argument made by someone else, our narrator here recalls what Brás Cubas did in *BC*, chapter 7 of his novel.
6. Michael Wood, "Master among the Ruins," in *The Author as Plagiarist—The Case of Machado de Assis*, guest ed. João Cézar de Castro Rocha, Portuguese Literary & Cultural Studies 13/14 (Dartmouth, MA: Center for Portuguese Studies and Culture, the University of Massachusetts Dartmouth, 2005), 299.
7. In 2017 and 2018, we are much concerned with what is termed "fake news," not the kind late-night comics promote openly as the basis of their shows and that they use to satirize the

events, empty posturings, and hypocrisies of the day but the more insidious kind, the deliberate and calculated promotion of lies, deceits, and false information that are intended not to amuse people but to fool them, to get them to believe (and thus vote in favor of) assertions and "facts" that are simply not true.

8. Paul B. Dixon, *Retired Dreams: Dom Casmurro, Myth and Modernity* (West Lafayette, IN: Purdue University Press, 1989), 1–13.

9. More pertinent, perhaps, to the plot of *Dom Casmurro* and the importance that the act of imitation plays in it is what else Aristotle says about why we like to view imitations of people and things: "mankind's pleasure in beholding likenesses of objects is due to this: as they contemplate reproductions of objects they find themselves gaining knowledge as they try to reason out what each thing is" (*Poetics*, 6). Just as the narrator, "Dom Casmurro," tries to "reason out" his life in an attempt to figure out who and what he is (or, perhaps, to expiate the guilt he feels late in life for the terrible things he did as a young man, things that may well have involved misinterpretations of the things happening around him and the needless suffering of others), so, too, does the reader do the same thing to the text that is *Dom Casmurro*. The question of "Dom Casmurro's" possible desire to be exonerated by his readers was first proposed by Helen Caldwell in her *The Brazilian Othello of Machado de Assis: A Study of Dom Casmurro* (Berkeley: University of California Press, 1960), 149.

10. Again, we have an example of how much this text stresses how, in art as in life, one thing can "seem" like another, the word "seem" becoming, finally, a basic motif of the novel and its structuring.

11. Some of the chapters in which the word "illusion" occurs are 2, 34, 126, 129, and 139, among others.

12. The words "Divine art!" are used twice, in rapid succession, and to emphasize the same point—the skill of the barber/artist/musician and the passion with which he plays his music (that of a violin), a passion that, as the chapter makes clear, goes beyond the appeal of money.

13. Lucas, "Uma ambigüidade insolúvel," 6.

14. J. Hillis Miller, "The Two Rhetorics: George Eliot's *Bestiary*," in *Writing and Reading Differently: The Deconstruction and the Teaching of Composition and Literature*, ed. G. Douglas Atkins and Michael L. Johnson (Lawrence: University Press of Kansas, 1985), 101, 102, 106–7.

15. This is because, for Machado, Bento carries within himself the natures of both Othello and Iago; he is, in a sense, both these characters.

16. As Caldwell has shown, the pernicious presence of Iago within Bento is evidenced, as a function of language, even in his name, Bento SantIAGO (*Brazilian Othello of Machado de Assis*, 11–61 and passim, emphasis mine).

CHAPTER 5. ESAU AND JACOB

1. Helen Caldwell, "Translator's Introduction," in *Counselor Ayres' Memorial*, by Machado de Assis, trans. Helen Caldwell (Berkeley: University of California Press, 1972), v.

2. Caldwell, "Translator's Introduction," vi.

3. Caldwell, "Translator's Introduction," vi.

4. Caldwell, "Translator's Introduction," xii, emphasis original.

5. As we have already seen, this same idea serves as the basis for Ferdinand de Saussure's linguistics, which the Swiss researcher is beginning to expound in his classes at about the time this novel is being published.

6. Caldwell, "Translator's Introduction," vii–viii.

7. Caldwell, "Translator's Introduction," ix.

8. It should be noted that, in Brazil, this distinction had already been questioned, if not obliterated, in Euclides da Cunha's seminal 1902 text *Os sertões*, translated as *Rebellion in the Backlands*, trans. Samuel Putnam (Chicago: University of Chicago Press, 1944).
9. Ayres has just suggested that the shop be renamed the *Confeitaria do Custodio*.
10. See also Idelber Avelar, "Machado de Assis on Popular Music: A Case for Cultural Studies in Nineteenth-Century Latin America," in *The Author as Plagiarist—The Case of Machado de Assis*, guest ed. João Cézar de Castro Rocha, Portuguese Literary & Cultural Studies 13/14 (Dartmouth, MA: Center for Portuguese Studies and Culture, the University of Massachusetts Dartmouth, 2005), 161–75.
11. See also Emir Rodríguez Monegal, "The New Latin American Novelists," in *The TriQuarterly Anthology of Contemporary Latin American Literature*, ed. José Donoso and William Henkin (New York: E. P. Dutton, 1969), 17–28.
12. In chapter 108, for example, which takes up the issue of Flora's death, we learn that a character named Nobrega (who, as a former suitor, is here cogitating about the lavish funeral he would have given Flora) "sketched in imagination the hearse, the most expensive horses, the coffin, an infinity of things that, by dint of inventing he made real" (*EJ*, 262).
13. G. Douglas Atkins and Michael L. Johnson, "Introduction," in *Writing and Reading Differently: The Deconstruction and the Teaching of Composition and Literature*, ed. Atkins and Johnson (Lawrence: University Press of Kansas, 1985), 2.
14. Elizabeth A. Drew, *The Novel: A Modern Guide to Fifteen English Masterpieces* (New York: Dell, 1963), 13.

CHAPTER 6. COUNSELOR AYRES' MEMORIAL

1. From the very last line of the preface to *Counselor Ayres' Memorial*, "The rest will appear some day, if some day comes" (*CA*, 5), it is also possible to think that Machado was already planning an additional novel.
2. Helen Caldwell, "Translator's Introduction," in *Counselor Ayres' Memorial*, by Machado de Assis, trans. Helen Caldwell (Berkeley: University of California Press, 1972), ix.
3. In the original Portuguese, which better illustrates Machado's concern with verisimilitude, the word is *inverosímil* (53).
4. Aristotle, *The Poetics*, trans. Preston H. Epps (Chapel Hill: University of North Carolina Press, 1942), 53, 56, 60.
5. Aristotle, *Poetics*, 53.
6. Aristotle, *Poetics*, 53.
7. Hazard Adams, "Aristotle," in *Critical Theory since Plato*, rev. ed., ed. Hazard Adams (New York: Harcourt Brace Jovanovich, 1992), 49, emphasis original.
8. Earl E. Fitz, *Machado de Assis and Female Characterization: The Novels* (Lewisburg, PA: Bucknell University Press, 2015), 1–36, and passim.
9. In the entry for September 21, 1888, Ayres once again suggests the power of pleasure that is connected to narrative imitation. Here, he writes about the irresistibility of "pure aesthetic pleasure," which, as in contemplating Machado's late novels, we always feel in the presence of superior art (*CA*, 109). See also Aristotle, *Poetics*, 5–6.
10. With respect to *Ecclesiastes* and its connections to Machado de Assis, William L. Grossman reports that an American nun, Sister M. John Berchmans Kocher, has written a doctoral dissertation that compares the two ("Introduction," in *The Psychiatrist and Other Stories*, by Machado de Assis, trans. Grossman and Caldwell [Berkeley: University of California Press, 1963], ix).
11. Aristotle, *Poetics*, 53, 60.

12. For more examples of this, and especially as these turn up as the narrative draws to its stopping point, its final entry (one that, not surprisingly, opens itself up to a number of possible readings), see *CA*, 167, 169, 171, 174, 176, 179, 180, 195, and 196.
13. C. Hugh Holman and William Harmon, eds., *A Handbook to Literature*, 6th ed. (New York: Collier Macmillan, 1992), 361–62.

CONCLUSION

1. K. David Jackson, *Machado de Assis: A Literary Life* (New Haven, CT: Yale University Press, 2015); and Paul B. Dixon, ed., "Preliminary Note," Special Issue: "Machado de Assis: The Nation and the World," *Santa Barbara Portuguese Studies* 8 (2004): 10.
2. David T. Haberly, "Introduction," in *Quincas Borba*, trans. Gregory Rabassa (Oxford: Oxford University Press, 1998), xxv.
3. Haberly, "Introduction," xxv–xxvi.
4. Louis Menand, "The Defense of Poetry," *New Yorker*, July 31, 2017, 64–69, https://www.newyorker.com/magazine/2017/07/31/can-poetry-change-your-life, 69.
5. J. Hillis Miller, "The Two Rhetorics: George Eliot's *Bestiary*," in *Writing and Reading Differently: The Deconstruction and the Teaching of Composition and Literature*, ed. G. Douglas Atkins and Michael L. Johnson (Lawrence: University Press of Kansas, 1985), 101.
6. Andrew P. Debicki, "New Criticisms and Deconstruction: Two Attitudes in Teaching Poetry," in Atkins and Johnson, *Writing and Reading Differently*, 178.
7. Debicki, "New Criticisms and Deconstruction," 178.
8. Debicki, "New Criticisms and Deconstruction," 178.
9. Today, it appears that, even in English departments, the positions taken by the deconstructionists have emerged victorious. For some, the victory can be judged to be pyrrhic in nature but a victory it does seem to be. More and more people, from literature and language, of course, but also from politics to history and from economics to anthropology, are coming to grips with the fact that our societies are built around words and what we want them to mean. The concept of meaning turns out to be much more slippery and relative than we had long thought. This realization has shaken the confidence of many. Words matter, and we use them to create our lives and social institutions, but today we accept that they are much less stable, in terms of what we want them to mean, than we used to believe. Words lead us not to certainty but to more words. This truism has consequences in all aspects of life. Historian Deborah Cohen, for example, writes that "like the best writers working in a biographical vein (many of whom eschew the conventions and certainties of biography)," Simon A. Goldhill, the author of *A Very Queer Family Indeed: Sex, Religion, and the Bensons in Victorian Britain* (Chicago: University of Chicago Press, 2017), "uses the inner conflicts of his subjects to immerse his readers in an unfamiliar and disorienting world" (41). Returning to my thesis here, I hasten to point out that what Professor Cohen describes here about what Mr. Goldhill does in his book is what Machado de Assis sought to do, between 1880 and 1908, in his novels. Machado's new, language-based Realism is more realistic, that is, a truer imitation of human existence, than the old Realism was.
10. Emir Rodríguez Monegal, "The New Latin American Novelists," in *The TriQuarterly Anthology of Contemporary Latin American Literature*, ed. José Donoso and William Henkin (New York: E. P. Dutton, 1969), 27.
11. G. Douglas Atkins and Michael L. Johnson, "Introduction," in Atkins and Johnson, *Writing and Reading Differently*, 3.
12. Rodríguez Monegal, "New Latin American Novelists," 13, 21.
13. Rodríguez Monegal, "New Latin American Novelists," 20, emphasis original.

14. J. Hillis Miller, "Composition and Decomposition: Deconstruction and the Teaching of Writing," in *Composition and Literature: Bridging the Gap*, ed. Winifred Bryan Horner (Chicago: University of Chicago Press, 1983), 41.
15. Miller, "Composition and Decomposition," 41.
16. Roberto González Echevarría et al., "Introduction," in *The Cambridge History of Latin American Literature*, vol. 3, *Brazilian Literature* (Cambridge: Cambridge University Press, 2008), 1.
17. Rodríguez Monegal, "New Latin American Novelists," 22, see also 23.
18. Rodríguez Monegal, "New Latin American Novelists," 22, see also 23.
19. J. Hillis Miller, "The Function of Rhetorical Study at the Present Time," Special Issue, *ADE Bulletin* 62 (September–November 1979): 13. My point is that it is this very quality, the "figurative nature of language," and its mining by the new novelists of Brazil and Spanish America, that Rodríguez Monegal is talking about in his 1969 essay. He uses different language, but this is his point. But it is also, I maintain, what Machado de Assis was exploring for the twenty-eight years between 1880 and 1908.
20. Roberto González Echevarría, "Latin American and Comparative Literatures," in *Comparative Cultural Studies and Latin America*, ed. Sophia A. McClennen and Earl E. Fitz (West Lafayette, IN: Purdue University Press, 2004), 89–104.
21. G. Douglas Atkins and Michael L. Johnson, "Introduction," in Atkins and Johnson, *Writing and Reading Differently*, 2.
22. Raúl Antelo, "Machado and Modernism," in *The Author as Plagiarist—The Case of Machado de Assis*, guest ed. João Cézar de Castro Rocha, Portuguese Literary & Cultural Studies 13/14 (Dartmouth, MA: Center for Portuguese Studies and Culture, the University of Massachusetts Dartmouth, 2005), 143.
23. Denis Donoghue, quoted in C. Hugh Holman and William Harmon, eds., *A Handbook to Literature*, 6th ed. (New York: Collier Macmillan, 1992), 475.
24. Debicki, "New Criticisms and Deconstruction," 170.
25. Vincent B. Leitch, "Deconstruction and Pedagogy," in Atkins and Johnson, *Writing and Reading Differently*, 19.
26. Alfred J. Mac Adam and Flora H. Schiminovich, "Latin American Literature in the Postmodern Era," in *The Postmodern Moment: A Handbook of Contemporary Innovation in the Arts*, ed. Stanley Trachtenberg (Westport, CT: Greenwood, 1985), 256.
27. Mac Adam and Schiminovich, "Latin American Literature in the Postmodern Era," 256.
28. Zephyr L. Frank, *Reading Rio de Janeiro: Literature and Society in the Nineteenth Century* (Stanford, CA: Stanford University Press, 2016), 43.
29. Franco Moretti, quoted in Frank, *Reading Rio de Janeiro*, 183.
30. Roberto González Echevarría, ed., *The Oxford Book of Latin American Short Stories* (Oxford: Oxford University Press, 1997), 16.
31. Gilberto Pinheiro Passos, "Afterword," trans. Barbara Jamison, in *The Posthumous Memoirs of Brás Cubas*, trans. Gregory Rabassa (Oxford: Oxford University Press, 1997), 206, 210.
32. Atkins and Johnson, "Introduction," 8.
33. George Steiner, *After Babel: Aspects of Language and Translation* (Oxford: Oxford University Press, 1977), 217.
34. Steiner, *After Babel*, 217.
35. Atkins and Johnson, "Introduction," 6.

BIBLIOGRAPHY

Abrams, M. H. *A Glossary of Literary Terms.* 3rd ed. New York: Holt, Rinehart and Winston, 1971.

Adams, Hazard. "Aristotle." In *Critical Theory since Plato,* rev. ed., edited by Hazard Adams, 49–50. New York: Harcourt Brace Jovanovich, 1992.

———. *Critical Theory since Plato.* Rev. ed. New York: Harcourt Brace Jovanovich, 1992.

Antelo, Raúl. "Machado and Modernism." In *The Author as Plagiarist—The Case of Machado de Assis,* guest edited by João Cézar de Castro Rocha, 143–60. Portuguese Literary & Cultural Studies 13/14. Dartmouth, MA: Center for Portuguese Studies and Culture, the University of Massachusetts Dartmouth, 2005.

Aristotle. *The Poetics.* Translated by Preston H. Epps. Chapel Hill: University of North Carolina Press, 1942.

Armstrong, Nancy, and Warren Montag. "The Figure in the Carpet." *PMLA* 132, no. 3 (2017): 613–19.

Ashcroft, Bill, Gareth Griffiths, and Helen Tiffin. *The Empire Writes Back: Theory and Practice in Post-colonial Literatures.* London: Routledge, 1989.

Assis, Machado de. *Counselor Ayres' Memorial.* Translated by Helen Caldwell. Berkeley: University of California Press, 1972.

———. *Dom Casmurro.* Translated by Helen Caldwell. Foreword by Elizabeth Hardwick. New York: Farrar, Straus and Giroux, 1991.

———. "Eça de Queirós: *O Primo Basílio.*" In *Obra Completa,* vol. 3, edited by Afrânio Coutinho, 903–13. Rio de Janeiro: Editôra José Aguilar, 1962.

———. *Epitaph of a Small Winner.* Translated by William L. Grossman. 1952. New York: Noonday Press, 1990.

———. *Esau and Jacob.* Translated by Helen Caldwell. Berkeley: University of California Press, 1966.

———. *Iaiá Garcia.* Translated by Albert I. Bagby Jr. Lexington: University Press of Kentucky, 1977.

———. *Memorial de Aires.* 2nd ed. São Paulo: Martin/Claret, 2003.

———. *Memórias Póstumas de Brás Cubas.* 18th ed. São Paulo: Série Bom Livro/Editôra Ática, 1992.

———. *Obra Completa.* 3 vols. Edited by Afrânio Coutinho. Rio de Janeiro: Editôra José Aguilar, 1962.

———. *The Posthumous Memoirs of Brás Cubas.* Translated by Gregory Rabassa. Oxford: Oxford University Press, 1997.

———. *The Psychiatrist and Other Stories.* Translated by William L. Grossman and Helen Caldwell. Berkeley: University of California Press, 1963.

———. *Quincas Borba.* Translated by Gregory Rabassa. Oxford: Oxford University Press, 1998.

Atkins, G. Douglas, and Michael L. Johnson. "Introduction." In *Writing and Reading Differently: The Deconstruction and the Teaching of Composition and Literature,* edited by G. Douglas Atkins and Michael L. Johnson, 1–14. Lawrence: University Press of Kansas, 1985.

Auerbach, Erich. *Mimesis: The Representation of Reality in Western Literature.* Translated by Willard Trask. Garden City, NY: Doubleday, 1957.

Avelar, Idelber. "Machado de Assis on Popular Music: A Case for Cultural Studies in Nineteenth-Century Latin America." In *The Author as Plagiarist—The Case of Machado de Assis*, guest edited by João Cézar de Castro Rocha, 161–75. Portuguese Literary & Cultural Studies 13/14. Dartmouth, MA: Center for Portuguese Studies and Culture, the University of Massachusetts Dartmouth, 2005.

Bagby, Albert I., Jr. "Introduction." In *Iaiá Garcia*, by Machado de Assis, translated by Albert I Bagby Jr., vii–xx. Lexington: University Press of Kentucky, 1977.

Barbieri, Ivo. "Under the Guise of Science." In *The Author as Plagiarist—The Case of Machado de Assis*, guest edited by João Cézar de Castro Rocha, 473–505. Portuguese Literary & Cultural Studies 13/14. Dartmouth, MA: Center for Portuguese Studies and Culture, the University of Massachusetts Dartmouth, 2005.

Caldwell, Helen. *The Brazilian Othello of Machado de Assis: A Study of Dom Casmurro*. Berkeley: University of California Press, 1960.

———. *Machado de Assis: The Brazilian Master and His Novels*. Berkeley: University of California Press, 1970.

———. "Translator's Introduction." In *Counselor Ayres' Memorial*, by Machado de Assis, translated by Helen Caldwell, v–ix. Berkeley: University of California Press, 1972.

Casanova, Pascale. *The World Republic of Literature*. Translated by M. B. DeBevoise. Cambridge, MA: Harvard University Press, 2004.

Castro Rocha, João Cézar de, guest ed. *The Author as Plagiarist—The Case of Machado de Assis*. Portuguese Literary & Cultural Studies 13/14. Dartmouth, MA: Center for Portuguese Studies and Culture, the University of Massachusetts Dartmouth, 2005.

Cohen, Deborah. "Before Straight and Gay: The Discreet, Disorienting Passions of the Victorian Era." *Atlantic Monthly* 319, no. 2 (March 2017): 40–42.

Coleman, Alexander. *Eça de Queirós and European Realism*. New York: New York University Press, 1980.

Comley, Nancy R., and Robert Scholes. "Literature, Composition, and the Structure of English." In *Composition and Literature: Bridging the Gap*, edited by Winifred Bryan Horner, 96–109. Chicago: University of Chicago Press, 1983.

Cortázar, Julio. *Hopscotch*. Translated by Gregory Rabassa. 1963. New York: Random House, 1966.

Coutinho, Afrânio. *An Introduction to Literature in Brazil*. Translated by Gregory Rabassa. New York: Columbia University Press, 1969.

Cunha, Euclides da. *Rebellion in the Backlands* [*Os sertões*, 1902]. Translated by Samuel Putnam. Chicago: University of Chicago Press, 1944.

Damrosch, David. *What Is World Literature?* Princeton, NJ: Princeton University Press, 2003.

Davis, Robert Con, and Ronald Schleifer. *Criticism and Culture: The Role of Critique in Modern Literary Theory*. Essex, UK: Longman, 1991.

Debicki, Andrew P. "New Criticisms and Deconstruction: Two Attitudes in Teaching Poetry." In *Writing and Reading Differently: The Deconstruction and the Teaching of Composition and Literature*, edited by G. Douglas Atkins and Michael L. Johnson, 169–84. Lawrence: University Press of Kansas, 1985.

Dixon, Paul B., ed. "Preliminary Note." Special Issue: "Machado de Assis: The Nation and the World." *Santa Barbara Portuguese Studies* 8 (2004): 9–11.

———. *Retired Dreams: Dom Casmurro, Myth and Modernity*. West Lafayette, IN: Purdue University Press, 1989.

Drew, Elizabeth A. *The Novel: A Modern Guide to Fifteen English Masterpieces*. New York: Dell, 1963.

Eliot, T. S. "Tradition and the Individual Talent." In *The Sacred Wood: Essays on Poetry and Criticism*, 47–59. London: Methuen, 1928.

Faraco, Carlos. "Machado de Assis: Um Mundo Que Se Mostra Por Dentro E Se Esconde Por Fora." In *Memórias Póstumas de Brás Cubas*, 18th ed., by Machado de Assis, 1–30. São Paulo: Série Bom Livro/Editôra Ática, 1992.

Favaretto, Celso. "The Misadventures of Unity: An Afterword." Translated by David T. Haberly. In *Quincas Borba*, translated by Gregory Rabassa, 273–90. Oxford: Oxford University Press, 1998.

Fitz, Earl E. *Machado de Assis*. Boston: Twayne/G. K. Hall, 1989.

———. *Machado de Assis and Female Characterization: The Novels*. Lewisburg, PA: Bucknell University Press, 2015.

———. "Machado de Assis' Reception and the Transformation of the Modern European Novel." In *The Author as Plagiarist—The Case of Machado de Assis*, guest edited by João Cézar de Castro Rocha, 43–57. Portuguese Literary & Cultural Studies 13/14. Dartmouth, MA: Center for Portuguese Studies and Culture, the University of Massachusetts Dartmouth, 2005.

———. "The *Memórias Póstumas de Brás Cubas* as (Proto) Type of the Modernist Novel: A Problem in Literary History and Interpretation." *Latin American Literary Review* 18, no. 36 (July–December 1990): 7–25.

Frank, Zephyr L. *Reading Rio de Janeiro: Literature and Society in the Nineteenth Century*. Stanford, CA: Stanford University Press, 2016.

Freedman, Ralph. *The Lyrical Novel*. Princeton, NJ: Princeton University Press, 1963.

Fuentes, Carlos. *Machado de la Mancha*. México: Fondo de Cultura Económica, 2001.

Gledson, John. *The Deceptive Realism of Machado de Assis: A Dissenting Interpretation of Dom Casmurro*. Liverpool: Francis Cairns, 1984.

———. "Introduction." In *Misplaced Ideas: Essays on Brazilian Culture*, by Roberto Schwarz, edited by John Gledson, ix–xix. London: Verso Books, 1992.

———. *Machado de Assis: Ficção e História*. Rio de Janeiro: Paz e Terra, 1968.

Goldhill, Simon. *A Very Queer Family Indeed: Sex, Religion, and the Bensons in Victorian Britain*. Chicago: University of Chicago Press, 2017.

Gomes, Eugênio. "O Testamento Estético de Machado de Assis." In *Obra Completa*, by Machado de Assis, vol. 3, edited by Afrânio Coutinho, 1097–120. Rio de Janeiro: Editôra José Agilar, 1962.

González Echevarría, Roberto. "Latin American and Comparative Literatures." In *Comparative Cultural Studies and Latin America*, edited by Sophia A. McClennen and Earl E. Fitz, 89–104. West Lafayette, IN: Purdue University Press, 2004.

———, ed. *The Oxford Book of Latin American Short Stories*. Oxford: Oxford University Press, 1997.

González Echevarría, Roberto, Enrique Pupo-Walker, and David Haberly, eds. "Introduction." In *The Cambridge History of Latin American Literature*. Vol. 3. *Brazilian Literature*, 1–10. Cambridge: Cambridge University Press, 2008.

Grossman, William L. "Introduction." In *The Psychiatrist and Other Stories*, by Machado de Assis, translated by William L. Grossman and Helen Caldwell, vii–x. Berkeley: University of California Press, 1963.

Guimarães, Hélio de Seixas. "Fictionalization of the Reader in Machado de Assis' Novels." In *The Author as Plagiarist—The Case of Machado de Assis*, guest edited by João Cézar de Castro Rocha, 205–17. Portuguese Literary & Cultural Studies 13/14. Dartmouth, MA: Center for Portuguese Studies and Culture, the University of Massachusetts Dartmouth, 2005.

Haberly, David T. "Introduction." In *Quincas Borba*, translated by Gregory Rabassa, xi–xxvi. Oxford: Oxford University Press, 1998.

Holman, C. Hugh, and William Harmon, eds. *A Handbook to Literature*. 6th ed. New York: Collier Macmillan, 1992.

Horner, Winifred Bryan, ed. *Composition and Literature: Bridging the Gap*. Chicago: University of Chicago Press, 1983.

Hoyos, Héctor. *Beyond Bolaño: The Global Latin American Novel*. New York: Columbia University Press, 2015.

Jackson, K. David. *Machado de Assis: A Literary Life*. New Haven, CT: Yale University Press, 2015.

———. "Madness in a Tropical Manner." *New York Times Literary Supplement*, February 22, 1998, 14–15.

Jameson, Fredric. *The Prison-House of Language: A Critical Account of Structuralism and Russian Formalism*. 2nd ed. Princeton, NJ: Princeton University Press, 1972.

Johnson, Barbara. *The Critical Difference: Essays in the Contemporary Rhetoric of Reading*. Baltimore: Johns Hopkins University Press, 1980.

———. "Translator's Introduction." In *Dissemination*, by Jacques Derrida, translated by Barbara Johnson, xiii. Chicago: University of Chicago Press, 1981.

Kinnear, John C. "Machado de Assis: To Believe or Not to Believe." *Modern Language Review* 71, no. 1 (1976): 54–65.

Lajolo, Marisa, and Regina Zilberman. "Machado and the Cost of Reading." In *The Author as Plagiarist—The Case of Machado de Assis*, guest edited by João Cézar de Castro Rocha, 249–62. Portuguese Literary & Cultural Studies 13/14. Dartmouth, MA: Center for Portuguese Studies and Culture, the University of Massachusetts Dartmouth, 2005.

Latimer, Dan, ed. *Contemporary Critical Theory*. New York: Harcourt Brace Jovanovich, 1989.

Lawall, Sarah, ed. *Reading World Literature: Theory, History, Practice*. Austin: University of Texas Press, 1994.

Leitch, Vincent B. *American Literary Criticism from the Thirties to the Eighties*. New York: Columbia University Press, 1988.

———. "Deconstruction and Pedagogy." In *Writing and Reading Differently: The Deconstruction and the Teaching of Composition and Literature*, edited by G. Douglas Atkins and Michael L. Johnson, 16–26. Lawrence: University of Kansas Press, 1985.

Lepore, Jill. "Just the Facts, Ma'am: Fake Memoirs, Factual Fictions, and the History of History." *New Yorker*, March 24, 2008, 79–83. https://www.newyorker.com/magazine/2008/03/24/just-the-facts-maam.

Levin, Harry. "Realism in Perspective." In *Approaches to the Novel: Materials for a Poetics*, rev. ed., edited by Robert Scholes, 101–20. Scranton, PA: Chandler, 1966.

Lucas, Fábio. "Uma ambigüidade insolúvel." In *Dom Casmurro*, 39th ed., 3–7. São Paulo: Editôra Ática, 1971.

Mac Adam, Alfred J. *Textual Confrontations: Comparative Readings in Latin American Literature*. Chicago: University of Chicago Press, 1987.

Mac Adam, Alfred J., and Flora H. Schiminovich. "Latin American Literature in the Postmodern Era." In *The Postmodern Moment: A Handbook of Contemporary Innovation in the Arts*, edited by Stanley Trachtenberg, 251–62. Westport, CT: Greenwood, 1985.

McLuhan, Marshall. *The Medium Is the Message*. London: Penguin, 1967.

Menand, Louis. "The Defense of Poetry." *New Yorker*, July 31, 2017, 64–69. https://www.newyorker.com/magazine/2017/07/31/can-poetry-change-your-life.

Merquior, J. G. "The Brazilian and the Spanish American Literary Traditions: A Contrastive View." In *Cambridge History of Latin American Literature*, vol. 3, edited by Roberto González Echevarría and Enrique Pupo-Walker. Oxford: Cambridge University Press, 1996.

Miller, J. Hillis. “Composition and Decomposition: Deconstruction and the Teaching of Writing.” In *Composition and Literature: Bridging the Gap*, edited by Winifred Bryan Horner, 35–56. Chicago: University of Chicago Press, 1983.

———. “The Function of Rhetorical Study at the Present Time.” Special Issue. *ADE Bulletin* 62 (September–November 1979): 10–18.

———. “The Two Rhetorics: George Eliot’s *Bestiary*.” In *Writing and Reading Differently: The Deconstruction and the Teaching of Composition and Literature*, edited by G. Douglas Atkins and Michael L. Johnson, 101–14. Lawrence: University Press of Kansas, 1985.

Moretti, Franco. *Distant Reading*. London: Verso Press, 2013.

Nietzsche, Friedrich. *Gesammelte Werke*. 23 vols. Munich: Musarion-Ausgabe, 1926–29.

Northam, Paul. “Heuristics and Beyond: Deconstruction/Inspiration and the Teaching of Writing Invention.” In *Writing and Reading Differently: The Deconstruction and the Teaching of Composition and Literature*, edited by G. Douglas Atkins and Michael L. Johnson, 115–28. Lawrence: University Press of Kansas, 1985.

Nunes, Maria Luisa. *The Craft of an Absolute Winner: Characterization and Narratology in the Novels of Machado de Assis*. Westport, CT: Greenwood, 1983.

Passos, Gilberto Pinheiro. “Afterword.” Translated by Barbara Jamison. In *The Posthumous Memoirs of Brás Cubas*, translated by Gregory Rabassa, 205–19. Oxford: Oxford University Press, 1997.

Passos, José Luiz. “Realism and Moral Reasoning: An Analysis of Machado de Assis’ Criticism of Eça de Queiroz.” *Estudos Portugueses e Africanos* (Campinas) 36 (July–December 2000): 5–20.

Power, Chris. “A Brief Survey of the Short Story, Part 47: Machado de Assis.” *Guardian*, March 1, 2013. https://www.theguardian.com/books/booksblog/2013/mar/01/survey-short-story-machado.

Rabassa, Gregory. “A Comparative Look at the Literatures of Spanish America and Brazil: The Dangers of Deception.” In *Ibero-American Letters in a Comparative Perspective*, edited by Wolodymyr T. Zyla and Wendell M. Aycock, 119–31. Lubbock: Texas Tech University Press, 1978.

———. “Osman Lins and Avalovara: The Shape and Shaping of the Novel.” *World Literature Today* 53, no. 1 (Winter 1979): 30–35.

Rodríguez Monegal, Emir. *El Boom de la novela latinoamericana*. Caracas: Tiempo Nuevo, 1972.

———. “The New Latin American Novelists.” In *The TriQuarterly Anthology of Contemporary Latin American Literature*, edited by José Donoso and William Henkin, 9–28. New York: E. P. Dutton, 1969.

Rodríguez Monegal, Emir, and Thomas Colchie, eds. *The Borzoi Anthology of Latin American Literature*. 2 vols. New York: Knopf, 1984.

Salvatore, Mariolina. “Reading and Writing a Text: Correlations between Reading and Writing Patterns.” *College English* 45, no. 7 (November 1983): 657–66.

Saussure, Ferdinand de. *Course in General Linguistics*. Translated by Wade Baskin. New York: McGraw-Hill, 1959.

Scholes, Robert, ed. *Approaches to the Novel: Materials for a Poetics*. Rev. ed. Scranton, PA: Chandler, 1966.

Scholes, Robert, and Robert L. Kellogg. *The Nature of Narrative*. New York: Oxford University Press, 1966.

Schorer, Mark. “Technique as Discovery.” In *The Theory of the Novel*, edited by Philip Stevick, 65–84. New York: Free Press, 1967.

Schwarz, Roberto. “Former Colonies: Local or Universal?” *Novel: A Forum on Fiction* 43, no. 1 (2010): 100–106.

———. *A Master on the Periphery of Capitalism: Machado de Assis*. Translated by John Gledson. Durham, NC: Duke University Press, 2001.

———. *Misplaced Ideas: Essays on Brazilian Culture*. Edited by John Gledson. London: Verso Books, 1992.

Selden, Raman. *A Reader's Guide to Contemporary Literary Theory*. 2nd ed. Lexington: University Press of Kentucky, 1989.

Sena, Jorge de. "Machado de Assis and His *Carioca* Quintet." Translated by Isabel de Sena. *Latin American Literary Review* 14, no. 27 (January–June 1986): 9–18.

Sontag, Susan. "Afterlives: The Case of Machado de Assis." *New Yorker*, May 7, 1990, 102–8. https://www.newyorker.com/magazine/1990/05/07/afterlives-the-case-of-machado-de-assis.

———. "Foreword." In *Epitaph of a Small Winner*, translated by William L. Grossman, xi–xx. New York: Noonday Press, 1990.

Steiner, George. *After Babel: Aspects of Language and Translation*. Oxford: Oxford University Press, 1977.

Stevick, Philip, ed. *The Theory of the Novel*. New York: Free Press, 1967.

Wellek, René. "The Concept of Realism in Literary Scholarship." In *Concepts of Criticism*, edited by Stephen G. Nichols Jr., 222–55. New Haven, CT: Yale University Press, 1963.

White, Edward M. "Post-structural Literary Criticism and the Response to Student Writing." *College Composition and Communication* 35, no. 2 (1984): 186–95.

White, Hayden. *Tropics of Discourse: Essays in Cultural Criticism*. Baltimore: Johns Hopkins University Press, 1978.

Wilkie, Brian, and James Hurt, eds. *Literature of the Western World*. 2 vols. New York: Macmillan, 1984.

Wood, Michael. "Master among the Ruins." In *The Author as Plagiarist—The Case of Machado de Assis*, guest edited by João Cézar de Castro Rocha, 293–303. Portuguese Literary & Cultural Studies 13/14. Dartmouth, MA: Center for Portuguese Studies and Culture, the University of Massachusetts Dartmouth, 2005.

Xirau, Ramón. *Octavio Paz: El sentido de la palabra*. México: J. Mortiz, 1970.

INDEX

ABOUT THE AUTHOR

EARL E. FITZ is a professor of Portuguese, Spanish, and comparative literature at Vanderbilt University. He is the author of *Machado de Assis and Female Characterization,* also published by Bucknell University Press (2015).